Annihilation

Also by Christopher Belshaw and
published by McGill-Queen's University Press

Environmental Philosophy: Reason, Nature and Human Concern

Annihilation

The Sense and Significance of Death

Christopher Belshaw

McGill-Queen's University Press
Montreal & Kingston • Ithaca

ISBN: 978-0-7735-3552-7 (hardcover)
ISBN: 978-0-7735-3553-4 (paperback)

Legal deposit first quarter 2009
Bibliothèque nationale du Québec

Published simultaneously outside North America by Acumen Publishing Limited

McGill-Queen's University Press acknowledges the financial support of the Government of
Canada through the Book Publishing Development Program (BPIDP) for its activities.

Library and Archives Canada Cataloguing in Publication

Belshaw, Christopher, 1952-
      Annihilation : the sense and significance of death / Christopher Belshaw.

Includes bibliographical references and index.
ISBN 978-0-7735-3552-7 (bound).--ISBN 978-0-7735-3553-4 (pbk.)

      1. Death. 2. Immortality (Philosophy). I. Title.

BD444.B44 2009   128'.5   C2008-907197-2

Printed in the UK by the MPG Books Group

Contents

... by convention hot, by convention cold ...: in reality atoms and void.

(Democritus)

Preface

No one died. The motivation for this book does not stem from personal encounters with what, too poetically, they call the grim reaper. There have been no premature deaths among people I have been close to, nor with those expiring closer to full term have I been up against the awfulness of dying, either because it has not been awful, or because I have been elsewhere, in another country. Perhaps I have, so far, been very lucky. Rather, it was in California in the mid-1980s that, in a much more abstract way, I first became interested in some of the topics discussed here. A lazy but uneasy summer in the Santa Barbara foothills when I first discovered Derek Parfit's *Reasons and Persons*. Reading, and soon after replying to, a provocative paper on a birth–death asymmetry by Anthony Brueckner and John Fischer. The finishing of a dissertation on Hume, and the need for something new. I worked on a longish paper on the evils of death, but set it aside, although always with the intention of taking it up again some day. Other projects have somehow been easier to address, and allowed me to put off this one without feeling too guilty about it. But they are also now finished. And time is running out.

This book addresses two main questions: what is death; and is it bad that we die? Thus, the sense and significance of the title. Chapters 1–3 deal with the first of these questions, Chapters 4–7 with the second. Chapter 9, in wondering how we might hope to avoid death, considers the sorts of things that we are. The short Chapter 8 asks whether it is worse if more die. It stands somewhat aside from the main flow, but it is of not unrelated interest, and, like a cheese course before dessert or the porter scene in *Macbeth*, does something for the pace.

In ending, rather than starting with some questions about identity, this book contrasts with certain others on these topics. It contrasts too in focusing very much on the badness of dying, and hardly at all on the wrongness of killing. So there is very little here about abortion, euthanasia or suicide. But what I have just said might be misleading. There is very little, also, about the process, as opposed to the event, of dying. These restrictions make the book somewhat narrow in scope, but, in compensation, should give it a fairly wide appeal. For death, it appears, will come to us all. How can it not be of concern? But we will not all undergo a drawn out dying process. Nor will we all have to face the moral dilemmas involved in thinking about what should be done in the light of death.

I begin with some widespread views about what death is and, distinguishing between literal and metaphorical uses of the term, ask about its relations to life, and to non-existence. I offer a unified and biological account of death and being dead, and so reject those who ally it, in our case, to a loss of consciousness. And, in line with this account, I deny that death brings about non-existence. Thus the annihilation of the title is not, I admit, entirely apt. Chapter 2 considers whether we might define death, and how definitions and criteria are related. I am somewhat sceptical about our being able to give a definition, and sceptical too about the need. In Chapter 3 the focus falls for the first time on human death in particular. It asks how our death relates to the so-called death of that key organ, the brain. As are growing numbers of others, I am unpersuaded by the brain death account. You can be brain dead, and still alive. And you can be brain alive, yet dead.

Chapters 4 and 5 are considerably longer than the others. Together they explore the common-sense view that death is often bad for us, along with its denial. They explore too the sorts of circumstances that might make it bad, issues about the ranking of different deaths, and our grounds for thinking that one is worse than another. I argue here, against the Epicureans and with the people, that death is often bad. But the questions of just when it is bad, and how bad it then is, are harder to answer. We can rank deaths against each other, but not in any clear way against other evils, notably pain. Chapters 6 and 7 deal with the related matters first of whether we can be harmed after we die, and second whether we can be harmed before we are born by, in particular, not being born earlier, and so having overall a longer life. I deny that there are posthumous harms. And I deny also that we are harmed by missing out on an earlier birth. Someone born at a different time would not, in one important sense, be me.

I said above that my concern is with death's badness, rather than killing's wrongness. This distinction, or at least one closely related, that between what happens and what we do, is central to Chapter 8. For, or so I claim, although it is fairly clearly worse if more die, it is less clear that we should prevent more deaths. So numbers count in assessing outcomes but not, or not as straight-forwardly, in determining action.

I said above, also, that death comes to us all. Yet, as I explain in Chapter 9, although I am pretty sure this is true of past and present people, I am less sure about the future. Technology might stave it off. But this is not because, *qua* animals or biological things, we might live forever. Rather, it is because we might survive the death of the animal with which we are closely related. Do I claim here, then, that we are not animals but are instead some other kind of thing – persons, or minds, or souls? No. Wanting to revive and defend a closest continuer account of identity, I argue instead that there is nothing, or nothing in particular, that we are.

Philosophy, generally, continues to trouble me. Is it hard, or easy? It by no means stands alone, but especially with a subject like death, always with us, it can be a real puzzle as to how there might remain some progress to be made, some genuinely difficult questions still to be answered, other than, of course, those that chemists, biologists or psychologists might address. So if the question "Is death bad?" is hard to answer, even harder is the question of how that question can be hard to answer. Perhaps, then, it is easy enough to say something true: harder to say something both true and interesting. I have tried to go for truth. Although there are a handful of exceptions the conclusions here, on the whole, strike me as fairly obvious and non-controversial. I still find it odd that others should disagree. And I have tried also to keep in mind the thought that our subject has a history, periods, fashions. Perhaps it is easier to say something not uninteresting if the aim is to enter what is at bottom a merely contemporary debate, one that is buoyant only for contingent reasons, rather than to engage with perennial problems, and the wisdom of the ages. As with our lives, so also our interests and concerns are but passing.

Some of what I have said here will be seen as bearing on a noticeable undercurrent to the book. There is, more or less throughout, an insistence that we are dealing with words, rather than concepts; a wariness of both the need for and availability of definitions; a disinclination to assume that our troublesome questions are well formed, admitting of yes/no answers; and a scepticism about metaphysics. An upshot of this is that certain of my conclusions may be less than fully clear. Sometimes this is a regrettable shortcoming on my part, and I have failed to say what I mean. But at others it is because I do not have a precise view, and that in turn is because I suspect there is no precise view there to be had. Two other things can be mentioned here. There are some repetitions. Again, no doubt some are unintended, but others I have allowed to stand just because they will, I think, help keep things moving. And there are occasions where views I might have taken from others are not fully described as such in the text. It is once more to do with flow, and I hope there are proper acknowledgements in the notes.

The Open University has provided me with several months' research leave in order to work on this book. That support has been much appreciated. In 2008, it, along with the University of York and the Royal Institute of Philosophy, generously funded a conference, "Death: What it is and Why it Matters", from which I benefited in many ways. Some of the views expressed in this book have surfaced elsewhere, in different form. But the argument of Chapter 7 derives fairly closely from two papers in particular, "Asymmetry and Non-Existence" (*Philosophical Studies* **70** [1993]: 103–16) and "Death, Pain and Time" (*Philosophical Studies* **97** [2000]: 317–41), which are recycled here with kind permission of the editor and Springer Science and Business Media.

I have many people to thank, including Parfit, Brueckner and Fischer, for that initial motivation. Fischer, on many occasions since, and in relation to a number of projects, has given encouragement and advice. He, along with Steven Luper, read the whole manuscript. They have both made invaluable suggestions, and are responsible for many improvements. A number of people have read and offered comments on various draft chapters. They include Steve Holland, Carolyn Price, Matthew Hanser, Gary Kemp, Christian Piller, Andrew Ward, Katie Chicot, Ann Gallagher, Barry Lee. Others have discussed parts of the book and its themes with me, often at length. Here I should mention again both Christian Piller, whose enthusiasm for talk on John Taurek is boundless, and Andrew Ward, who has a similar energy for Eric Olson. Richard Law and Calvin Dytham, biologists, have helped me get to elementary school level with some aspects of their subject. I have given talks on parts of the material represented here at the Open University, and at the universities of York, Santa Barbara, Lancaster, Hull, Glasgow and Oxford. The audiences here have known, more or less, what they were in for. I have benefited always from their comments. But as death is a topic close to us all, so it has been perfectly possible to quiz others about it. Thanks, then, to all those who, although having expected and preferred a more light-hearted intercourse, have tolerated my pressing them on mortality. Ben Bradley and Steven Luper have provided a good deal of stimulus both through their published and unpublished work, and through correspondence. Their death books are appearing more or less simultaneously with this one. Most unfortunately, I have not had time to read them. So apologies to these authors if, in drawing often on their earlier work, I have misrepresented their current position. And finally I want to thank Steven Gerrard and Kate Williams at Acumen for their support, advice and patience.

1
Death

What is death? It will surely seem appropriate to address this question in a book like this. It is, after all, a book about death. And so it is a book about a subject that is of considerable interest to all of us, as it has been for thousands of years. It may well seem appropriate, then, to address the question more widely, and to recognize that this is not simply of philosophical but of quite general concern. And I shall ask, and give an answer to, the question here. There is a second question. Does it matter that we discover what death is? It might simply be taken for granted that this does matter, and that it is not only here appropriate, but also generally important to ask and to answer this first question. So it might be thought that this second question is not one that needs in any further way to be addressed. But, of course, mattering comes in degrees, and the "we" of the question might be philosophers, or other people having a professional interest in death, or those – surely almost everyone – having a non-professional interest in the matter. As the question cannot then, have a simple yes/no answer, I shall consider it and give it in the end a less simple answer here.

What is death? I shall say that it is the irreversible breakdown of, or loss of function in, the organism as a whole.[1] But that should be taken only as a sketch of an answer; there is much that needs to be explained, and a number of qualifications that will need to remain in place. Does it matter that we discover what death is? I shall say that it does matter, and matters a lot, that we know a good deal about death. But we already do know a good deal. It matters that doctors and scientists know even more, and that they look further into its causes, its nature and the ways in which it might be countered. They are doing that. As many of the questions about death are important, and philosophically

1

challenging, so it matters too that philosophers address these questions. If I did not think that mattered, I would not have written the book. Even so, I think it is possible to exaggerate the importance of all this. And in particular, I shall want to suggest that it does not much matter that we settle on a strict definition of death, or that we discover or decide of all cases just when and where it comes.

Candidates

We will die. So too will our parents, children, pets, birds that visit our gardens, insects they feed on, daffodils that cheer up the spring and trees that we plant now with an eye to posterity. It is a mistake to think that death comes only to human beings. Rather, it is a widespread phenomenon throughout the natural world. But it is a mistake too to think that what death involves is in any detail the same wherever it occurs. Our deaths involve heart failure, brain damage and collapsing lungs. Trees have none of these organs, but they die all the same. Even so, what death involves is in some ways the same whenever it occurs. It always involves, as I have suggested above, an irreversible breakdown in the organism as a whole. I mean to imply here, as I have hinted above, that death is something that affects living things: something that is visited on animals, plants and on other biological organisms. These things operate or function in certain ways. Very roughly, when, irreversibly, that functioning ceases, they are dead.[2]

Does it affect only living things, only biological organisms? People talk of death in other contexts. We talk of batteries, telephones, hairdryers, seas, volcanoes, stars, being dead. And we talk as well of the death of ideas, of democracy, or liberalism in America, or culture. Function fits in here. These things, when dead, no longer work, no longer play an active role in our lives. So too does life fit in. The batteries that were once dead, like the ideas now defunct, once had some life in them. But none of these things are organisms. So there appears already to be something wrong with what I have said death is. But I can, of course, appeal to a familiar distinction. Animals and plants are literally alive, and will literally die, whereas machines and ideas are only metaphorically alive, and die only in some metaphorical or figurative sense.

But what is this distinction between the literal and metaphorical use of terms? What determines, and how can we tell, just how a term is used? This is not straightforward. I knew a girl in California who cultivated some interesting turns of phrase. She spoke of someone involved in traffic accident:

"Motorbikes, they're life killers, man". This was intended to be funny. What else can be killed but a living thing? "And afterwards, in hospital, he was a vegetable, literally a vegetable." This too was supposed to amuse, affected hyperbole. But did it succeed? Doctors – and philosophers – will refer to the brain dead as human vegetables. These people lack sentience, and movement. So is it, perhaps, literally true that an animal can turn into a vegetable? Or think of music. Do sopranos literally or metaphorically have higher voices than tenors? And what of an instrument's sounding bright? I think we can only say that there are some clearly literal uses of a word, some clearly metaphorical, and much room for finessing in between.

Consider another case. Nietzsche, famously, wrote that God is dead. Was he speaking literally or metaphorically here? Many people think that God exists. Perhaps many of them think that God is alive. None of these believers think that God's ceasing to exist, or ceasing to live, is even possible. And Nietzsche too was not suggesting that God once existed, once lived, but now exists, or lives, no longer. What he meant was that the idea of God, or belief in God, is no longer doing the kind of work, or playing the kind of role, it did. He could claim that this is literally true. Even so, that the idea of God is dead is, I think, only metaphorically true. Ideas are only metaphorically alive. But consider the believers further. They think that God is alive, but will not and cannot die. Do they think that God is literally alive, or only metaphorically so? Perhaps it is just not clear what they think. But certainly people do seem to have believed in fantastical creatures, gods and monsters, and to have believed that these things are literally alive, and in many cases able literally to die. Does this make sense? The only uncontroversially living and dying things that we know of are biological entities: carbon-based, DNA- or RNA-containing, genetically linked with all other living things. But must living and dying things be this way? Or could there be creatures with a different chemistry, say silicon-based, or highly complex and self-replicating machines, that also, and literally, live and die?

That is one area to consider further. It concerns creatures that have a merely hypothetical existence. It is speculative. Here is another area, concerning now things that do exist, and with which we are all familiar. Biological organisms, I have said, are the kinds of things that are literally alive, and that literally die. What about parts of organisms? What about, say, a human kidney, a headless chicken, a tomato, the branch of a tree? Are any of these literally alive? Will any of them literally die?

In attempting to answer this question, there are various things to note. First, in some of these cases we do talk frequently, and confidently, in terms of life and death. We talk of a still-living heart or kidney. We say that there remains life in a damaged branch, and refer to old cut flowers as dead and now ready to throw away. In other cases – tomatoes, carrots, seeds, joints of meat – we are little inclined to use such terms. In still other cases – hair, nails, an oyster shell – these terms seem even less apt. I shall suggest some reasons as to why this might be below. Second, in all these cases we can, at least in principle, describe the biochemical condition of the thing in full detail. And we can say just how it relates to the organism as a whole, how it has developed into the thing it is, and how it might or might not assist with the functioning of that organism, or give rise to further organisms of the same or a similar kind. Hearts, pieces of skin, individual cells, acorns and feathers can all be accounted for in these ways. Are any of these things dead or alive? If so, this will follow from just these sorts of facts then coupled with accounts developed by biologists and others as to what death is. It will not depend (or so most of us now believe) on further and different sorts of facts, whether the things contain souls, or have the life force within them, or some such. And it is clear, I think, that none of these things is as evidently alive as is some paradigm organism – you, a magpie, an oak tree – or as clearly lacking in life as a book or a stone. It is clear too that all, or almost all, of these things can exist in different conditions such that they are more appropriately described as alive in some, and more appropriately described as dead in others. So if anything is a living kidney then it is one whose functioning is not irretrievably lost, one that can again operate within an organism after a transplant. If anything is a dead kidney it is one whose functioning is altogether lost, one that is useless for transplant purposes. But is a so-called living kidney literally alive? Some think, or appear to think it is, others that it is not. There seems not to be full agreement here.

A kidney is, in a fairly clear sense, a part of an organism. Clearly too organisms can contain other organisms, as when I swallow an oyster, or when the cat suffers from worms. But the smaller organisms here are not really parts of the larger. Can one organism be genuinely a part of another, so that the two function together, as if in the maintenance of one system? Unlike kidneys, individual cells can reproduce. And this is often taken to be a characteristic of living things. Perhaps, as some maintain, cells are both themselves organisms and parts of larger and more complex organisms. Thus cells, unlike organs, might be literally alive, and destined literally to die.[3]

I think that only organisms are literally alive, so rule out organs. And I do not know enough about cells to know whether they are really organisms. But the important point here is that I think organisms are alive, organs not, only because this seems to be the way we mostly, usually coherently, and often confidently speak about such things. I do not think organs lack life and that

4

this can be shown by appeal to some observations in biology, but these are things many people have failed to notice. Similarly, the suggestion that cells might be literally alive implies not that there might be further facts about cells of which we are unaware, but only that there might already be a settled way of talking about such things, a pattern to our language, which has so far passed me by. And this important point is fairly general. Although there are, of course, some exceptions, most of the puzzles I shall be concerned with are, or so I claim, linguistic rather than scientific.[4]

Life and death

These terms are obviously connected, but how? I have suggested that only living things can die. The things that can die literally are, at some earlier time, literally alive. And similarly for things that can die metaphorically.[5] So all that is now dead was once alive.

That might appear to be an altogether uncontroversial claim. But it has been challenged. This challenge is, I think, successful but uninteresting.[6] Suppose the five-minute hypothesis is true. The world is only five minutes old. And we only seem to remember the middle of last week. Then there are many dead things – on battlefields, in butchers' shops, in morgues – that were never alive. We either say that, or we say that these things only appear to be dead. I prefer the former option. And so the seemingly uncontroversial claim is false. Fair enough. But, setting such sceptical hypotheses to one side, this claim – call it the *death from life thesis* – is surely true.

Here is a second claim, again apparently uncontroversial, but again no doubt susceptible to some elaborate counter-example: nothing is, at one and the same time, and in the same way, both dead and alive. The terms are exclusive.

Two questions remain. Is everything that is at some time alive destined at some later time to be dead? And is everything alive or dead? That is, are the terms exhaustive?

Life to death

The answer to the first question, concerning what we can call the *life to death thesis*, falls into two parts. Perhaps we can at least imagine some beings, literally alive, that will live forever. We can at least imagine immortality. Of course, many people think that God is such a being, and many think that we are, or at least have, immortal souls. Apart from the obvious questions about their existence there is, as I have suggested, the further question of whether such beings – let us assume they are understood as non-physical – are literally alive. But certainly there seems nothing obviously incoherent about supposing that a genuinely living thing, some biological entity, should continue to live forever. That is one, and a familiar, form of immortality. But could there be another? Could a living thing cease to live without dying? Is a so-called deathless exit[7] possible?

Some have argued that this is possible, because it is, and frequently, actual. The amoeba does not die, but rather divides. And the caterpillar does not die but turns into a butterfly.[8] So fission and metamorphosis are two ways in which things can cease to exist, and so cease to live, while yet avoiding death. But although importantly different, neither example is altogether happy. The difficulties for the caterpillar case are evident. There is, it seems, nothing here that ceases to live, or ceases to exist. A caterpillar is not itself a thing. Rather it is a stage in the history of a thing, and is to the butterfly very much as an awkward and spotty teenager is to a mature adult. The objector appeals here to a strong intuition that the caterpillar is a phase in an animal's life, rather than itself a particular animal. No similarly strong intuition figures in the amoeba case. We do not believe the amoeba continues to exist, after the divide, either as one, or as both of the resulting organisms.[9] But then neither do we believe, perhaps, that the amoeba is a particular thing that with fission ceases to exist, yet does not die. That is, or so I suspect, we just do not have here any firm beliefs either way. When something divides into two in this way it neither continues, nor ceases, to exist. And if that is right, then even the amoeba case does not clearly refute the life to death thesis.[10]

Consider now some imaginary cases. Many of the stories in Ovid suggest deathless exits. But distinguish those where someone seems to continue living, but is trapped in a different body (Actaeon, Callisto as a bear), and those where someone is altogether transformed, and both physically and psychologically nothing of the original person remains (Narcissus, Callisto as a constellation). In both types of story we certainly start out with someone who is literally alive. But the first sort of case resembles that of the caterpillar. The youth or nymph or god continues to exist, but in very much a different form. Yet whereas the caterpillar turns naturally into the butterfly, these transformations are unnatural, resulting only from intervention elsewhere. In the second it is much more tempting to say that the youth, the nymph, ceases to exist. In a more recent story,[11] the Queen turns into a swan, and similarly ceases to exist. Yet I am disinclined to say that any deaths have occurred. And if that is right, then these cases, although imaginary, do involve deathless exits, and counter the life to death thesis. But think about some details. Perhaps part of my reluctance to suppose that the Queen is dead is because I suspect that if she can be turned into a swan, this process can be reversed, and the swan turned back into a queen. And as, controversially, I believe there can be two beginnings of existence[12] then this could be the very same queen, and thus the Queen. Suppose we turn her into a swan and then kill the swan. There is a dead swan, the Queen is now gone forever, but even so she never died. Suppose the magical transformation is, for some reason, from the outset irreversible. We turn a nymph into a cake stand. This may be just an outré way of murdering someone.

What should we conclude from this? Suppose you do think that the amoeba exits deathlessly. Should we say death does not occur when, in fission, new organisms are formed? No. Fred Feldman imagines a machine that separates a mouse into its component cells.[13] Each cell is, he maintains, an organism. But this kills the mouse. Suppose you think Callisto exits deathlessly, when transformed into stars. Should we say death does not occur unless there is a corpse? No. The mouse separator produces no corpse. Nor, in the actual world, does a very proximate nuclear bomb. Should we think there can be deathless exits? In the actual world it seems as if living things all die. None of them cease to exist instead of, or prior to, dying. Only the behaviour of the amoeba, and perhaps some other single-celled organisms, puts any strain on this. But we can imagine cases, and tell stories, where talk of a deathless exit seems more appropriate. And there are, as well, immortality stories where no exit occurs.

There is, then, a range of cases to consider: something might live forever; it might cease to exist, and so cease to live, without dying; it might continue to exist, but in a non-living form; or it might continue to exist, and to live, but in a different living form. Examples might be, respectively: Jesus; the amoeba; Callisto as stars; Callisto as a bear, or a caterpillar/butterfly. There is a further distinction to add. We might say, of Callisto (and similarly for the Queen/swan) that the human being or nymph has ceased to exist, and without dying, but that the person lives on. There are amoeba, and caterpillars. But the other examples are, to different degrees, less than clearly real. The life to death thesis appears to be more or less true in fact, but nevertheless false in principle.[14]

Life or death

Are the terms exhaustive? In two ways, clearly not. There are many things, physical and non-physical, that are never alive or dead. And there are many times when living things do not exist, such that for at least some of those times they are then neither alive nor dead. But we can ask: are those things that are at any time alive or dead, alive or dead at all times at which they exist? This is a question of some complexity.

One quick response needs reasonably careful consideration. It might be claimed that as well as the living and the dead there are the dying. And they occupy an intermediate position. In one way that reveals a certain elementary mistake. At least in most cases, the dying are certainly alive. Yet they are in a condition where, without intervention, they will relatively soon be dead.[15] But is it so clear that the dying are certainly alive? Anyone insisting on exhaustivity will think so. No one thinks you can be, at one and the same time, both dying and dead.

Now it may be that it is some thought about others' confusion of death with dying that leads certain writers to insist that death is an event and not a process. According to James Bernat (2002: 331), this is a "fact" that "results automatically" from the exhaustivity thesis.[16] But this is in several ways at least potentially confusing. Let us agree that dying is a process and that it needs to be distinguished from death. But where do we go from there? If, as Bernat also insists, death is a state then it persists through time. And so, if an event begins and ends in a moment, if it is instantaneous, then death is not an event. Either there is or is not relevant change in that time during which something is dead. Often there is.[17] So it is not easy to see why someone should deny that death is a process. Moreover, at least on the ordinary understanding, events themselves often take time, and so involve processes. But we can usefully introduce a further distinction here: that between the apparently instantaneous coming about of one's death, that dateable moment of extinction, and the ongoing and endless state of one's being dead.[18] So then the near-sloganeering of "event and not a process" applies only to the former of the two. And the idea here, that there is a moment of death – that, even if for a while they have been dimming, the lights go out in an instant – is widely believed to be true.

Is it true? Is death, in this sense, an event? Does death's being, in this sense, an event, follow from the exhaustivity thesis? And is the exhaustivity thesis itself true? The middle question is the easiest. And I think Bernat is right to insist on a connection here. If organisms are either alive or dead then their ceasing to be alive, and becoming dead, must occur in an instant. So now there is only one question that needs to be addressed. But although Bernat insists, also, that the exhaustivity thesis is true, he offers little by way of argument. Is there an argument? One, although flawed, has already been hinted at. Someone might think that having pointed out that dying is a process that occurs in life, it follows that the shift from life to death occurs in an instant. But that too could be a process, one that occurs between life and death. Perhaps then we should insist on exhaustivity simply on empirical grounds; we can just see that things are at one moment alive, and at the next dead. But I doubt we can just see this. And even if we could see this we could not just see that things have to be that way. Suppose death were defined as the absence of life. Would the exhaustivity thesis follow? No. There might still be a period in which it is indeterminate whether life is absent.

Consider what the exhaustivity thesis implies. If it is true then there can be no third state between or besides life and death. And the life/death boundary cannot be indeterminate or fuzzy. These are separate points. For a third state might have sharp or fuzzy boundaries. Suppose the former. Then death is an event – it occurs in an instant – even though the exhaustivity thesis is false. Consider now some less abstract implications. I referred above to states between or besides life and death. Assuming that, for any individual, life both precedes and cannot succeed death, then this thesis implies that a living thing cannot exist before it is alive, and cannot exist after life, excepting it be then dead. For if it were at either time to exist it would have to be in some third condition, neither living nor dead. And this the thesis disallows. But Frankenstein builds his creature and then, with electricity, gets life into him. Someone might insist that only with life did this thing begin to exist. But surely it is more natural to suppose that he first came into existence, and then acquired life. And remember Callisto, turned into stars. Some will say she continues to exist but, as she is no longer an organism, is neither living nor dead.

There are less fantastical cases to be considered concerning intermediate states. Just as someone whose membership is put on hold is neither a member nor not a member of his club, so, plausibly, someone in suspended animation is neither alive nor dead. And my claim here is of a piece with the account of death I offered at the outset. For if life implies some sort of overall functioning, and death involves an irreversible loss of function, then there seems to be, too, at least the possibility of a state in which function is lost, but reversibly so. Yet someone wedded to exhaustivity will insist either that these thus far imaginary cases fail to challenge a merely empirical claim, or that you simply remain alive in suspended animation, no matter how much functioning is then lost. But are the cases imaginary? Perhaps none of us can as yet be shut down, and then revived, but we are talking here of death in general, and so need to consider other animals, and plants.[19] And even if the disjunction can be insisted on, unless it corresponds to an overall robust distinction within the organism's states, it remains unmotivated.

Existence

The living exist. But what about the dead? There is a widespread view that they do not.[20] This is most curious, for the dead would seem to be all around us, in butchers' shops, cemeteries, second-rate garden centres, wreckers' yards, spent battery stores and so on. Occasionally death and non-existence begin together, as when people and animals and batteries all stand too close to a big bomb. But usually death comes first, with non-existence following on some time behind, when the body is, for example, eaten, or cremated, or melted down.[21] Why should anyone hold to a different view?

There are two reasons. Many of those considering this matter are focused on our deaths. They often now refer to the *termination thesis*, or the view that we cease to exist at death.[22] But what are we? If we are human beings, or animals, or biological organisms, this view seems at first sight to have no plausibility. If we are minds, or non-immortal souls, or persons, where these terms all refer to something substantially different from human beings, or animals, or organisms, then this non-existence view might now seem plausible after all. For you might think that with death there is just nothing at all left of the mind or the psychology, even if there is something left of the body that gave rise to this psychology. But I fear we have only traded one problem for another. Just as someone might think that batteries are, at best, only metaphorically dead or alive, so too for persons, if persons are entities of this distinctively non-biological kind. So even if it is true that we cease to exist at the time that our bodies die, it is false, or at least not literally true, that we cease to exist when we die.[23] For if we are not biological organisms it is at least moot as to whether we do literally die, and whether we are literally alive. A number of writers who subscribe to some version of this person view appear simply to assume that dying and ceasing to exist can be used of us interchangeably. But this is to be regretted. Several further points could be made here, but as I discuss person views in more detail in a later chapter, I shall defer them.

Holding to this person–organism distinction is one reason, albeit not a good one, for believing we cease to exist when we die. A second reason, maybe even worse, is in holding that all organisms cease to exist when they die. This second reason is sufficiently different to warrant a different name. Persons, if there are any, certainly cease to exist but only controversially do they die. Organisms, and there are many, certainly die, but only controversially do they then cease to exist. I shall call this the *disappearance thesis*.

Its best-known proponent is Eric Olson, but there are several other writers who favour this view.[24] It is not quite as strange as it first appears. Olson does not believe that things, when they die, simply vanish, their atoms scattered, the place they occupied suddenly empty. Rather, he believes that the things typically called dead animals are better referred to just as corpses, or as the remains of dead animals, or perhaps as bodies.[25] And he has no argument with most ordinary claims about why these corpses are as, and where, they are, or about their likely futures.[26] Of course, there are some ordinary claims that are at odds with the disappearance thesis; Olson thinks it just wrong to hold that the corpse, these remains, were earlier living, breathing and walking around. But is it wrong? The dispute here can appear empty, with Olson urging an albeit possible deviation from standard terminology with little or no motivation, and with no evident gain. But there is more to it. And he believes that the living animal is a distinctive thing, or substance, that goes out of existence with death, even if the raw matter that makes it up remains. And so the claim that living organisms continue to exist after death is deeply false, rather than merely infelicitous.

Suppose there are substances. Why think the substance here disappears with death, rather than that it continues to exist, although in a considerably different condition? For certainly, just as we might think of persons as phases in the history of an organism, rather than as distinct things, so we might similarly believe that organisms have a phase in which they are alive, followed by, usually, a further phase in which life is absent. There are two main components to Olson's view. First, he thinks that the changes that an organism undergoes when it dies are undeniably profound: at one moment it is a complex integrated thing, all its parts involved in certain metabolic processes, at the next mere lumps of matter, stable, inert, with no resistance to entropy.[27] We might overlook this if we attend only to a thing's grosser surface properties, for at that level the difference between the living and the dead is not always clear. But, he says, we need instead to be concerned with inner workings, and microstructure. And then the profundity of the differences can hardly be denied.

Yet this is not obviously right. It may be more or less right for most animals, most of the time. But it is not right for trees, which can be alive even though large parts are dead and expendable. And it is not right for many of those human beings whose death is impinged on by sophisticated medical technologies. For on current accounts of death, a human being can be dead even while many of the dynamic processes associated with life continue. So the changes involved in the shift from life to death are far less dramatic and weighty, at least over a wide range of cases, than Olson claims. And the reasons for holding that with death animals and other organisms immediately cease to exist are noticeably undermined.

The second component follows from the first, but has a more technical feel. Suppose there are, at least at the micro-level, the profound differences that Olson cites. What it takes for a corpse to continue to exist is that its particles continue to exist, in roughly the same number and location as at present. The persistence conditions for a dead body are similar to those of an artefact. But the "metabolic turnover" we observe in a living thing indicates that its persistence conditions are of a radically different kind. An organism can continue to be alive even while none of its particles remain the same, and even while it takes on a wholly different shape and size. As Olson puts it, two organisms, or organism phases, are one and the same, or phases of one and the same organism, when they share in the same life.[28] Surely, though, one and the same thing cannot, in this way, have two quite different sets of persistence conditions.

This argument is not strong. We can claim that two organisms x and y are one and the same either when x and y share in a life or when y's particles are most of x's particles, and are arranged as they were when x died. That is not the simplest or most elegant account of a thing's persistence, but it is not at all clear why we should expect simplicity here.

As I have suggested, Olson seems to believe in some sort of metaphysical substances. Are there such things? I deny it, but need to hold out on explaining that denial until Chapter 9. If I am right, then the disappearance thesis is doubly flawed: the living and the dead could not be related as claimed. And even if they could be, there is no good reason to think they are. This is not quite the end of the matter, for this thesis infects certain of the purported definitions of death to be considered below. But there is not going to be reason, via such consideration, to revise these negative verdicts.[29]

Value

If death is, as I suggest, an irreversible breakdown, or loss of integrated functioning, in the organism as a whole, then, perhaps, the notion of death carries with it some indication of a decline in value. When artefacts cease to function – when, metaphorically, they die – this is bad for us. When organisms cease to function this is bad for them. So the badness of death is no news.

Someone may want to reject this entirely. Perhaps it does not matter at all that some device or machine breaks down. It might be hard to sustain the view that for things other than persons, it is good for that thing to continue living.[30] And in many cases human death is not bad for the one who dies. Suicide might be rational, and euthanasia – ending someone's life in order to benefit them – possible. If life is no longer worth living, then, apparently, death might be good. But I am not suggesting the connection here is thoroughgoing. I mean only that there is a widespread and natural tendency to link life and value, death and disvalue, over a wide range of cases, and perhaps especially those in which our own interests are implicated. And if I am right about this, it helps explain some of the puzzles noted above. I said that we do not suppose that tomatoes or strawberries or joints of meat, even though they are parts of organisms, are alive or dead. In general, we do not want to think of the food we eat as living or dead, nor that we kill things, shellfish apart, in cooking them. We talk of dead wood on a tree, or when it is rotten or decayed, but we do not naturally think of the solid timber in a church or house as alive or dead. So long as they are useful, that things are dead is unlikely to be insisted on.

An attendant association, perhaps, is one of life and potency. Death takes away value, and so is often bad, but it also neutralizes: strips things of their power. We kill – people, animals, bacteria – to protect ourselves. But if some power is good, or can be used for good, we might try to keep things alive. And so a thought, often, is that so long as things are alive then power and value might be restored. Thus only with death should we, and will we, give up hope. This can be good. For, in fact, the chances of recovery can be slim, or null. But only with death, many of us think, is it legitimate to end treatment, appropriate to begin grieving, possible to continue with the business of life.

I certainly do not claim that these associated notions are part of death's meaning. An organism is dead when it ceases to function, irreversibly, as an integrated whole. That often implies a loss of value, and of power, but death occurs whether or not the links obtain, and whether or not we do any thinking about them. But without the links, our thinking about death, and what we say and do about it, is sometimes less than straightforward and confident. And they might fail to obtain in two ways. First, something might die, even though, in important respects, value and power remain. Perhaps this is the way to think of the kidneys we eat, the wood with which we build. And there are imaginary cases. If my personality survives, perhaps in heaven, perhaps embedded in some machine, then it may be true both that I have died and that what matters about me survives. Second, a thing might lose value, and power, even before it dies. There are, in increasing numbers, real cases. Someone in a persistent vegetative state (PVS) has lost, and irreversibly, that for which they are mostly valued, and lost as well their ability to value themselves, but they are nevertheless alive. Perhaps some of those counted as brain dead are in the same category. And I have suggested that we should think of the imaginary magical disappearance – gone forever, but not dead – in the same way.

13

The suggestion here, then, is that there is something that death is, something that implies certain structural changes in a biological organism, that this can occur without its customary associations, and that without these associations our speaking of death, although continuing to be correct, often finds itself under some strain. But what if it is objected that this has things the wrong way round? As is well known, there is a significant level of disagreement about the PVS case, with some arguing that when consciousness is irretrievably lost then a death has occurred. For those making such a claim the link between death and value is more prominent, and more fully embedded in death's meaning, than I have wanted to allow. What is to be said against this contrary view? Any argument here has to claim either that this is at odds with death's true nature, or that it is impossible to speak consistently and coherently in this way, or that this is in fact in tension with the way in which most of us do speak, and consistently so, and, further, that there is no good case for revision. Only the last of these, I think, has any hope of success.

Summary

I have said what death is: an irreversible breakdown in integrated functioning in the organism as whole. I have suggested that this is how the term is literally or strictly used, but of course allowed that it has metaphorical and looser uses elsewhere. And I have discussed and, I hope, thrown some light on the connections between death and certainly commonly associated notions: life, existence, value. I should say something now about the limits on these claims, and something also about their status.

The focus has been on a biological account of death. And I shall refer to such an account in the chapters that follow. Certain writers refer to, articulate and criticize a *biological paradigm* of death. This paradigm has many components.[31] My account is much narrower, and I am not going to accept that all the criticisms of the paradigm bear on it. On the contrary, some of these criticisms I am more than willing to endorse.

Friends of the biological account will include *animalists*. I have already referred to the most famous animalist, Eric Olson, and his strange view about disappearance. This view is not, I think, at the centre of their position. That centre comprises two claims: that we are animals; and that animals die when they cease to function as integrated wholes. Now, although I am pretty much fully committed to the second claim, I am less committed to the first. I discuss the issues in Chapter 9, but meanwhile it might be worth thinking of the difference like this: animalists think we are essentially animals, while I think the relationship here is contingent.

Death is a biological phenomenon. Do I think it is *simply*, or *merely*, or *only* or *just* a biological phenomenon? Well, I think death in the literal sense is confined to certain biological entities, namely organisms, and that these things die when and only when there are certain changes to their biological structure. But, unsurprisingly, I do not think that is all there is to say about death. Sociologists, psychologists, historians and culture critics can say much more, and much that is true, interesting and important. But while conceding that, we might note – and in a sense I here allude to the point above – that there remains an important difference: death is in every case a biological phenomenon, but is not in every case a sociological, or cultural, or psychological, or whatever else phenomenon.[32]

What is the status of these claims? How am I to defend my view if, for example, someone insists that persons as well as organisms are literally alive, and can literally die, or that the dead do not exist, or that death involves something more, or something less than overall loss of function? The point made towards the end of the previous section is salient here. I am not claiming to offer some sort of demonstration or proof that, irrespective of what people might think about the matter, death has these features rather than these. Rather, I have taken myself to be, first, simply noting and reporting on the ways in which we actually think and speak about these matters, second, to some extent systematizing and clarifying what we have to say, and third, making certain predictions as to how we would speak, were circumstances to be changed. I do not think that what people say about death is the final arbiter of what is true about it. But it is at least the starting-point.

2

Definitions

I have said that death is the irreversible breakdown of the organism as a whole. And I've now made a number of further claims about death, and some of its relations to biology, to life and to existence all of which, I hope, are consistent with the first claim. Is this first claim a definition? We can ask, what, in general, is a definition? And what, in particular, is a definition of death? Only a few of the philosophers writing on death consider these sorts of questions. Several of these writers are concerned principally with matters concerning value. They often seem to think we know well enough what death is, and are unconcerned to give a definition. Others, focusing on some of the more technical issues about human death, speak often, and confidently, about the definition of death. But only rarely have they thought much about what a definition would be. One of a handful of exceptions is Fred Feldman. In the opening chapters of *Confrontations with the Reaper* (1992), Feldman considers these questions in both detail and depth. I want to attend to two aspects of his discussion in particular: his distinction between an analysis and a criterion; and his attempt to define death. Alongside this, I shall take into account also the endeavours of certain other writers. Their suggestions will help throw further light on what death is.

Analysis and criterion

Feldman starts by observing that the question "What is death?" can be taken in a number of different ways. We might, he says, be asking what "death" means, or we might be enquiring after the nature of death, or, again, we might be looking for a philosophical analysis of the concept of death.[1] Although he does not make it clear at this stage, Feldman seems to think there are here three ways of asking the same question, rather than three different questions that stand in danger of being confused. Even so, he wants to focus on the last of these. And he suggests that we construe attempts at analysis in terms of definitions. Thus to unpack the concept of death is satisfactorily to complete the following:

x dies at t = df. x ...

What is needed here? A definition has to get the uncontroversial cases right, and so not be susceptible to obvious counter-examples, either actual or conceivable. It may offer surprising verdicts on certain controversial cases but, according to Feldman, that is not clearly a mark against it, and "would merely show that we can learn things from good philosophy" (1992: 13). It needs to avoid circularity, either explicit or implicit. There is no point in defining death in terms of thanatological termination, for example (*ibid.*: 14). It needs, further, to avoid "use of any terms that are as obscure in meaning as the term being analyzed itself" (*ibid.*: 13). For then we will not learn anything. Now, assuming we can uncover a definition that fits with these conditions we will, according to Feldman, have succeeded in analysing the concept of death, we will have a grasp of its nature, and we will know what the term "death" means.

Contrast this account of an analysis with that of a criterion. It is often important to be able to distinguish between the living and dead. Doctors and lawyers need to do this. And so they need to appeal to some mark or sign or criterion of death, "a fairly easily recognisable property that serves as an indicator of death" (*ibid.*: 14–15). Absence of heart beat, or respiration, or persistent low body temperature have long been taken as reliable criteria of human and animal death. And thus to have a grasp of a criterion of death is to know that some such sentence as this is true:

x dies at t iff ...

Yet schematically, at least, it looks now as if what is needed here might strongly resemble that involved in a definition, such that the distinction between an analysis and a criterion is less than clear. And, as is often noted, many of the terms appealed to here are perhaps rather too widely used.[2] But certainly, there is an important difference in knowing what "death" means, or what it is for someone or something to be dead, and in being able to tell, in a particular case, whether someone or something is dead or alive. Take my suggestion: to be dead is to have undergone irreversible breakdown in the organism as a whole. Someone may agree with this but be at a loss as to how to tell whether such a breakdown has actually occurred. Or consider spies. You probably know what a spy is, but are nevertheless unable to identify one. So there is indeed a distinction to be made here. And Feldman discusses the differences between an analysis and a criterion in some detail, and at some length. Much of that detail is provided in a summary that follows on from this discussion. I give it here in full.

1. A criterion of death purports to help us locate the moment when death comes. An analysis of death purports to tell us what death is.
2. A criterion of death may be formulated in such a way as to apply only to human beings. An analysis of death must apply equally to anything that can die.
3. A criterion of death may be quite useful even if only contingently true. Indeed it might be quite useful even if there are a few rare counterexamples. An analysis of death, if true at all, is necessarily true. There cannot be even so much as a *possible* falsifying instance.
4. A criterion of death may be "in force" during a certain time and then, with advances in technology, abandoned. An analysis of death, on the other hand, is eternally true if true at all.
5. A criterion of death is a success if enough people, thinking it would be useful, decide to adopt it. An analysis of death is a success if it is true – even if no one adopts it.   (*Ibid.*: 17)

Start with his explication of a criterion. As I discuss some of this further in the next chapter, I can be relatively brief here. First, in relation to (1), it is worth noting that even without a clear mark of death's moment, some lesser signs might be useful. Some, but not all, the dead have been decapitated. If someone has been decapitated, doctors can certainly cease their endeavours. That is useful information.[3] So as well as a single criterion there might be multiple criteria. A second point to note here is that Feldman seems to be assuming that death comes at a precise instant, rather than gradually, over a period. I have discussed this above, and I shall return to it below. On (2), Feldman is right to make the point that a criterion might be less than general. Signs of death in a human being will be different from those in trees. But useful criteria are unlikely to be species specific; lack of heartbeat and respiration are

18

as much signs of death in apes as in humans. Points (3) and (4) are evidently connected. What needs most to be noted here is that what functions as a reliable indicator of death can change over time, as technology changes. Again, I return to this in Chapter 3. The last point, (5) is puzzling. We might agree that a criterion is successful only if adopted. But if most people adopt a criterion, is its success assured? They will believe it successful, but surely they could be wrong. There were widely adopted criteria for witches, but as there never were any witches it is hard to see how these criteria were ever successful. Or imagine a disease, well known and rightly feared. People associate certain symptoms with the disease, taking these as sure signs that infection has occurred. But there might be symptoms without the disease, and disease without the symptoms.[4]

I have more to say about analysis. Go back. We can, via a philosophical analysis, unpack the concept of death, find about its nature, discover what "death" means, and provide the term with a definition. This seems to presuppose that the notion of a concept is unproblematic, that death is something that has a nature, and that the meaning of this apparently everyday term is discovered not by looking in a dictionary, or by asking, say, doctors and priests for guidance, but through some sort of philosophical enquiry. And, given the couching of definitions in terms of logically necessary and sufficient conditions, it seems to presuppose too both that what death is is the same in all possible worlds, and that we do not know what "death" means until we know how correctly to describe certain happenings in all those worlds. Yet little here is straightforward.

Contrast two broad-brush approaches to a term like death. Under the first this term names something, some phenomenon, that has an unchanging and unchangeable structure or nature: one thing that is the same in all possible worlds. And to find out what death is, and what "death" means, to unravel the thing's nature, requires philosophers to investigate and analyse – by some sort of *a priori* activity – the concept of death. Under the second there are, in the actual world, a good number of phenomena that are involved in the development or history of living things. These can, in principle at least, be individually described in some detail. Some of these phenomena, or certain concatenations of such phenomena, strike us, not unreasonably, as having considerable importance. Given our interests, we elect to mark these off. When certain of these phenomena occur, we say the thing has died. And the question "What is death?" might be understood in two ways: a non-English speaker is asking about what is to him an unfamiliar term; an English speaker is asking for more information about the phenomena implicated – are, say, the dead gone forever, or might they return?

I favour the second approach; I shall say considerably more about it as things go along. Feldman seems to favour the first, as his discussions and summary remarks indicate. Thus in (1) his claim that an analysis will "tell us what death is" means not that we will learn more about the physiological processes involved, but that we will somehow penetrate its essential nature. His next point (2) can appear innocuous, given what I have already conceded about the analysis–criterion distinction, and what I have said about "death" being univocal. But there is room for hesitation about the modal terms. It is one thing to say that, as a matter of contingent fact, the term is univocal, but perhaps another to insist, as it appears here, that it must be univocal. "Death" and cognate terms might have had two literal, even if linked, meanings, rather than, as it seems, one literal meaning, and certain attendant metaphorical meanings. Again (3) and (4) are connected. And here the case for attributing the first approach to Feldman is at its strongest. The idea seems to be that there is something that death is, in all possible worlds, and for all time. And a correct analysis will reveal this. Finally, note the reference to "success" in (5). Feldman might insist that an analysis is correct if true, but the notion of success seems to be linked to some satisfied aim, such that an analysis would be successful only if it reveals the truth to us. Yet the view here seems to be that someone might successfully analyse death, say what death is and what "death" means, even though neither she nor anyone else believes the analysis is correct. Note also that there seems to be some tension between the view expressed here and the earlier insistence that an analysis needs to avoid obscure terms, on pain of being unhelpful.

In sum, Feldman seems to hold to some sort of Platonist or realist view about meaning. Even though it is contingently true that particular words – "death", "dead", "dying" – are used in particular ways, they do, when so used, pick out or refer to unchanging and unchangeable concepts and natures. Further, these concepts and natures are sharp edged, such that every actual and every possible thing in the universe is either dead or not dead, and that we do not know what death is, or what "death" means, unless we know whether all these things are dead or not dead. Further still, grasping the meaning, knowing the nature, are philosophical tasks, and are fully completed by giving logically necessary and sufficient conditions, or a definition, of death. But this is implausible. It sets the stakes for meaning rather high. Anyone who, knowing all the scientific facts, is uncertain whether some creature is dead or alive thereby reveals themselves as not knowing what "dead" means. On my view, in contrast, a word can have a meaning, and that meaning can be grasped, without this. And our response to certain puzzle cases ought to be not that we are uncertain as to which of two claims obtains, but rather we are as yet undecided as to what best to say about it. In contrast, the conditions on knowing a thing's nature might seem on Feldman's account to be set rather low. It may be unclear exactly what is to count as knowing what some natural object or phenomenon is, but it is far from evident that one could claim that just in virtue of knowing some necessary and sufficient condition for something's being such an object, or phenomenon.[5] Bitzer, in Charles Dickens's *Hard Times*, is famously able to define "horse" while yet knowing very little about horses.

Definitions

I want to say more about one aspect of this in particular. Feldman insists, remember, that a good definition first gets the uncontroversial cases right, and so is not susceptible to straightforward refutation. But then it deals also with the puzzling and borderline cases, the things about which we are so far undecided. Hence "we can learn things from good philosophy". But there should be reservations here. Let me first put this in a somewhat abstract form. Suppose there are two purported definitions, each of which deals altogether satisfactorily with the uncontroversial cases, but they have different implications for those remaining. How could there be reason to prefer one of these accounts over its rival? If we are already, or almost, decided about the borderline cases then one of the two is already on the way to being preferred. Waverers might be encouraged to come on board. If we need to make a decision, even if arbitrary, then a stipulative definition might thereafter terminate debate. But in neither case are we learning from the definition, so much as constructing the definition around what, independently and antecedently, we want to say. And it may just be that we are genuinely undecided.

Let us put some flesh on this. I said earlier that someone who is dying is on the way to death. Clearly that is not a definition. But then what is it, really, for someone to be dying? Feldman devotes a chapter to this. This is a worthwhile topic, and his discussion is genuinely illuminating. But it is, once again, structured around the attempt to find a definition of what it is for someone to be dying at t, and it follows the perhaps too familiar strategy of offering, countering and then refining a series of candidates. This is the end point:

x is dying at t = df. at t, x is engaged in a process that would be terminal for x, if it were allowed to reach its conclusion without interference.

(Feldman 1992: 84)[6]

21

Feldman acknowledges that this account contains several "soft spots" (*ibid*.: 85). Even so, it is the best he can come up with, and better than many alternatives. One of its alleged virtues is its handling of Ninian Smart's shrapnel case. A man is wounded. He recovers, but some shrapnel remains inside him. This does not currently cause any difficulties but it will, in time, work its way towards his heart, interfere with normal circulation, and soon thereafter kill him.[7] There is no need to worry about the details of their accounts, but for Smart the man is dying before, for Feldman only when, the shrapnel interferes with heart function. The latter is, he says, the better account: "This seems right to me" (*ibid*.: 85). Perhaps it would seem right to everyone, Smart included, on reflection. But in this case there is no genuine controversy. Perhaps though (as it seems to me) Smart's position remains defensible. But then we still do not have a definition.

We might come at this problem from the other direction. Can we define life? At one point Feldman suggests:

x is alive at *t* = df. *x* is animated at *t* by some DNA or RNA in *x*'s
        cells.   (*Ibid*.: 48)

There are, as he acknowledges, several ways this might be criticized. But consider the points he makes about some imaginary situation, where a "little green man" steps out of a flying saucer and performs in various human-like ways, including offering to scientists here a sample of his "skin", which proves to contain neither of the substances mentioned above. The scientists say:

The Martian is alive, but he contains no DNA or RNA.   (*Ibid*.: 50)

And for Feldman this seems not to be self-contradictory. It could be true, and hence the failure of the definition. But could it be true that the Martian is alive? Or might he be only metaphorically alive, as might be an android or a robot? I just do not see how this could be established, either way, and so do not see how the appearance of controversy could be altogether avoided here. In the dying case Feldman wants to defend his definition. Here he is on the attack. But in both the strategy makes suspect appeals to intuition and relies on spurious assumptions of clarity. And they illustrate the difference between our approaches. Whereas Feldman seems to think there are, albeit sometimes deeply hidden, facts of the matter as to whether things are alive or dead, in rude health or about to expire, on my account there are, in these puzzle cases, at best interest-driven better and worse things to say. And unless we already agree, then neither the counter-example, as in this case, nor the offer of completeness, as in that above, can carry the day.

Analogies

It is going to be useful to look briefly at three further cases, the last two of which have excited considerable philosophical discussion. They throw further light on what we should think and say about death.

Vixens are female foxes. I have little difficulty in thinking that this is true, is always and everywhere true; that "vixen" (as it happens) means "female fox"; that the former can be defined as the latter or even, although this is beginning now to sound rather elevated, that the former can be analysed in terms of the latter. Someone asks, "What's a vixen?" "A female fox" is a good answer. But it would be odd to think that in any of this we are getting hard information about what vixens are, as opposed to what "vixen" means: odd to think we are finding out anything about the nature or essence of vixens.

Many people have asked for a definition of art. They have believed both that it is possible to give logically necessary and sufficient conditions of whether something is a work of art, and to divide the stuff in the world into two kinds: the art and the non-art. And they have believed too that unless we can do this, we do not know, or do not really know, what art is. This all seems to me to be wrong. A number of points can be made. First, unclarity at the margins does not make for unclarity *tout court*. We know that the *Mona Lisa* is a work of art, that bombing Fallujah is not, and we know these things even while being uncertain what to say about a number of problem works. Perhaps if we discovered certain further facts – Leonardo copied, Fallujah was planned by the Chapman brothers – then these judgements would need to be revised. But absenting such discoveries, nothing could persuade us that we are wrong about these cases. Second, uncertainty can be dealt with in different ways. Perhaps the discovery of further facts – this thing is natural and not an artefact – will settle matters. Perhaps we can decide, say for financial reasons, to count something as art. But in many cases it just may be stubbornly indeterminate as to a thing's status. And rather than thinking we do not really know what art is until we have decided about all such cases, we should instead think we do not understand art so long as we believe a decision is needed. So we might grasp all the salient facts about some object without, first, it following, as a derivative fact, that it is, or is not art, and without, second, this being some independent, further and deeper fact about it. Third, it seems clear that whether or not a thing is art depends not on its internal properties alone, but also (and as suggested in the examples above) on its relational properties: how, why and by whom or by what it was made.

A further complexity arises here. What counts as, is classified as, art changes over time. The Pre-Raphaelites would not have thought of conceptual art as art. Must we say either that they or we are wrong about this, or that one concept and definition of art has ceased to exist, and has been replaced by another concept, allowing now for another definition, pointing to another nature? Perhaps it is at least as true simply to say that what art is, and what counts as art, is not always and everywhere the same. And consider a spectrum of cases; there is disagreement as to what art is within a community, or between communities, or across time. If we should think in the last case that there are distinct concepts in play, then it is unclear why we should not think this also in the first. But this is not tempting. What we should think, I suggest, is that the distinctions between rival, and contested, concepts are far from clear.

Consider a different case. "Water is H_2O" is a claim that many of us now will take to be necessarily true, something always and everywhere true, true in all possible worlds. Being H_2O is a necessary and sufficient condition of something's being water. And substances, if unmixed, either are or are not water. There are, and can be, no genuinely indeterminate cases. So whether something is water depends on its internal properties alone, and not on our beliefs about, or interests in the thing. But have we, in assenting to this identity claim, succeeded in analysing the concept of water, so that "water" can now be defined, so that we know what "water" means? Hardly. And we can question any meaning claim on two grounds. Competent language-speakers had a proper grasp of the term "water" before the advent of modern chemistry. And what we now know about water is the result of scientific investigation, rather than philosophical analysis.[8] In learning that water is H_2O, we learn something of what water is, something about its nature, and not something about the concept of water, or what "water" means.[9]

I need to clarify an important point. Current orthodoxy has it that we need to invoke, in making our claims about water and H_2O, a distinction between natural and logical necessities. I think this is broadly right. But, whatever the details of the accounts that others might provide, I want to unpack this in the following way. In saying that water is H_2O in all possible worlds my claim is in fact defeasible. What I believe is that the kind of stuff that we call water – stuff that, knowing it well, we find to behave as we expect water to behave – will turn out to have just this chemical formula. For I believe there is a good degree of fit between this stuff's micro- and macro-properties. So its being

H_2O gives rise to its further properties: its boiling and freezing points, its being – for us – colourless and odourless, its complex relations to life. And were that not so, then there would be no reason for upholding the necessity claim. For suppose there is something with all the important properties of water, but a wholly different chemical constitution. Rather than holding that, because it is not H_2O, this is at best ersatz or fool's water, such stuff gives the lie to the necessity claim. But there is good reason to think there is not and in fact cannot be such stuff.[10]

Compare and contrast these cases. "Vixen" is, for most of us, a quasi-technical term. It can be defined. But in learning what "vixen" means, we do not learn much at all about what a vixen is. The other terms here are non-technical. Perhaps we know well enough what "water" means. And in discovering, via science, that it is H_2O we are finding out important things about what water is, about its nature or essence, rather than more about meaning. Art does not in the same way have a nature or essence; there is not a certain deep structure common to works of art that gives rise to and explains their surface appeal. There are, of course, various activities and processes related to art and art-making that can be further investigated, but to look into the nature of bronze, or linseed oil, is not to explore art's nature. Do we nevertheless know what "art" means? If meaning is allowed to be somewhat vague, and soft-focused then we should say yes. But there does not seem to be, in Feldman's sense, a definition.

What about death? As with art, there is something wide-ranging here, with the one notion pulling together multiple phenomena. Inevitably there are puzzle cases. But in contrast to art, where there is something to be said for exploiting these puzzles and undermining several of the distinctions already in place, most of those dealing with death would, for legal, moral and organizational reasons, prefer to resolve them. As with water, investigations into death are the concern mainly of natural scientists. But even though several of the associated phenomena – putrefaction, entropy, rigor mortis – might have a nature, death itself, in virtue of being so multifaceted, surely does not.[11] Could we nevertheless decide to sharpen up our use of the term, make decisions on the puzzle cases and give a definition of death about as clear as the one we have for vixen? We could, but there is no clear reason to do this; we can introduce new technical terms as needs emerge. Nor is there reason to think that if only we work a little harder we shall discover that there is already a definition in place, already something that death is.

A final point here. A number of writers have suggested that death might be some sort of cluster concept, with the term "death" used in a number of overlapping and criss-crossing ways such that its resistance to ordinary definition can at least thus far be explained.[12] Am I sympathetic? Not very. First, I think we are actually closer to an ordinary definition than the cluster concept allows. Second, and relatedly, aspects of the case for such a concept can be undermined by appeal to the distinction between literal and meta-phorical uses. Third, the starting-point to this, that the notion of a cluster concept is broadly coherent, is one that might be challenged.

Defining death

Feldman sets high standards for a satisfactory definition. Can his demands be met? Clearly, he thinks that in principle they can, and so thinks there are a number of terms that can be satisfactorily defined. But his best endeavours to provide a definition of death all hit problems: "So, though death looms large in our emotional lives, though we hate it, and fear it, and are dismayed by the thought that it will someday overtake us and those we love, we really don't know precisely what death is. The Reaper remains mysterious" (1992: 71). Nevertheless, some suggestions are better, come closer, than others. Here is one:

x dies at t = df. x ceases permanently and irreversibly to be alive at t.
(*Ibid*.: 64)[13]

The objection to this is involved, but in the end uninteresting. Nevertheless it should be considered. The cryonics factory suffers some mishap on Thursday. Thereafter its clients cannot live again. Consider someone who entered on Tuesday. Because of what happened on Thursday, his ceasing to live on Tuesday was permanent. But he did not irreversibly cease to live until Thursday. Thus there is no one time at which he permanently and irreversibly ceased to live. Hence the failure of the definition. Interestingly, Feldman does not consider the modified definition, cutting the reference to permanence. That might appear to hold out more hope. But he does, later, suggest another:

x dies at t = df. (i) x ceases to be alive at or before t and (ii) at t internal changes occur in x that make it physically impossible for x ever to live again.   (*Ibid*.: 65)

This, Feldman thinks, "comes pretty close" to avoiding suspended anima-tion problems. And it comes pretty close to capturing, as well, my rough formulation in terms of irreversible loss of function.[14] The difference between us, of course, is that I think it neither possible nor desirable to get closer than close, whereas Feldman continues to hanker after more.

What about other definitions? Although many writers have had things to say about death, not all of them are offering a definition, in the sense explicated by Feldman. So they can avoid certain criticisms that might otherwise be levelled. Some are. Joel Feinberg is blunt here: "Actually, death is defined as the first moment of subject's non-existence" (1984: 80). This seems wrong on various counts. I shall need to return to it. Another example is John Lizza, who in a recent book identifies and modifies an earlier account offered by Jay Rosenberg.[15] And he maintains that death is a "change in kind of (a) living entity marked by the loss of an essential property" (Lizza 2006: 32).[16]

Lizza's account, like Rosenberg's, is unpersuasive. They both imply that living things are essentially alive, such that, with death, these living things cease to exist.[17] We have considered this above. Olson at least acknowledges the peculiarity of this view, and attempts to defend it. Rosenberg and Lizza offer no such discussion and put forward this essentialist thesis with only minimal comment. But even if we were essentially alive there are, for Lizza's account, still further problems. Do living things exhibit only one essential property, that of being alive? He might say no, but insist that if a thing loses any essential property then it ceases to exist. So if a living thing loses any such property it ceases to be a living thing. But how does this connect with death? A magician turns the Queen into a swan. She ceases to exist, but it is not clear that she dies. And, in contrast to Rosenberg, Lizza makes no mention of irreversibility. The next day the magician turns the swan into a queen, and a queen who is qualitatively identical to the Queen. It is tempting to say the Queen ceased to exist but was then brought back into existence. But it is not tempting, I think, to suppose that she died, and was then brought back to life. Finally there is an element of redundancy in the account. For surely every change in kind is marked by the loss of an essential property, and vice versa. But Lizza's position might be explained, if not defended. Although it does not show in the definition, he is principally concerned with persons. Suppose persons are essentially conscious beings. Then it may be plausible to connect person death, supposing persons are things that can literally die, with the loss of this essential property and with ceasing to be. But it is hard to see, first, why we should think that persons can die, or second how this even begins to be viable as an account of death in general.

There are further purported definitions that are explicitly concerned with human death. I postpone their consideration until Chapter 3.

What death is

Death is the irreversible breakdown of, or loss of integrated functioning in, the organism as a whole. Is this, then, a definition? It is, I think, and, as I have suggested, something close, and perhaps as close as one can expect to get. In grasping this we grasp at least something of what death is. Correct use of the term links it to just this phenomenon, for all actual and ordinarily possible cases. And there is a considerable degree of resilience to the claim: it could not become false overnight, as a result of some advances in science or technology. But certainly we do not have here all that Feldman demands of a definition. I am not sure that this claim is eternally true, or even eternally true for this concept; nor that it would be true (or indeed what it would be for it to be true) even if no one adopts it. I do not think we arrive at this result by *a priori* philosophical analysis so much as by attending to what people say, and engaging in some rudimentary fieldwork. Nor do I think that armed with this definition we can handle the entire range of puzzle cases. Nor, finally, is it clear that we overcome the obscurity condition, with all the terms in the *definiens* perspicuous. Feldman's point here is itself a little obscure. He says that terms figuring in the analysis must not be "as obscure as the term being analyzed" (1992: 13). This suggests that lesser degrees of obscurity are compatible with a definition's success. Yet elsewhere he implies that anything less than perspicuity will to some degree undermine the definition. But then there is a quite general difficulty to be overcome. A bachelor is an unmarried man. But this leaves open the issue of whether there are Martian bachelors and, more mundanely, invites questions about the boy–man divide. A vixen is a female fox, but precisely what it is to be female and what it is to be a fox might be thought somewhat unclear. If we need complete perspicuity then even these terms are not yet successfully defined. Indeed, it is beginning to look as if we cannot define anything unless we can define everything. And if we need perspicuity then I have not defined death. For there are puzzles about organisms, about functioning and about irreversibility. I turn to these now.

Organisms

Almost all the things that we encounter can confidently and successfully be divided into organisms and non-organisms. We know that cats, trees and bacteria are organisms, while mountains, bicycles and tennis matches are not. We know also, or so I have claimed, that organs and pieces of tissue are not organisms, even if they might contain organisms, individual cells, bacteria and so on within them.

But there are puzzles about certain of the margins, and about a handful of anomalous cases. One puzzle is about whether what exists after death is itself an organism, although dead, or some other sort of naturally occurring stuff. I have signalled my view on this. Another is whether all living organisms will, and literally, die. I have left the amoeba issue unresolved. We can kill them. But it seems, also, that they might be able to cease to exist without dying.[18]

There are further problems. One concerns numbers. Is some underground fungus one big organism with a number of local eruptions, or a network of individuals, somehow joined together? Similarly for suckering trees and shrubs, such as the rhododendrons, or rhododendron, in my garden. This has a bearing on death, for it is not clear, in digging something up, whether we are killing one thing or merely damaging something larger. And there is a problem about boundaries. Although most parts of an organism are not themselves organisms there are two sorts of puzzle case. One concerns those small bits of organisms that appear not to be organisms of the host kind, and appear, also, not to be clearly alive. But they can turn into organisms. I am thinking of acorns, grass seed, little bits of twig or leaf. Are these organisms? The other involves those pared down organisms that might still be claimed to be the very same thing they earlier were. A cat can lose a tail, a tree a branch, and yet remain an organism. How far might this paring down go? I would exist, and be an organism, without my arms and legs. Could I exist without a head, or conversely, as a head alone? More generally, must we retain a certain quantity of the original parts, or does the quality of the parts also matter, with some parts counting for more than others?

These problems bear on known and actual cases. But there are further problems when imaginary and hypothetical cases are considered. The organisms we know are carbon based. Might they not be, with alternatively structured living things encountered in space or fabricated on earth? Consider two versions of such fabrication. We might try to build a living thing just from metal. Or we might take living things, say human beings, and endeavour to forge links between them such that they become a superorganism. Could we succeed?[19]

I raise these questions in order to suggest that it is not altogether clear just what an organism is. By that I do not mean, of course, that there are facts about organisms that we have not yet discovered (although certainly there are many such undiscovered facts about individual organisms) but rather that we have not altogether decided what to say about such cases. Does this matter? If we need definitions to know what things are, and what words mean, and if definitions need to adjudicate over all actual and possible cases, then it matters a lot. But there is no such pair of needs.[20] And we can, I think, profitably employ our useful even if incomplete grasp of what an organism is in a similarly useful though incomplete "definition" of what death is.

Functioning

What is it for something to function? We can point to paradigm cases of functioning and non-functioning: you and I are functioning organisms; Tutankhamen and Lenin are not. Similarly for artefacts: there are clear examples of functioning and non-functioning televisions, and cars, and vacuum cleaners. But even if we suppose that light bulbs, for example, either work or do not, surely, for any complex entity, functioning can occur to a degree: and in at least two ways. All the parts can be working, and working together, but not all of them well. Or the parts might individually be working, but not well connected together.

Your television is not in perfect running order, but it is functioning in part. Certainly we can, in principle at least, and very probably in practice, say just which parts are working, and to what degree. In principle, at least, this is straightforward. But is it similarly straightforward to decide when it is functioning as an integrated whole? This might at first appear so, and we could perhaps make it so by, for example, stipulating that such functioning occurs only when all the parts are working to some degree, and they are all working together. But it seems that, in fact, some judgement is needed as to when to apply such a phrase. Is it so working when it will receive only one or two channels, or when there is no sound, or when you keep losing the picture? We might give an answer, and be able to defend it, but equally we might acknowledge that the answer is, over a range of cases, somewhat arbitrary.

Similarly for organisms. Perhaps we can imagine that organisms, like light bulbs, flip between two clearly contrasting states in an instant. But they do not. Almost always there are deteriorations both before and after death, with some function loss before, and at least some residual functioning after the thing has died. Clearly an organism can lose some of its parts – an arm, a branch – and yet still be functioning as an entirety. So, as is often said, we should not confuse the organism as a whole with the whole organism.[21] But suppose those parts remain. I have in my mouth what is at least described as a dead tooth. If, as it seems, this is still a part of the whole then, or so it seems, I am no longer functioning as an integrated whole. But I am not dead. So, clearly,

30

something here has to give. In another puzzle case all the parts are working, and are linked, but the link goes via some external mechanism. The sound and picture are synchronized, but only if the engineer is constantly tweaking the controls. Or someone remains alive, but only if an array of machines coordinate the functioning of the different organs.

Suppose we try to circumvent these problems by suggesting that for integrated holistic functioning all that is needed is that a thing do, to some degree, what it is supposed to do. So non-integrated parts and external mechanisms are not in themselves problematic. But it is not really clear what organisms are supposed to do and, in so far as this is clear, unclear that death altogether prevents them from doing it. I shall say more about this, related to human beings in particular, in Chapter 3.

We should note some of the real differences between plants and animals here. But perhaps that is too crude, and the distinction we want is that between plants and higher animals, say vertebrates. The suggestion that a human being, a sheep or an eel is a living organism when and only when it functions as an integrated whole has, in spite of its problems, some plausibility. There is a brain, a central nervous system and a series of demands on the organism that require a coordinated and sophisticated response. But the situation is surely very different with a sponge or an oak tree. A tree can be alive when most of its parts are dead. And the call for integration is faint.[22]

My account of what death is makes reference to this integrated functioning. Such a notion is, I think, tolerably clear over a wide range of cases. But as with the organism, there are several local difficulties. Nevertheless, so long as we remain sensitive to this, appeal to such functioning can, and usefully, figure in the "definition".

Irreversibility

What does it mean to say that death is irreversible? Does it mean that it is logically impossible for the dead to live again? Suppose that the dead do not exist, and that there cannot be two beginnings of existence. Then it is logically impossible for the dead to live again. On this view death is very strongly irreversible. But we should not believe either that death brings about non-existence, or that existence cannot begin twice. And most of us do not believe that death is strongly irreversible, and that it is logically impossible for someone to return from the dead. If we did believe this then many of the stories in the Bible – the resurrection of Jesus, the raising of Lazarus – would strike us as unintelligible or incoherent. But, typically, they do not strike us that way, even if they do strike us as far-fetched. Even if God cannot square the circle, or create married bachelors, he can (if there is a God) raise the dead. And if he did restore Jesus, and Lazarus, he can restore any one of us. So if we persist in the view that death is logically irreversible, then no one is dead. The strong reading should go.

We might say, instead, that if someone or something has died then it is physically impossible that they should live again. So neither doctors nor ordinary good fortune are able to bring someone back from the dead. Doctors might revive people after certain vital signs – respiration, heartbeat, reflex responses – have been lost, but some such signs can be lost before death sets in. For some such signs can be lost without a breakdown occurring in the organism as a whole. They might even be able to revive people after integrated functioning has ceased, if that ceasing is but temporary, as in cryonics. And, as I have suggested, where plants are concerned there already are dormant states where there is nothing going on. But again, reversals here will not count as raising the dead. Death is, in fact, final. And we should treat so-called near-death experiences as precisely that, and so altogether unilluminating about what it might be like to be dead.

On this second view, whether someone is dead can, in principle at least, be ascertained by knowledge both of the laws of physics and of the current internal condition of the person's body. And, assuming that the laws of physics are fixed, this implies that what it is to be dead, what is involved in that, is invariant over time and place. Invent a time machine, and zap someone who is dead in an eighth-century Scandinavian village into a twenty-first-century New York hospital and, whatever the doctors do to him, he remains dead. There might seem to be a complication here. You might think that we need to take the physical environment into account. Perhaps someone in a certain condition might not be dead on Jupiter where temperatures are low and pressures high, but would be dead on earth, where conditions are otherwise. But this is a mistake. First, Jupiter is a red herring; we can simulate these conditions in the New York hospital. Second, we should not confuse the conditions in which someone might die with those in which he is already dead. On the current view, if someone is dead, then their body is in a certain condition. And if it is for any moment in that condition then no change in external circumstances could restore the person to life, even if such changes could then make a difference to the corpse's future, and even if, had they been in that condition prior to death, they would not have died.

Does this physically irreversible view imply, also, that the criteria for being dead are, for a given kind of thing, similarly invariant? Here there are complications. Follow, more or less, Feldman's account of criteria, and we still need to note, first, that even if it is unlikely the signs themselves may vary – different environments might give rise to different marks of death – and, second, that the easily recognized signs will vary – technological developments allow us in some times or places to detect marks that are elsewhere and at other times undetectable.

There is a difficulty for this view. If we appeal to what is logically irreversible none of those we think of as dead are truly dead. But if we appeal to physical irreversibility many of those who were diagnosed as dead were not then dead and, for many more, the diagnosis is unreliable. For, as a matter of fact, we know relatively little of the complex physiological processes involved, and so know relatively little about what is and what is not physically possible for an organism in some critical state. Misdiagnosis might not much matter if we are sorting through chrysanthemums in the garden, but surely does matter when we are dealing with people. We need to be able to tell whether someone is dead or alive.

Yet the difficulty here may be exaggerated. The currently prevailing view is that brain death is the criterion of human death. So we think that those people diagnosed as dead before brain death occurs are misdiagnosed. In millions of cases people have been diagnosed as dead when heartbeat and breathing stopped, but before brain death set in. Yet in almost all of those cases brain death was in fact inevitable, and inevitable only a few minutes later. There just was not any possibility of intervening, and preventing death. So, even though they were declared dead ahead of time, this misdiagnosis was not of practical importance. But now as people were always wrong to think of heart death as death, for heart death is reversible, so we might be wrong to think of brain death as death, for brain death too might be reversible. It is not yet, or here, reversible in practice; it is technologically impossible to recover from brain death, but it does not follow from that that it is not reversible in principle, or physically possible. And this possibility might take two forms. There might always be a very remote chance of someone's recovering naturally or spontaneously from brain death. And there might come to be, as technologies are improved, a more or less routine procedure for reversing what is now known as, and identified as, brain death.[23] Moreover, because of technologies already in place, we cannot say that here too death is inevitable only a few minutes later. Most diagnoses of brain death occur in technology-rich hospital situations. And it is possible there to arrest a good deal of further decay, either at room temperature with complex machines, or by freezing. Perhaps, if we sustain them as best we can, we shall find that in time the supposedly brain dead might be more fully revived. But there are, as well, more immediate difficulties. Suppose that it is not physically possible to reverse the disassembly brought about by cremation. Perhaps those who are cremated are dead. But it may be that in cremating people we are killing them, rather than disposing of their remains.

There seem to be problems, then, in holding to this second account. Perhaps only a handful of those declared dead are truly dead. For perhaps death comes much more slowly, and demands much more devastation, than we currently believe. And so a third view is that we should make technological possibilities the yardstick: an organism is dead when it suffers an overall functional breakdown, and when this is not reversed naturally, and cannot now in practice be reversed artificially. So death is determined by appeal to what is technologically possible. There are clear advantages. A declaration of death will properly be made when integrated functioning ceases, and when, in fact, it is appropriate to give up hope, and to cease treatment. And setting aside a handful of cases in which the signs are misread, our current diagnoses in terms of brain death, along with earlier appeals to pulse and breathing, will be rendered correct. For, in fact, we can do nothing now to reverse this condition, no matter what might in the future be possible, just as, in the past, people could do nothing, then, to reverse conditions that now are reversible. On the other hand, as this last point itself suggests, the proposal introduces an element of relativism: your being dead will not depend on your internal condition alone, but also on where and when you happen to be. Someone might be dead in the Amazon jungle when the very same person, in the same physical condition would not be dead were they in the middle of São Paulo. And someone might be alive in London today while, in the very same city, and the very same condition, they would have been dead some two centuries ago.

Is this problematic? You might think not. There are related notions – those of a fatal disease or terminal illness and, more generally, just that of dying – whose applications vary with circumstances. So why not also for death? Further, some of the links between death and value loss might suggest that technological possibilities are the ones that count. There are legal, and for relatives psychological, consequences of declaring someone dead. It seems appropriate to bring these consequences into play when, in fact, nothing more can be done to reverse a condition, even if it is still physically possible that it be reversed. Still, many will think it odd to suggest that whether someone is dead can depend on things other than the condition of their body, and to suppose that accidents of history and geography can make the difference.

The Becker–Hershenov model

These puzzles about irreversibility have prompted David Hershenov, in a recent paper (2003), to revisit an account of death proposed some time ago by Lawrence Becker (1975). Becker appeals to a distinction that I have been making above, between those cases where, after some trauma, an organism recovers normal functioning on its own, and those where outside intervention is needed. I have not wanted to exploit this distinction; Becker does. So consider, as in Hershenov's illustration, two people who fall off a ship and take in enough water to prevent normal functioning in their hearts and lungs. Both are fished out. Alfie needs, and is given, CPR, after which breathing recommences. Babs recovers on her own. According to Becker and Hershenov, this self-restarting makes all the difference. Babs, as intuitively we mostly agree, never died. Not so Alfie. He did die, just because he was unable, on his own, to recover from his mishap, and to restart the operation of his heart and lungs. The doctors brought him back to life.

Surely, this exaggerates the powers of medicine. We might grant someone's being brought back to life in special circumstances, by divine intervention. But there are millions of cases where doctors arrest and reverse a decline. We are happy to say of such cases that the patient was near to death, and that without medical assistance would certainly have died. We are disinclined to say that they are already, although as it turns out temporarily, dead. So why make such a suggestion?

Hershenov acknowledges the counterintuitive component here. But he thinks that even so, Becker's proposal fits best overall with the central desiderata in an account of death. For death is a biological notion, and is "best thought of as a non-relational alteration in an individual's body or organs" (Hershenov 2003: 93). Becker's account seems to fit the bill here, as whether or not a body self-starts will, apparently, depend on its internal condition. In contrast, an account that links reversibility to technology will, as noted above, imply that whether or not someone is dead might vary with their location. But even granted that there is considerable appeal in a non-relational account, what does Becker's proposal have over the competing non-relational account, which holds that death occurs when loss of integrated functioning is physically impossible to reverse?

Hershenov imagines a cryogenics programme where bodies are frozen after cardiopulmonary failure, but before further decay sets in. But now:

> Do we really want to say that they are not dead because it is possible that some day science will know how not only to reverse

the cancer or heart disease that caused their lungs and heart to cease, but will also have the technology to thaw them out without tissue damage and also to restart their vital organs? ... it seems that in such a future the only people who could be declared dead are those whose lives end as a result of terrible explosions or collisions, or due to some other violence that prevents them from being preserved intact. Millions, even billions of people would be alive for centuries. (*Ibid.*: 92)

There are some puzzles about this case. Freezing occurs before brain or brainstem damage sets in. And so, on the current understanding of death these people are clearly not dead even if, as Hershenov allows, they are not clearly alive. And there seems to be some conflation of epistemic and physical possibilities in play here. People are not dead, on one plausible account, if it is genuinely physically possible to reverse their condition. No one is suggesting that our ignorance of what is physically possible is enough to render someone alive. Nor is it clear where Hershenov gets his extremely high numbers. Even if people are declared dead prematurely, excepting those cases where freezing occurs, death-inducing decay will inevitably occur in a matter of hours or days. But perhaps these are details. The central claim is that on the view that you are alive so long as it is physically possible for your condition to be reversed, it is highly likely that considerable numbers continue to be declared dead prematurely. The determination of death is, as it were, no longer in our grasp. And that is an unwelcome result.

The Becker model hopes to avoid this problem. It is assumed that we know enough about physiology to be reasonably confident about those cases where self-restarting is possible.[24] And so the question "Is she dead or alive?" can, in most cases, be answered with reasonable certainty. But, of course, in most cases doubt will last for seconds or minutes at most. Either bodies will restart or they will not. So, either way, there is no longer the risk of serious miscounting. But there are problems for this view. First, if doctors intervene early they may muddy the waters. We count someone as dead and restored when, if they had been left alone for a while longer, they would have restarted on their own, and so never have been dead at all. Second, the distinction between self- and non-self-restarting is not clear. It is not as if people either recover altogether on their own, or need the full resources of modern technology to get them back on their feet. Someone might recover if they are given mouth to mouth resuscitation, or they are turned over so that water can escape, or they are slapped, or they are brought from the cold into the warmth. Imagine two people on a hillside suffering from hypothermia.

Their hearts have stopped. One of them happens to roll downhill, to a camp fire. The other is dragged to the fire. Both recover. It does not seem right to think that one of them, but just one of them, died. Third, a general point follows from this. Whether someone self-restarts will depend not only on their bodily state, but on the environment in which they are located. So what was attractive about the view that death depends just on someone's internal condition is not, in fact, in place. Fourth, the self-restarting account is both radically and gratuitously revisionary. We have forever thought of death as the end, as final, as a condition where, miracles apart, there is no possibility of a revival. And we are already accommodated to believing that when someone is revived, a misdiagnosis must have occurred. The Becker–Hershenov view asks us to give up on all this and to adopt such locutions as "she was dead for a few hours last week", "he keeps dying" and the like. Further, as there will continue to be situations where doctors cannot help, and where burial or cremation is called for, then there will, surely, be a need for new terms to replace those we already have. The dead cannot be revived. Neither, I think can Becker's proposal.

We can agree, then, that death is irreversible. But the competing claims of the physical and technological interpretations have not yet been altogether resolved. I want to make just two points. First, consider the prevailing view that the brain dead are dead. Brain death is technologically irreversible, but is unlikely, I think, to be physically irreversible. So here the two interpretations come apart. Yet suppose that this prevailing view is false, and that death involves significantly greater systemic deterioration. Then the chances for physical reversibility will begin to seem less likely, and the interpretations will more clearly converge. Second, suppose there remains, nevertheless, some measure of discrepancy. Perhaps people just have not thought through the fine detail of these competing accounts. But then, even if less so than the self-restarting model considered above, any suggestion as to a resolution will be revisionary. And it is not clear how that could be warranted. Some unclarity at the boundaries can, and should, be tolerated.

Summary

I might appear to have suggested, in the above, that we do need to get clear about the precise role of irreversibility within the notion of death. But this is not really so. Our ordinary notion gives space to irreversibility, for we think that death is the final end, and the suggestion that people might return from the dead, excepting special circumstances and divine intervention,[25] is one that puts this notion under strain. But "might return" here is intentionally ambiguous. Strain is considerable if we imagine actual cases featuring such returns. It is minor, and perhaps bearable, if we consider only that the remote physical possibility of such return cannot be ruled out. Our ordinary thinking about death has not extended that far.

In the end, then, we are reasonably clear about the reversibility condition. And I think we are clearer about this than about the other two matters discussed above, concerning organisms and functioning. So even though I have given a general account of death, and said what in all actual and many possible cases it involves, we are, in view of this unclarity, a good way from a definition. Is this a problem? We are altogether clear, in almost every case, whether someone is dead or alive. Often, when we are not clear, we need just a little more information of a straightforward kind. We are similarly clear about higher animals. We are rather less clear, I suggest, about plants. One issue here is whether the processes occurring within a plant are taken, or should be taken, as signs of life. Another is whether, assuming there is life, this is a property of the original plant, or some successor. And we are less clear about fictional and imaginary cases. But, of course, I do not mean that the little green man is in fact alive, or dead, or in some third condition, but that we have not yet discovered which. Rather, I mean that nothing we say about life and death, none of the distinctions we currently draw, determine what we should say about this case and, until we decide what to say, there just is no fact of the matter as to which of these conditions he is in. What this suggests, I think, and what is in any event worth spelling out, is that there are facts elsewhere. So it is a fact that Lenin is dead and that Putin, at least as I write, is alive.

In sum, we know a lot about death. There are some puzzles around the margins, and we are unable strictly to define it. But this is not to say that death is deeply mysterious, or enigmatic, or that we really do not know what it is.

3

Human beings

Allow that we know something about what death, in general, is. What, now, can we know about human death? This is a matter of considerable importance, for human death, is, of course, our death. What is involved in our deaths? When do we die?

In this chapter I want to present and defend an account of human death. Death is the irreversible breakdown of the organism as a whole. There are human organisms. They die when they suffer irreversible breakdown as a whole. When does that occur? A now familiar, even if not fully established, view is that human death, and indeed all higher vertebrate death, occurs when there is irreversible breakdown in just one organ, the brain. Many people talk of brain death. I have signalled, already, my reservations about speaking of organ, as opposed to organism, death. But this phrase is widely used, and it would be inconvenient to try to avoid it here. So the view I want to consider is that we die when, and only when, our brains die.

In the section that follows I sketch something of the substance and development of the brain death account of human death. Our organisms are complex, and the brain particularly so, and there is a good deal of technical, scientific and indeed historical information involved in fully describing the goings on here. Much of this has, by many of us, simply to be taken on trust, and much of it is not directly relevant to the philosophical problems that are here the main concern. So my account focuses, as far as possible, on the uncontroversial key elements of the story. A more detailed account is given in the Appendix. In subsequent sections I consider objections to the brain death account. The major objections might usefully be divided into two groups. There are, first, those that target the definition of death and aim, on various grounds, to resist the account I gave in Chapter 2. Some of these objections insist that this account is altogether wrong while others, and these are the more interesting, hold that it is wrong for creatures like us. As the brain death criterion assumes a general account of what death is, so, if that account fails, the criterion fails along with it. But all these objections, I argue, are unimpressive. The definition still stands. The second set of objections accepts this, but take issue with the brain death criterion. The failure of the one organ is not to be straightforwardly equated with death of the organism. Certain of the objections here, or so I claim, carry some weight.

A particular issue that threads through the chapter is that of the relation between death and the loss of value. Unsurprisingly, interest in this relation is pronounced where human death is concerned. In a final section I consider this relation in some detail.

Brain death, and human death

What happens when someone dies? How can we tell whether a person is alive or dead? These are connected, but nevertheless distinct, questions. Many complex physiological changes are involved in human death. Most of us, including doctors, have no need of knowledge of them all. But some of us, especially doctors, need to be able to distinguish between the living and the dead.

Until relatively recently loss of heartbeat and respiration, temporary interruptions aside, were sure signs that someone had died. These signs were linked with others: loss of consciousness, failure of responses, a drop in body temperature. So there was in place a cardio-respiratory criterion of death. Someone was dead when and only when their heart and lungs were unable to function.

Towards the middle of the twentieth century the development of various resuscitation and ventilation techniques, along with progress in transplant surgery, led to the undermining of this established criterion. It became possible to sustain various functions of the body for extended periods even while the heart and lungs were inoperative. In some cases, as with a successful heart transplant, all of the functions could later be restored, and the patient returned to full health. These patients were not dead and, on almost all views, had never died. In others, as with those having suffered severe brain damage, heart and lung function could, with assistance, be sustained even though it seemed to some that, as consciousness could not be restored, the patient was already dead. The cardio-respiratory criterion was in trouble.

How is this to be resolved, and a coherent account of what death involves to be reintroduced into clinical practice? There are various prognoses following an accident, a head injury, or a setback on the operating table. In the best cases there is full recovery. But contrast two cases in which recovery is far from complete and consciousness is forever lost. In the first of these there is some brain damage, but not enough to prevent the patient, unaided, from breathing, regulating body temperature and so on. In the second case the injuries to the brain are more severe, and these basic functions can be sustained only with machines. The first patient here is, on widespread current understanding, in a deep coma or PVS.[1] But she is nevertheless alive. The second patient, on the same understanding, is brain dead. Thus he is dead.

The brain is a highly complex organ. But its basics can, for present purposes, be made reasonably clear. Consciousness resides in the upper brain, or cerebrum. The lower brain, or brainstem, controls most of the functioning in the rest of the body. It controls, as well, functioning in the upper brain. If there are certain sorts of irreversible damage to either the brainstem or to the whole brain then both consciousness and control are irretrievably lost. If such damage is restricted to the upper brain, then even if consciousness is lost, organization and control can continue.

Brain death theorists, those who support the brain death criterion of human death, hold first that when and only when the brain is dead is integrated functioning of the organism as a whole irretrievably lost. Then they hold, second, and in line with the biological account, that without this integrated functioning the patient is dead. Brain death is, then, necessary and sufficient for organism death. Those patients in whom cardio-respiratory activity is altogether reliant on machines are not functioning as wholes, and so are dead. These theorists hold, also, that consciousness is not essential to human life. Thus damage to the upper brain does not, in itself, render the patient dead, for such damage does not, in itself, prevent overall integrated functioning from continuing. Hence those in deep coma and PVS remain alive.

That is a sketch. It invites a number of questions about a number of topics. In the following four subsections I shall endeavour to anticipate and deal with several of these.

The brain

What is so special about the brain? Why single out one organ, and say that its death is necessary and sufficient for the death of the organism as a whole? It needs to be noted that the brain is distinctive in a number of different ways.

41

First, in so far as it controls functioning elsewhere it can rightly be claimed to be that without which the body fails to function as a whole. Let us say that it is analogous to the programming box in a heating system. No other organ plays such a role. Second, it cannot be replaced with either an organic transplant or a mechanical substitute. So it looks as if it is altogether plausible to hold that in order to survive we need both what the brain does, and the brain to do it. Most other organs are either clearly expendable – the eyes, one kidney – or are replaceable – the heart, the second kidney.

Even if it is accepted that the brain is necessary for life, it might be less clearly sufficient. To go back to the analogy, there is more to heating than the programmer. And there is more to an organism than a functioning brain. But, at least regarding real-world clinical situations, this betrays some misunderstanding. And the analogy can only be pushed so far. For problems elsewhere in the organism can themselves bring about brain death. If, through failure of the cardio-respiratory system, the brain is deprived of oxygen for several minutes it will be irreparably damaged.[2] It is as if when the heating system breaks down, so too does the programmer. The two elements stand or fall together. And so we do not, at least just yet, need to consider the hypothetical situation where the brain in isolation remains alive and so, on the account offered so far, lays claim itself to be a living organism.

The brain is said to be special in a further way. Consider the heart. Loss of heart function causes brain death. But there is a time lag here. So loss of heart function is not in itself death, even if it is a precursor. But there is no corresponding time lag between loss of brain function and loss of function in the organism as whole.[3] Hence the view of at least some brain death theorists seems to be that brain death *is* organism death, rather than leads to it, or causes it. The details of the argument here, and some reservations about it, are considered more fully below.

One final point. As I said, the brain houses overall functioning and consciousness. Brain death theorists differentiate here: functioning is necessary for life, consciousness is not. Both are sufficient for life, just because functioning is sufficient, and functioning is necessary for consciousness. The upper brain will not work on its own. Yet suppose that consciousness were housed in a separate organ, such that it could continue even when the brain was dead. We can imagine that might put the brain death criterion under pressure.

Definitions, criteria and tests

I want to persist with a "definition" of death that is thoroughly general, and applies to all the things that can literally die. Most of these have no brain. And so, if we are unpacking the meaning of the term "death" the brain in particular needs no mention. But as we can define, or quasi-define, death in general, so we can also define, or quasi-define, brain death. That is a legitimate enterprise. And it remains legitimate, I think, even if we hold that the brain, as an organ rather than an organism, cannot literally die. So I shall allow, at least as a metaphor, that when it ceases irreversibly to function as an integrated whole, the brain is dead. But it is one thing to define brain death, and quite another to refer to the brain within a definition of death. Several writers do this, many of them thinking we have now a new definition, or a redefinition of what death is. This is a mistake. It comes about in part as a result of considerable imprecision in talking of definitions, and in part because organism death follows on from brain death without a time lag. But to explain is not to excuse. And we should think of brain death as a mark or sign that the human being has died, and so should think of it as a criterion of death in such cases.

However, it should be noted that this does not mesh altogether well with Feldman's account of criteria. For brain death, on two counts, is not amenable to direct observation, and so is not "a fairly easily recognisable property that serves as an indicator of death" (Feldman 1992: 14–15).

The first concerns irreversibility. Even if we can directly observe that some condition obtains we cannot in the same way observe that it must obtain, or that having once obtained must now continue to obtain. So given the link between death and irreversibility we cannot directly observe that the brain is dead. Nevertheless, it is clear that we can often have good grounds for inferring, from the condition of something, the trajectory of its future condition, and so can easily see, even if we cannot directly see, that an organ or organism is dead. The second is more important. Often, the condition of the brain cannot be directly observed. Even though we can look closely at an extracted brain in a laboratory, we cannot do this in those cases where diagnosis of its condition most matters, and where there is still a question about whether patients or victims are alive or dead. In these circumstances, then, the condition of the brain does not offer an easily detectable criterion of some further condition's obtaining. And a number of theorists have insisted on the need here for a threefold distinction, between definitions, criteria and tests, and thus distinguish between the brain death criterion for organism death, and the battery of empirical tests needed for diagnosing brain death.[4] What are these? Interestingly, the standard tests for brain death are just those employed in connection with the cardio-respiratory criterion: absence of breathing, pulse, reflex responses, pupil dilation. And an upshot here is that in a number of jurisdictions there are currently two criteria in place: the patient is declared dead when tests show her to be either brain dead or to have lost, and irreversibly, cardio-respiratory function.

Organs and function

An important distinction needs to be noted. Our normal concern, in matters of human health, is not for an organ as such, but for the continuation of the role that organ plays in our organism's overall functioning. Often, the distinction here is academic. If you lose your eyes, you cannot see.[5] But increasingly an organ's function can be replaced, either by a transplanted organ, or by some mechanical substitute. Thus the death of the heart was once, but is no longer, sufficient for death of the animal.

This again makes for certain complications in understanding the position of the brain death criterion. Consider a particular animal, or organism, whose prognosis is in question. What is wrong with the cardio-respiratory criterion? Heart death and lung death – the irreversible breakdown of these organs – is not sufficient for organism death. For we might make use of transplants. Nevertheless, it surely seems as if irreversible loss of cardio-respiratory function is sufficient. No animal can survive the loss of these organs together with both the absence of transplants and the failure to provide some mechanical substitute. So the irreversible loss of these particular organs is not, while irreversible loss of their function is, sufficient for death. (Note, though, an ambiguity here. It is the overall loss of heart function that is sufficient for death, not the loss of function in a particular organ. You can, at least in this case, survive a transplant.) Conversely, the presence of the living organ is not sufficient for organism life, as is evidenced, clearly, in transplant surgery. What about the organ's function? Here there is an ambiguity. You might think that a living and healthy heart is itself a functioning heart. Or you might think a heart only functions when it performs, within an organism, the role the heart standardly performs. But either way, heart function is not sufficient for life. Even if the living heart, on its way between donor and recipient, is a functioning heart, still it is not at that time supporting life. Nor is it necessarily supporting life when it, or a mechanical substitute, is again implanted and pumping blood. First, it may be functioning, and supporting life, after a transplant, in a different body. The original organism is dead. Second, and more importantly, it may be functioning, although machine assisted, within a brain-dead organism. And in this case, on the standard view, it is again not supporting life. For, as it is not functioning as an integrated whole, so, allegedly, the organism is dead.[6]

It is similar, but not altogether the same, for the brain. Again, there is a distinction between organ death and function loss. As with the heart, irreversible loss of brain function is sufficient for death. But here there are available neither transplants nor mechanical substitutes. So brain death is sufficient for the irreversible loss of brain function and so, in turn, sufficient for organism death. Matters concerning the living brain, and the presence of brain function are more complicated. As there are no substitutes, brain function can be supplied only by the brain. Suppose, as with the heart, that we contrast a detached living brain, on the one hand, with a brain *in situ*, on the other. Shall we say, of the latter, that even though there is brain function, you might not be alive? Clearly not. This is sufficient for integrated organism functioning. In the real-world clinical situation, then, as long as the brain is alive so too is the patient whose brain it is. What about the detached brain? Is it, when alive, functioning? Some people think that the puzzle present in the heart case is absent here. For they deny that the brain is just another, albeit important, organ. We can lose certain parts – eyes, a kidney – and still survive. How far can we take this? On some views a detached brain is simply a maximally pared down organism. So wherever there is a living brain there is a living organism, and thus brain function. Wherever there is brain function there is a living organism, and, as only the brain can supply brain function, a living brain. Evidently, some organisms do not have brains. But wherever there is a human organism there is, on the view expressed here, a living and functioning brain. And wherever there is such a brain, there is a human organism. It does not immediately or obviously follow from this that the organism to be found where your brain is to be found is you. Nevertheless, those believing that a detached brain is an organism mostly believe that no identity shift is involved in the paring down. I return to some of theses issues both briefly below and, in more detail, in Chapter 9.

The view outlined just above is a further optional component within animalism. Both animalists and non-animalists might reject it. And few supporters of the brain death criterion go this far. On the standard view, the brain is an organ, and not an organism. So, at least in theory, the brain can be alive while the organism that housed it is dead.

Innovation and motivation

There is considerable dispute about just how innovative or radical the intro-duction of the brain death criterion has been. As I have noted, some have claimed that we are now working with a new definition of death.[7] That would indeed be radical. But this is just a mistake. Rather, at best, a new criterion is in play.

But is the criterion of death really different, now that explicit attention to the condition of the brain plays such a central role? In my sketch of the current picture I reported on the various changes supposedly brought about by the shift from the cardio-respiratory to the brain death criterion of human death. But, in light of the clarifications made above, certain of these should now be seen as exaggerated. And, as noted, the old and new criteria are often employed in tandem. So we need to consider in a little more detail just how the old and the new accounts might best be interpreted.

Did people in the past believe that loss of heart function was sufficient for death? No. For it has long been known that the heart can stop beating for a short period, and then start, or be started, again. They believed that irrevers-ible loss of such function was sufficient for death and believed too that if the heart stopped beating for several minutes, or if it was damaged in such a way as to preclude its restarting, then heart function was irreversibly lost. So heart death was believed sufficient for human death. The former belief is still in place today. The latter belief, construed in terms of technological impossibili-ties, was true. I do not know how many people ever thought it was physically impossible to replace one heart with another.

Did people in the past believe that the condition of the brain was in no way implicated in human death? No. They believed that when we die almost all our organs cease irreversibly to function, even if there is residual activity in certain of these organs. They believed that human death is sufficient for brain death. And so they believed heart death was sufficient for brain death.

This so far overlooks details as to timings. We believe that there can be a time lag between heart death, on the one hand, and brain and organism death, on the other. And whether or not it is technologically possible, it is physically possible to reverse the organism's loss of function, and the brain's loss of function, for some minutes after heart death. Perhaps people in the past did not believe this.

Consider now the present. The dominant belief is that brain death is neces-sary and sufficient for human death. The first component is uncontroversial. That someone should be alive so long as there is significant brain activity, and so should be alive even after the heart has stopped, represents a modification of, but no radical departure from, the older view. But it is the second component over which people profoundly disagree. For the brain death theorist, a hospital patient who in many respects appears to be alive – there is, although aided, heart beat, respiration, a near-normal body temperature, and near-normal metabolic activity – is in reality no more than an artificially ventilated corpse. Supporters of the old criterion cannot accept this.

My scepticism about the degree of change here leads to a similarly diffident position on questions of motivation. It is often said that support for the brain death criterion is motivated by a desire to "harvest" organs for transplant purposes.[8] A car crash victim, brain dead, is sustained on machines. Most other organs remain in good condition. Given the so-called dead donor rule and that killing people is disallowed[9] the insistence that this man is no longer alive might permit certain of these organs to be removed, and then used elsewhere. But that there is an overall beneficial consequence of the brain death criterion does not at all show that its advocates are motivated by this consequence. They might just as easily be motivated by a desire, for the patient's sake, to end treatment when all hope is gone.[10] Or they might be motivated by a desire for truth. Further, there are other, consciousness-related accounts of death that would better serve the harvesters. For if those in PVS could be considered dead then even more organs would be made available.

Objections

The dominant belief is that human beings are dead – integrated functioning is irreversibly lost – when, and only when, their brains are dead: when and only when that organ ceases, and irreversibly, to function as an integrated whole.[11] This account has, then, two main components. Both can be challenged. I shall consider here three areas of challenge. First, there are objections made to the precise criteriological status of the brain death account. The claim here is that although this gets things right for standard and central cases, there are at least theoretical problems along the margins. These objections are misconceived, and they fail. They can be dealt with fairly quickly. But, when modified, they begin to take on the shape of further objections. Thus, second, there are criticisms of the definition or quasi-definition of death; it can be insisted that we die later or, more interestingly, earlier than this account allows. Interesting or not, these also fail. Third, and finally, there is more bullish resistance to the brain death criterion, and argument about its handling even of central cases. The objections here cannot so easily be dismissed. One important point should be noted. Objections to the biological or organism account of death will, in practice if not in principle, imply at least reservations about the brain death criterion. The criterion is supposed to tell us when some condition obtains. The very same criterion could succeed in picking out some quite different condition, but this would be highly fortuitous. Why is this important? Some components in objections to the definition can resurface, with a narrower construal, in relation to the criterion. It would be a mistake to think their shortcomings in the former context makes for failure in the second.

Objections I: misunderstandings

Start with some predictable complaints. Brain death is neither necessary nor sufficient for organism death. It is not necessary, because we can conceive of a case where the organism is clearly dead, but the brain remains alive, perhaps in a jar, perhaps in some other organism. And it is not sufficient because we can conceive of a case where although your brain is dead you clearly remain alive, perhaps supported by large-scale hospital machinery, or perhaps by some inserted artificial brain, or brain transplant.[12]

These objections, as here stated, miss the point. Brain death is a criterion, or sign, or mark of death in the actual world. That it is logically possible that someone should live without a brain, or that the brain should live, while the organism is dead, does nothing to undermine the position of the brain death theorist. So merely conceivable counter-examples are irrelevant.

Suppose the objections are differently cast. It is insisted that it is not merely logically, but also physically possible for there to be detached brains, or brain-stems, kept alive while the rest of the animal dies. And it is similarly physically possible for there to be brainstem transplants, or mechanical stems, such that someone might be alive while their own brainstem is dead. It is hard to believe that such things are not physically possible. Is the brain death criterion thereby refuted? I think not. Properly understood, the criterion is supposed to give us a way of telling, in current real world circumstances, whether someone is alive. We might say, even though such things are possible, they are not actual.[13] Appeal to this criterion remains an altogether accurate procedure for determining someone's status. And this reply remains in force even if the objection should again be recast, this time in terms of technological possibilities. Even if it is possible for someone to build a mechanical brain or brainstem now, and even if they build such items in the future, still the brain death criterion might remain perfectly reliable.

Suppose now that there are a handful of detached brains, still living, in laboratories at this time. And suppose there are as well, at least working prototypes of the mechanical brain, a few of which are managing to keep some animals alive. What now for the criterion? At least on a defensible interpretation, it remains in place. Recall Feldman's insistence that a criterion can be useful even though there are a few counter-examples. Assuming we know well enough just where these new developments are taking place, and can, where necessary, discount them, we can still apply the criterion to settle those cases in which a patient's status is in doubt. It is already true that in almost all cases appeal to this criterion is unnecessary; people are clearly dead, or clearly alive. It is employed in a handful of difficult cases where there is genuinely a puzzle as to a patient's condition and prognosis. That there should somewhere, even now, be experiments with brains does nothing to undermine this.

Whether or not the brain death criterion is susceptible to refutation by counter-example depends in part on how it is construed. I am suggesting here that it should be given a modest interpretation, as indicating a way of telling, for specifiable circumstances in the actual world, whether someone is dead or alive. So interpreted the criterion appears to remain, at least for now, secure. But suppose the brain death account is given a more ambitious reading. Still some will think it sees off, rather than sidesteps, the sorts of objections outlined above. Although I am not persuaded, the moves here need to be considered. Start with the sufficiency claim.

I allowed that there might, probably will, be artificial brains. Even so, brain death is, now and in fact, sufficient for death. This possibility has no bearing on the criteriological claim. But a number of writers deny there could be such brains.[14] Thus they are able to see brain death as much more strongly indicative of a death's having occurred. On the face of it this seems implausible. Surely it is only a matter of time until we make, or grow, a replacement brain in a laboratory. Surely then the criterion will be in trouble. This, though, might still be denied. And this flat rejection of the artificial brain might ask to be understood in one of two ways. First, emphasize consciousness and the practical. It might be thought that even if we will sooner or later be able to fabricate the brainstem, or the control mechanism, we will be up against the wall with the obviously far more difficult task of constructing some consciousness-supporting replica of the upper brain.[15] But, we might ask, even if it is harder will it really be impossible? And we might note that the emphasis on consciousness is in any event not so obviously relevant. Things do not need to be conscious in order to live. And so a substitute lower brain is the most that is needed here. Unsurprisingly, I shall need to return to some of this below. Second, forget consciousness and the practical, and take instead more of a theory-driven approach. Someone says that even if, superficially at least, you can mimic the operation of the brain with some machine, this is not going to be a genuine case in which the organism remains alive. A living organism cannot – in some strong sense – be regulated by an artefact.[16] The upshot here, again, is to insist that the brain is necessary for life in a much stronger sense than is warranted just by the criteriological account. The difficulty is in finding reason to accept such a claim.

There appears to be a fairly clear and fairly important distinction between these two versions of the no artificial brain view. The first, emphasizing consciousness, is perhaps leaning towards a different account or definition of death. The second, in contrast, appears not to be at odds with the biological account. It simply denies that a machine-regulated collection of organic parts constitutes an integrated whole. It does not constitute an organism. And so it is not alive. This same distinction is evident, also, in two ways of unpacking the second objection to the criteriological view.

Consider now the necessity claim: brain death is necessary for death. I allow that there might be brains, and living brains, in vats. Again, this possibility does not engage with the criteriological claim. But here, also, several writers want to make a stronger claim, holding that so long as your brain survives then your life continues. This looks implausible. But perhaps there are two ways that suspicion might be dispelled. On the first there is again an emphasis on consciousness. So long as your brain is alive, and fully functioning – when hooked up it communicates with scientists in the laboratory – then surely you are alive. As in the case above, the thought here puts pressure on the biological account; it seems life can continue even though there is no integrated and fully functioning organism still in existence. The second version sees things differently. Life can continue even without consciousness. For so long as even the brainstem survives then the organism survives and, given that I am this organism, I survive as well. On this view, the brainstem is just a maximally pared down organism. This version of the view accepts the biological account of what death is.

Objections II: the definition

The account or definition that I favour has death occurring when the body is, roughly, in a certain condition, and so roughly, and generally, at a certain time in the organism's history. But we need to consider rival accounts that place death either significantly earlier or significantly later than this, and so demand of the body a significantly different condition. And they imply a different definition of death.

Death comes later

The emphasis, in the prevailing account, is on a breakdown in the organism as a whole. Some writers want to insist on the difference between this phrase and the variant that refers to the whole organism.[17] I am not sure that they are right to believe that a breakdown in the whole organism requires a breakdown in every part, in every organ, but certainly they are right to say that such a breakdown is not required on the standard account. But what that account requires is, it is sometimes said, insufficient for death to have occurred.

Some will say you are dead only when all your organs have ceased, irreversibly, to function, only when there is a complete absence of vital signs, perhaps only when overall putrefaction has set in.[18] There can be versions of this view that identify death with the dispersal of the body, perhaps through cremation or digestion. And it implies that almost all current declarations of death are premature. Notice that this view does not represent a retreat to the cardio-respiratory criterion. That too will be charged with undue haste. Rather, it asks for a different definition of death. This is not uncomplicated, however, as different definitions might be suggested here.

We might think of death as a wholly, or partly, or not at all a biological phenomenon. Those wanting, as I want, a uniform account of death, one that covers all living things, will be mostly drawn to a thoroughgoing biological account. Only rarely do people think that animals and plants have non-biological parts. Suppose someone thinks that death occurs when and only when the whole organism is irreversibly non-functioning. This definition, or quasi-definition, although different from the one so far favoured, nevertheless constitutes a biological account of what death is. And it might be applied to all organisms. Animals, plants, bacteria are alive so long as any part of them is alive.[19] Others, and some of these will be attracted to or motivated by certain religious beliefs, want to separate off our deaths. Some of these think that as well as a biological organism human beings are, or have, non-biological parts – a soul or spirit or mind – but that the condition of the biological parts determines, or at least provides good evidence for, the condition of the non-biological parts. They might think the soul is at rest, or at peace, or no longer in existence only when all the vital signs are gone, or when the body is thoroughly destroyed and its parts dispersed. So the body's condition, here understood as further deteriorated than on the standard account, is indicative of the condition of the soul. What is it for one of us to be dead? It is for our soul to be at peace, or rest, or destroyed.

This definition, or quasi-definition, represents an alternative to a biological account.

Thus there are two views, and two rival definitions here. But neither is defensible. On the first, death is a general biological phenomenon. A human being – like a snake, like a tree, like a fungus – is dead only when all its parts, organs, cells are dead: when there is a complete absence of vital signs. What is wrong with this view? It does not, I suggest, at all represent the way we currently think and speak. Perhaps it claims to. But then it is mistaken. Perhaps it claims, instead, to be revisionary. But then we need reasons to embrace the changes proposed. And I do not know what they would be. On the second, there is rejection of the biological account. Our deaths, unlike those of animals and trees, involve the condition and location of our souls. There are communities of people who think and speak of such things. We might see how there is a good degree of internal consistency between their beliefs and practices, and so see how the belief that one is only fully or truly dead when all of one's body is in some way or other at rest plays a central role in their lives. Even so, we might detect, and regret a lack of consistency between, these beliefs and beliefs elsewhere. Either way, then, the view that death comes later has little to recommend it.

Death comes earlier

It will take considerably longer to deal with the converse view: that human death, or the death of the likes of us, occurs, often, considerably earlier than the biological account, as so far understood, would have it. This will take longer both because there is a good number of variants to consider, and because this view, in at least several of its forms, is well enough embedded in the tradition to demand to be taken seriously. I shall start with a sketch of how, in at least one of its forms, this view goes, and then consider first its motivation and second its justification.

Typically, those claiming that human beings can, and often do, die before the brain as a whole is dead, and before integrated functioning is lost, insist on consciousness as the critical component in our existence. They advance a consciousness-related account.[20] And they hold that we die, or cease to exist, when consciousness, or the capacity for consciousness, is irreversibly lost. What, and where, is consciousness? There are puzzles here. We think of ourselves as both self-conscious and conscious, of many animals as merely conscious, of plants as neither. Consciousness links with awareness, sentience, responsiveness.[21] But plants and fairly simple machines respond or react to stimuli, and it is not easy really to understand what it is to be the sort of thing that might be aware of its surrounding without being at least sometimes aware that it is aware, and so self-aware, and so self-conscious. The neologism *painience*[22] might do more work here than sentience; while cameras might sense what is in front of them, either literally or metaphorically, they do not even metaphorically feel pain when dropped. Yet even if the things that feel pain are conscious, it is again unclear how we make sense of painience altogether bereft of self-consciousness. But we have to set these puzzles aside. The concern here is with human life, and human death. And we should assume we have a grasp of what consciousness, for us, involves. The puzzles about location might be easier to deal with. Some people hold that thoughts, beliefs, awarenesses, have a temporal but not a spatial location. But surely I can at least say that the seat or ground of consciousness is up here, behind my eyes, in my head. And what most of us believe is that consciousness depends on the existence and condition not simply of the brain but of the cerebrum. Consciousness is irreversibly lost when that organ part is in certain ways irreversibly damaged. Thus, a higher brain account of death.

Why think this way? A starting-point, for many, is a belief in the importance of consciousness for creatures like us. The thought is, when that is gone, so are we. And thus there is disagreement with proponents of the standard account over real-world clinical cases, in particular those in permanent coma or PVS. On the standard view these patients are still alive, while on the consciousness view they are already dead. The claim here is that consciousness is necessary for life. But of course, that is a long way from being right. Trees are alive, but are not conscious. So the view needs to be modified; it holds either that consciousness is necessary for human life or, wider, for higher animal life. What about a sufficiency claim? Again, starting with the phenomenon's importance, there is a strong intuition that so long as you are conscious, you remain alive. As it stands, there is no tension here with the standard account; that account will readily allow that our being conscious is a good indicator of brain activity and overall functioning. But tension can arise certainly in theory, and possibly also in practice, by considering cases where consciousness is sustained even though overall functioning and at least some seemingly relevant aspects of brain activity are gone. I shall offer more detail on this below.

As I have said, consciousness views occur in variant forms. Here are some, starting with one extreme. The definition, or quasi-definition, of death – an irreversible breakdown in the organism as a whole – needs to be rejected, at least for creatures like us. We should say instead that death is the irreversible loss of consciousness. (Of course, we then need a different account of death for plants and for at least some non-human animals. Assume that can be done.) And this view allows for, although it does not require, dualism. Perhaps we are minds, or souls or thinking things. We live so long as those things continue to exist. And we die when they are gone. More plausibly, and less extremely, it might be supposed that consciousness is an emergent property, and is grounded either in some sorts of brain states or, more generally, in whatever configurations of matter can adequately replicate these brain states. At one extreme here is the view that I continue to exist so long as my thoughts, beliefs, psychology are manifested in, say, some computer program, while at the other is the contention that this mind can be supported only by this particular hunk of organic matter, my brain.

On any of these consciousness-based definitions we turn out, assuming that we are the sorts of things that live and die, to be not biological but psychological or mental things. And this is so whether we are distinct mental substances, on the one hand, or some collection of mental properties that emerge from physical substances. Either way, we exist when and only when the requisite consciousness is present. The most familiar of such views has it that we are persons. And I need to say something about this now.

Each of us is a person, first, in a seemingly non-controversial sense, where "person" is just another term for "human being", where its plural is "people" and where the number of people in a country or a town, or its population, comprises the number of live human beings, irrespective of their health or mental condition. That point about populations is, I think, just a useful convention: as I have suggested earlier, the sense of "person" here being considered at least allows for a person to continue existing after death; and thus allows that there are dead people. It clearly and on many grounds suits us, however, when counting people, to exclude the dead. But now each of us – the writer and the readers – is a person in a further and wholly non-controversial sense: each of us is a self-conscious and rational agent, is or has a mind, exhibits certain sorts of psychological continuities, and so on. Here, in this philosopher's sense, the plural is "persons"; the number in a country or town excludes, as well as the dead, the newborn, the anencephalics, some of the comatose, some of the demented. But it may, depending on what is going on inside, include the apes, the cetaceans and, if there are any, the gods.

Why do I say that it is non-controversial that we are persons in this second sense, but only seemingly non-controversial in the first? I have left it unclear as to whether "person" in this second sense itself denotes a separate item, a thing, a substance, as apparently does a term such as "human being", or whether it denotes a phase in the history of a thing, on a par, say, with "teenager". What is uncontroversial is that we are persons understood in one or other of these ways. But now if this second sense in which we are persons is understood in the first of these ways, so that a person is a thinking thing, something that is, rather than has, a mind, then arguably we are not also people, or human beings. For it seems to many to be reasonably clear that human beings are things, or substances, rather than phases, or stages, and reasonably clear also that we cannot be both of two substantial items, at least at the same time. So unless it is certain that we are not persons, or mental substances, it cannot be certain that we are people, or human beings. Thus, that we are human beings is not, contrary to first appearances, thoroughly uncontroversial. But certainly there are people, or human beings. And even if we are not such things we are intimately linked to such things. For on a secular view the death of the human being is sufficient for the ceasing to be of the person. On certain religious views this is not so. Still, the fate of the body is not a matter of indifference to the soul.

It is uncontroversial that consciousness, having a mind, a psychology, matters to us. And being a person, in the second sense, matters to us. But, of course, the conditions here are distinct. Most animals are conscious without being persons. Similarly for foetuses and babies. And in certain conditions a human being who was, uncontroversially, a person can cease to be a person without thereby ceasing to be conscious. So the claims that we die when we cease to be persons and that we die when we cease to be conscious are distinct. The focus here is on consciousness, and so on a view that allows we might continue to exist even when personhood is gone, but that denies we exist once consciousness, sentience, painience are gone. It should be noted that this is a little odd: although it is clear why the developed and sophisticated consciousness that figures in personhood matters to us, it is less clear, I think, why mere consciousness should matter. Nor can this oddity be quickly disposed of by revising the consciousness view, and simply claiming that we die when personhood is lost. Even if there is a fair degree of support for the claim that those in PVS are dead, there is hardly any at all for the similar claim made of those dementia sufferers who are no longer, in the philosopher's sense, persons, but who are considerably more than merely conscious.

I reject all these consciousness-based definitions. Death is a biological phenomenon that affects all and only organisms. We are organisms, and we die. Sometimes, before we die we irreversibly lose consciousness. That may be a tragedy, but it is not death. And I simply deny that we speak of those in PVS as dead. Of course I do not claim that none of us ever speak this way. But only vanishingly small numbers of us think, or say, after reflection and after being made clear as to the lower-level facts, that it is literally true that those in PVS are dead.[23] And surely no one thinks that the PVS patient is, without any further modification, already fit for burial or cremation. So suppose we are animals. We are for some time, perhaps for most of the time, conscious. But animals do not die when they cease, even irreversibly, to be conscious.

Suppose we are instead, and as many believe, persons. Persons invariably have an existence shorter than that of the human being with whom they are closely associated. For they never, in fact, continue to exist after the human being dies, and they always in fact come into existence after the human being is born. But no one suggests, or speaks as if, there are two births: first that of the human animal, and then, some months later, and more gradually, that of the person. Nor should they suggest that there are, for neither do we speak of there being, two deaths: that of the organism and, too frequently days or months or years earlier, that of the closely related person. So if we are persons then even though we have beginnings and ends to our existence, and even though PVS may signal such an end, we are not, I claim, the sorts of things that are born, live and then die.

Suppose it is objected that even if we do not, in fact, speak of those in PVS as dead, we should, either because irrespective of our beliefs those in PVS are dead, or because it will be better for us if we do. I deny that there are, in this sense, deep facts to death and deny as well that there are gains to be had from such a revision. I return to the second point below.

Thus consciousness is not necessary for life. Clearly it is not necessary in every case – there are living but non-conscious trees – and it is not, I have argued, necessary in our case – there are living but non-conscious human beings. Is it sufficient? Suppose it were. Then perhaps we could still offer a redefinition of death: death is an irreversible loss of functioning coupled with an irreversible loss of consciousness. Consider some actual cases.

There exists a rare but now well-known condition in which you are fully conscious, and self-conscious, but unable to manifest this in any of the normal ways.[24] Perhaps, if you are lucky, you will be able to control movement in one eyelid, and so signal your needs and desires to others. Some consciousness theorists have thought that locked-in syndrome can grist their mill. Whereas the PVS patient is alive given the standard account, but dead on the consciousness-related view, here this is reversed, with the patient dead according to the standard view, but clearly alive.

This may be elegant, but it is wrong. The locked-in patient, typically suffering the effects of a severe stroke, is seriously incapacitated. But she is clearly alive on the standard account, as there is integrated functioning through the organism, and there is life and functioning in both the upper and lower brain. Further, this overall functioning is mediated by the brain. Consider an allegedly more extreme case, a victim of severe Guillain–Barré syndrome.[25] Here the brainstem, although it is not dead, is unable to regulate the remainder of the organism. Heart and lung function is provided by machines. The patient is conscious. But here too the intuition that the patient remains alive is endorsed, rather than countered, by the verdict delivered from the standard definition. The organism as a whole continues to function. So there is no reason to abandon the standard definition and give instead a consciousness-based alternative. Nor does this case put incontrovertible pressure on the brain death criterion. For the brain is not dead. Still, there is pressure nevertheless. For at the centre of the brain theorist's account is the claim that organism function needs to be brain mediated. And that is not happening here. I come back to this point below.

There are further, and related, cases. Jeff McMahan considers a "hypothetical locked-in patient whose entire brain stem has died and has been replaced by an array of mechanical substitutes" (2002: 433). We might also consider a similar situation, so far fictional, in which the machines fail, and so bodily function is lost, but then the brain is removed from the body and kept alive in laboratory conditions. In each case consciousness persists. Does the patient remain alive through these cases? And consider a real case, but one that does not involve human beings. Several writers report on, and discuss experiments in which, decapitated monkeys were kept alive. Lizza is one. Although it is not immediately clear, he fairly soon makes it clear that it is the head, and not the body, that is kept alive, and that he thinks of as the monkey. Bernard Gert says of this: "When a monkey's severed head responds to sounds and sights, claiming that it is dead alters the ordinary understanding of death far more than claiming that the monkey is still alive" (1995: 26; discussed in Lizza 2006: 23). This may be right. If asked to choose between one of two terms to apply to this in some ways functioning and seemingly conscious monkey head – is it a living or a dead monkey? – we may prefer the former. But the better reaction, as well as some expression of antipathy or distaste, may be to think of this as a puzzle case; one that, like suspended animation, gives us reason to think that the terms "life" and "death" may not be exhaustive. We should think as well that the puzzle here is not particularly challenging. For what we clearly have are some important parts of what was a monkey, machine supported and, for now, at least metaphorically alive. And that is really all that needs to be said. Similarly for the imaginary cases concerning human beings. Consciousness is important. And if my brain survives, with my psychology intact, then there may well be reasons to care about its condition and its future. We might think that its future is my future. But it will not follow from any of this, I think, that a human being remains alive. As the procedure considered here is only imaginary, so these claims about our reactions are speculative. It may be that if such procedures become common, and perhaps are followed by rehousing the brain in some substitute, albeit artificial, body, then our talk of life and death will be accommodated. Even so, there is no reason, I claim, to think that our current definition, or quasi-definition, of death should, currently, be replaced by one that emphasizes consciousness. For consciousness is not sufficient for life.[26]

There is one further point to be noted here. A consciousness-emphasizing account could be differently construed, and understood in a way that offers much less of a challenge to the standard view. What is involved in overall functioning varies, of course, from species to species, or from kind to kind. Now it could be claimed that those organisms in which consciousness is important are not functioning properly, in an integrated fashion, in those cases where consciousness is irreversibly lost. Thus those in PVS are dead. But while the brain death criterion is in this case in need of amendment, the biology-based definition survives intact. Yet even if it appears conciliatory, there is no good reason to accept such a move. Although an irreversible loss of consciousness will, in nature, lead fairly quickly to an animal's death, the conditions are still distinct. And those in PVS can be, for a long time, alive.

Objections III: the criterion

I want finally to consider the claim that although death is, within the biological account, properly defined, it is not, even in actual clinical cases, well demarcated by the brain death criterion. It is not true, the claim goes, that the death, metaphorically, of the brain, is the sign or mark of death, literally, in the whole organism. Rejection of the brain theorist's position can take on different forms. I shall begin with some that are only minimally challenging, and move then to others that offer more of a threat, and need correspondingly more discussion.

Disjunctive and conjunctive accounts

As has been noted, the cardio-respiratory criterion and the brain death criterion are not worlds apart. In almost all cases someone will be dead, simultaneously, on both accounts. And the tests for the one very much resemble the tests for the other. Some brain theorists are less wedded to the radical and innovative character of their approach than others. Suppose it is suggested that irreversible cardio-respiratory breakdown and brain death are each sufficient for death. This is going to be acceptable to the brain theorist. What, of course, is not acceptable is the converse claim: he is not going to allow that both are necessary for death.

Could there be a further disjunct? Those consciousness theorists who want still to accommodate an overall biological approach may suggest that higher brain death is also sufficient for death. The brain theorist cannot accept this.

If it were true, then whole brain or brainstem death would not be necessary for death. And as I have indicated, I share in this rejection of the higher brain view.

Suppose someone holds that cardio-respiratory breakdown and brain death are jointly sufficient for death. This is going to be very widely acceptable. Someone who is seemingly dead on two counts is fairly assuredly dead. And evidently a higher brain component can be fitted into this conjunctive view. Again, the converse will be found contentious. The brain theorist allows that the dead are both brain dead and higher brain dead, but resists the claim that they have also suffered irreversible loss of cardio-respiratory function.

An alternative account

There is, then, a substantive dispute here. A central claim of the brain death theorists is that when brain function is gone, so too is function in the organism as a whole. Although, given mechanical ventilation and further ancillary support, heartbeat and respiration will continue, and further signs of death – a drop in body temperature, rigor mortis, organ decay – will all be arrested or delayed, the patient is already dead. What might look to be overall integrated functioning is no more than a simulacrum; rather than a living organism there is, in such a case, merely a bag of living organs. But this has been strongly denied. Machines, in part by sustaining cardio-respiratory function, can keep someone alive, in an integrated fashion, for some time. So supporters of this view think that while death implies brain death, the reverse does not hold: brain death is not sufficient for death. Who is right here?

It is worthwhile to revisit the discussion of Guillain–Barré syndrome. Even if this failed to lend support to a new definition of death it can rightly be seen as putting some pressure on the brain death criterion. Someone suffering from this condition is, as McMahan says, "undeniably alive" (2002: 433). So? As they are not brain dead, so the brain theorist might think himself unembarrassed. But this would be a mistake. For his central claim is that patients are dead when functioning is not brain-mediated. And it is not so mediated in these cases. Brain death is sufficient for, and the normal cause of, this mediation failure, but it is not necessary. Saving the day by insisting either that these patients are dead or that consciousness is here making the difference appears somewhat desperate in both cases.

The argument against the brain theorist does not rest on just a tiny handful of anomalous situations. And this consideration of Guillain–Barré syndrome should be seen as merely a softening up. For there are, of course, many cases where a patient is genuinely brain dead (and so here, of course, no longer conscious) but where integrated functioning appears to continue. There are the cases where someone is on life-support machines, so that these organs might be removed and transformed. Many think these patients are still alive. How can this seemingly intact human being – breathing, pink warm, and supple [27] – really be dead? How can a dead woman, as in several attested cases, continue the development of a foetus for several months, until in the end a normal healthy baby is born?[28] The problem for the brain death criterion is not that we can imagine that someone might be alive without a brainstem, nor that it is surely physically possible, and may at some time be technologically possible, to construct an artificial stem to do the brain's work; the problem, rather, is that even now functioning can occur, and the organism can remain alive, without the aid of the brainstem, without, even, the presence of a brain.[29] Put another way, the problem for the brain death account is not that an artificial stem is remotely possible. That is something they can accommodate. It is, rather, that they are already actual, exist in almost all hospitals, and are surprisingly simple to construct and to operate. For, of course, no one claims that the brain-dead patient will remain alive without any external support; that mechanical assistance is needed is undeniable. But then neither does the brain theorist allege that one is alive only if circulation and respiration are spontaneous, and unaided.

This is the dispute. For some, the evidence gleaned from these clinical cases renders the brain death criterion "spectacularly false" (McMahan 2002: 429). They claim that the traditional cardio-respiratory criterion should be reinstated. Failure here is not only sufficient, but also necessary for death. But brain theorists are fully aware of these cases, and interpret them differently. So how is the matter to be resolved? There are difficult and technical questions here about just what is going on within the bodies of certain brain-dead patients. I reserve these details for the Appendix. But I think the critics have the edge here. And I might make just two points. First, as I have said earlier, the notion of integrated functioning, within a structure of any complexity, is surely going to resist sharp and unambiguous delineation. There will need to be judgement as to when it occurs, and those judgements will, to some degree, represent and reflect certain of our interests. But then interests can conflict. Brain theorists are certainly guilty of painting things in black and white. Yet so too, perhaps, are some of their opponents. Second, one of the more general criticisms of this theory should be noted. For it has been argued that the brain criterion goes wrong in modelling the human body too much on machines.[30] I have done this, of course, in likening the brain to a programmer in a heating system. But it may be that such models, with their clearly differentiated and clearly replaceable parts, all of them having different histories, grossly distort our understanding of organisms, and how they work.

Death and value

Does it matter that we can distinguish between the living and the dead? Surely it does. And according to David Lamb, "It is as wrong to treat the living as dead as it is to treat the dead as alive" (1994: 1028). So there are two errors we might make, and they are equally to be avoided. Yet this does not seem quite right: to treat the living as dead might involve depriving them of food and water, burying them alive, removing their organs or switching off the machine ahead of time. If we treat the living as dead we will almost certainly kill them. But to treat the dead as alive seems, at worst, to waste time and resources. And so that in puzzle cases we should err on the side of caution, assume life until proved wrong, seems to be only good sense.[31]

Yet this too might not be altogether right, especially in relation to the sorts of cases figuring in the present discussion. Is it always wrong to treat the living as dead? Typically, we treat dead people with some respect, and do not think of them as merely waste matter entirely without value. To treat the living as dead is consistent, then, with acknowledging their value. Is it always wrong to deprive, even knowingly to deprive, a living person of food and water, or to switch off the machines, or to remove their organs? In most cases life is of immense value, and it is wrong to end it. But many people think there are exceptions, and it can be in someone's interests for their life to be ended. So consider those cases where life is no longer of value, and fairly clearly so, because consciousness, and personhood are irreversibly lost. Is it wrong to treat a PVS patient as dead and to remove their organs, so killing them? Many will think so, even if they think this would be less wrong than taking the organs of a perfectly healthy passer-by. They will think it wrong even if, beforehand, the patient gave permission for this to happen. But of those who think it would be wrong to take the organs of a still-living PVS patient, a considerable number think it not wrong to switch off the machines, and so, if not killing the patient, at least allowing her to die. And then, and immediately, organs might be removed.

Most of us, I have claimed, think the PVS patient is alive. Some deny this, and say that as consciousness is irreversibly lost she is dead. Curiously, David DeGrazia characterizes this as a position most often supported by "liberal intellectuals" (2007: §2.4). I do not see what is liberal about counting as dead, and presumably then refusing to support, those that many, including their relatives, will think of as alive. Perhaps, though, it is in some sense a modern and progressive position. But it is surely possible to acquire the benefits here – a freeing up of organs and other resources – without the intellectual sleight-of-hand needed to maintain that these patients are dead. Most of us, I suspect,

61

continue to think that the brain dead are dead, even if there are increasing numbers who have doubts. DeGrazia sees those wanting a return to the cardio-respiratory criterion as "religious conservatives" (*ibid.*: §1).[32] Perhaps some are. They think, having agreed that the brain dead are alive, we should now agree that they need to be cared for. But there need not be a link here. And, as with those in PVS, we might, while allowing that the brain dead are alive, still decide to bring their life to an end.

Some of the living might, then, legitimately be killed. They might be killed because it is in their interests, it might be better for them, to die. Or they might be killed because it is not against their interests and it is in our interests: better for us, in freeing up hospital resources, and in adding to the stock of transplantable organs. They might be killed, and their organs then removed. Lamb may well not have such cases in mind. For intentionally to kill a living patient is not, whether or not it is right or wrong, to treat that patient as dead, but rather to see them, and to treat them, as alive. But now as there are advantages to removing organs from a body in which circulation and respiration continue, rather than one that has been on ice for some time, so some people might be killed by removing their organs. Perhaps here we treat them as dead. And that too may be legitimate. Inevitably some, on hearing this, will think it an altogether horrific suggestion. Hence support for the dead donor rule. But, of course, I am not proposing any change whatsoever in our practice. The suggestion is only that we might, in pursuit of truth rather than convenience, reclassify the brain dead as living, and then do with them as we do now.

Summary

When do we die? When the organism as a whole ceases to function. Almost always it is perfectly clear when, or approximately when, this happens. It happens when the heart stops beating, breathing ceases and the brain is deprived of its flow of oxygenated blood. In a handful of cases the near-simultaneity of these central signs of death is overturned. And then there are puzzles and disputes about death. Brain death theorists insist that we die, that integration is lost, just when the brainstem, and thus the brain as a whole, dies or ceases to function. This brain death criterion is subject to many objections. Most, I have argued, miss their target. But there is one objection – that in fact overall organism functioning, and thus life, does not require the operation of the brainstem – that deserves to be taken seriously. I believe the critics here are right, that the brain death criterion is thus flawed, and that the traditional cardio-respiratory criteria have not been superseded. But I do not claim that this has been, or indeed that it can be, established beyond doubt.

I am assuming here that we are organisms. So we die when the organism dies. But some people deny that we are organisms, holding instead that we are souls, or minds, or persons. Even so, all of us are intimately related to a human being, or organism. I have argued that if this person view is right then, even though we exist, and might cease to exist, strictly we neither live nor die. So even if this is right, it warrants no revision of the definition of death. There are religious and secular versions of the person view. On some of the religious versions persons never cease to exist. On most secular versions we do cease to exist. When? On these secular views we cease to exist when consciousness is irreversibly lost. Whatever might, in the longer term, be possible for the persistence of consciousness, right now consciousness is irreversibly lost either before, or when, the body to which we are intimately related dies. Situations involving deep coma, or PVS, or ventilated brain death, are extremely rare. In almost all actual cases consciousness is irreversibly lost almost precisely when the body dies.

I have objected to the phrase "die or cease to exist" when used by proponents of the person view; these terms are not synonymous, and they should stick with the latter. But that phrase, employed disjunctively, does have a legitimate use. In almost all cases, when the body dies we die (if we are human beings, or organisms), or cease to exist (if instead we are minds or persons). Either way, we have reason to take death seriously.

4

Is it bad to die?

You are getting towards what should be your middle years, neither young nor old. Life has been good and, it seems, will continue to be so. But you are in the wrong place at the wrong time, and are blown to pieces by a bomb. Does anything bad happen to you; is it bad for you, when this bomb goes off? Most of us say yes. Just a few say no. But many of those saying yes acknowledge that there are difficulties in explaining how it can be that death is bad for the one who dies. I agree that there are difficulties here. But perhaps their number and their extent have been exaggerated. Some of the best known and most discussed puzzles about the evil of death can, at least in outline, be fairly easily solved. I deal with three of these here. But others are more resilient. I discuss several examples in Chapter 5.

Some clarification. First, the focus, for now, is on a case like that just sketched. I shall call it a *prime of life case*. Change any of the details – age, how life is going, circumstances – and what we say about death's badness may well be different. We can consider such changes later. Second, this idea of something's being bad will for now be assumed to be roughly intelligible. As things go on we can explore it further, and consider as well whether death might be a harm, or a misfortune, or a thing we might suffer, or an evil. Third, we are concerned with death, and not dying. There is little dispute about dying: that drawn out, often painful, often humiliating process that ends in death. That is bad for you, and would be bad for you even if at the last moment you made a miraculous recovery. In this prime of life case you die suddenly, painlessly, unexpectedly. So you avoid much of the badness associated with dying. The distinction here is relatively straightforward. But a number of writers have wanted to make a further distinction, useful even if less straightforward, between the supposedly momentary event of one's death, and the subsequent apparently endless state of being dead. Fourth, the question is whether your death is bad for you. Uncontroversially, it is often bad for others, harming them psychologically if they are partners, friends, relatives, or materially if they are partners, children or business associates. Now, whether it is bad for you or others, one way to think of death's badness is in instrumental terms: death has some bad effects, or bad consequences. But, and more controversially, it might be bad in a further way. Someone might think that death is intrinsically bad, or bad in itself, or bad for, or from the point of view of, the universe, or impersonally bad.[1] And they might think it bad in this way irrespective of its bad effects either on you or on others. They might think all deaths are bad in this way, or the view might be restricted to some subset of deaths: perhaps the deaths of sentient beings, or just those of human beings, or persons. But the question of whether your death is bad for you is distinct from that of whether it is bad in this further way. So we might, as has elsewhere been suggested, speak here of personal bads: the question is whether it is bad for the person that he or she dies.[2] Now it might be thought that the contrast implied here – things bad in themselves and things bad for you – is not stark. For some things, say botched dental work, will be instrumentally bad for you, while others, say pain, will be intrinsically bad for you. But we might wonder first whether, assuming pain is intrinsically bad, it is intrinsically bad for the person who feels pain, and second whether death is ever intrinsically bad. Again, I shall need to return later to these questions, and to some further questions that the above distinctions imply or suggest. Fifth, the assumption here is that death is the end, if not altogether of existence, at least of consciousness. There is no soul, or spirit, or life after death to take into account. In at least one important sense, death is nothingness. Some will want to challenge this. But all those I engage with make this assumption.

Three views

Is it bad for you that you die? Answers to this question about a particular death will connect with more general views about death's badness. It is going to be worthwhile, before going further into detail, to consider these views.

Always bad

Someone might think that death, or at least human death, is always bad, or bad in every case, or in all circumstances. So it is bad when it comes to both the young and healthy, and the old and sick. And so, of course, it is bad in the prime of life case. There are different versions of this view. I shall discuss four, only the first of which can be speedily dismissed.

Some think that life is sacred, or intrinsically valuable. Whenever life is ended, something of value is lost. So there is always something bad about, always a downside to, death. But this view need not claim either that it is overall bad that a death should occur, or that it is in any way bad for the person that their life should end. So unless further buttressing is in place, the sanctity view does not, contrary to a widespread belief, imply much about our reactions to death, or anything about our treatment of the dying.[3]

A second view, perhaps via some links with religion related to the first, is that life is always worth living, such that it is always worse for someone to die than to continue with their life. An extreme version of this view is that whatever someone's condition, however much pain they might be in, and however much they might think that death is preferable, it is better for them to continue living. A less extreme version is that whatever someone's condition, this condition can be improved, such that life is better than death. Hence palliative care. The first version, I shall assume, is false. The second is probably false.

A third view also claims that there is always something bad about death. Its proponents note that we rarely think of death as an unqualifiedly good thing. Even when it seems better than, or preferable to, life and puts an end to a life not worth living, our reactions suggest that we think of it as, at best, the lesser of two evils. So death, on this view, is sometimes better than life, sometimes worse, but still a bad thing either way. And so it is never unreservedly welcome. I come back to this.[4]

The fourth view is also one that gets much fuller discussion below, but it needs to be mentioned here. It relies on a distinction between particular, or token, deaths and death as a general phenomenon. Were there no death, we would be immortal. And that would be good. So it is bad for us that there is death. But it can be allowed, nevertheless, that some particular or token death might not be bad. If we assume that you will die anyway at eighty, then dying at seventy-nine, when, were you to live, you would have ahead of you only a year of painful dying, is not a bad thing. Some might think this death is good, others that it is the lesser of evils. But whereas the token death might be good in one way, bad in another, the general fact of death is bad through and through.

66

This discussion of ways in which death might always be bad has exposed an important distinction: that between *bad* and *worse*. For, as it appears here, it might in some ways be bad to die even while it is not worse to die than to live. Conversely, as will appear below, death might be worse than life, even while it is not bad. The prime of life case seems, on the face of it, to involve both. Dying then leaves you worse off than you would have been, had you continued to live. But you are not simply worse off; you are in no respect well off. It is bad for you that you die, and bad that you end up dead.

Never bad

There are people who think death is never bad. Some of these will simply take issue with the point made above. They think that even if death might be worse than life, it is never positively, or genuinely, or really, bad to be dead. What does this mean?

Suppose one situation is worse than another. It is worse to be without sight and hearing than to be without sight alone. And it is worse to earn £50,000 than £100,000 per annum. But we might think that to be without sight alone is bad, while to earn £50,000 is not bad. Someone blind is in a bad situation, even if a better situation than someone both blind and deaf, while someone earning £50,000 is in a good situation, even while not such a good situation as someone earning £100,000. A familiar view, then, is that one's situation might be overall good, overall bad, or overall neutral.

We can make the same point about things. One painting, or restaurant, or football team might be worse than another, while both are good. Or it might be worse while both are bad. And, of course, if one is good and the other bad, then the second is worse.

One objection to this is very general. Nothing is genuinely good or bad. Even though things can be ranked as better or worse than their competitors, there is no non-arbitrary divide between the so-called good and bad examples. Such, apparently, is John Broome's view.[5] Now this view is possibly more sustainable than at first you might think – perhaps there really are just better and worse paintings – but it does not seem plausible through and through. Surely pain is bad, and not merely worse than pleasure. Surely too we can think that some lives are worse than, while others are better than, nothing. And if so, then there is a non-arbitrary divide in place here.

The second objection focuses on death. Recall the assumption that death is nothingness. So there is no pain in death. Being in hell might be positively bad, heaven positively good, but being dead, as nothingness, is neutral. So it is not genuinely, positively, bad. And as the dead are located, if anywhere, at some zero level of welfare, their situation, if any, is neither good nor bad. So we can, without too much difficulty, understand the suggestion that death, even if it might be worse than life, is not bad.

But something here seems to be overlooked. It relates to the distinction between death, an event, and being dead, a state. Someone is worse off with a salary of £50,000 than £100,000. They get the lower salary as a result of a salary cut. Is it bad that a salary is cut? Plausibly, it is bad for you when things get worse, even if the situation in which you end up is not in itself bad. Similarly, it is good, or good for you, when things get better and make you better off, even if when better off you are still not in a good situation. So, plausibly, death is bad, even if being dead is not. Put this another way. Something that causes your situation to improve, or deteriorate, is instrumentally good, or bad, for you even if your end state is not intrinsically good, or bad, for you.[6] And so plausibly the event of death is, in many cases, instrumentally bad even though the state of being dead is not intrinsically bad.

Contrast this position – worse but not bad – with another. Some think that death is never bad. But they do not think simply that being dead is, in the way sketched above, of neutral value. They think also that death is in a much stronger sense in no way bad for the person who dies. No one is worse off being dead than alive. So death is not something to regret, or fear or avoid. It is not, ever, an evil.

Those who deny that we can be worse off being dead seem to have four options. Either they think life and death can be compared, but death never loses;[7] or they allow that life can be good, but then deny that any comparison can be made between the two states.[8] Or they allow that certain comparisons can be made, and allow also that death is in itself the worse state, but they deny that death is a worse state for a person to be in. Or, finally, they take issue with the idea that to be dead is to be in a neutral state, and so they deny there are two states to be compared.

I am going to assume, against the pessimists, that life can be good. I am going to assume, also, that when dead we are either in a neutral state, or in no state at all. So the first of these options can be set aside. The other three will resurface.

Sometimes bad

The standard view is that death is sometimes, but not always, bad for those who die. So some deaths are bad, and others not. Almost all those who think death is sometimes bad will think it bad in the prime of life case.

Before further explaining the view it is worth pointing out a certain ambiguity attaching to terms such as "always", "never", "sometimes". If we ask
"When is death bad?", we might be asking about the circumstances in which
it is bad, or we might be asking about the moment in time when its badness
begins, or the period in time for which its badness lasts. The concern here,
and again in Chapter 5, is with the circumstances in which death is bad; we
want to distinguish cases where it is bad from cases where it is not. A major
concern later in this chapter is with the temporal location of the badness, in
a case where at least its apparent badness is beyond dispute.

Now this standard view might usefully be couched in terms of certain
distinctions already drawn. It holds that death is bad, and worse than life, in
some circumstances, and not bad, not worse and maybe better than life, in
others. But the view does not hold that death is in some circumstances merely
worse than life, as if allowing it might be the lesser of two goods. Death is
often an overall bad thing. Distinguish again between events and states. The
event of death is bad, as it takes you from a good state – living a good life – to
a worse state – being dead – which is not only worse, but, even though it is
not bad, is not in itself a good state to be in. This standard view holds, then,
that the value of death – the event – varies from case to case, while the value
of being dead – the state – is always neutral. So death is sometimes, perhaps
often, overall bad. Suppose you think there is no being dead: no neutral state
the dead are in. Then we can put the matter thus: the event of death is bad,
when it is bad, in that it takes you from a good state – living a good life – and
annihilates you, ends your existence, leaves you nowhere, rather than leaving
you in some other state, good, bad or indifferent.

The Epicurean view

The idea that death is never bad, never an evil, for the person who dies is associated with Epicurus. He lived and died long ago, and was, by the Christian
world, very much neglected. But interest in Epicureanism, or the Epicurean
view, has resurfaced in the current, more secular age, and has been encouraged particularly by Thomas Nagel's well-known paper on the topic (1971). I
discuss several parts of this paper in what follows. But I begin with the founder.
He writes:

> Accustom thyself to believe that death is nothing to us, for good
> and evil imply sentience, and death is the privation of all sentience,

… Death, therefore, the most awful of evils, is nothing to us, seeing that, when we are, death is not come, and when death is come, we are not. It is nothing, then, either to the living or to the dead, for with the living it is not, and the dead exist no longer.

(Letter to Menoeceus, in Diogenes Laertius 1925: 126)

What does he mean? The so-called Epicurean view is standardly taken to presuppose both hedonism, or (roughly) the claim that goods and bads concern, respectively, pleasures and pains, and atomism, the belief that all that there is comprises various elaborations of material particles, and so expressly excludes immaterial beings, including certain familiar sorts of gods, souls, ghosts, angels and the like. So the idea here is that death signals the end of sentience or awareness, and thus the end of all possibility of pleasure or pain, or anything good or bad happening to us. While we are alive, while we exist, we can be hurt, or harmed, or subject to misfortune, but when we are dead, and exist no longer, we are beyond all this. So while dying can be bad, and a fear of death, like a fear of spiders, can compromise our everyday happiness, there can be nothing bad about death itself. Only mistakenly, then, are we at all concerned about it.[9]

Yet some have doubted that Epicurus was, in this sense, an Epicurean. He wrote at a time when, although he did not share them, beliefs in souls, spirits and the underworld were prevalent. And it may be that he was principally concerned to quell anxiety, or worry, or a fear about what death had in store for us, and to provide in his followers a more settled attitude, or *ataraxia*. You are captured by terrorists. There is much to fret about in what might soon happen. There will be future experiences, but they are unknown. Maybe there will be torture. For believers in Hades, or hell, death is like this. Persuade them that there is nothing after death, that there is then an "experiential blank"[10] and these emotions, these fears, are undermined. Epicurus might have had these aims without aiming, further, to persuade us that death is not in some way a bad thing, something that there is reason to avoid. He might have thought that death is worse than life, but not, in itself, a bad state to be in. Scholars can debate this.[11] I raise the matter here just to point out that we might not worry about being dead, but still care to avoid death.

Consider again the stronger claim: that death, or being dead, is neither bad nor worse than life. Most disagree. But many are at least tempted. They think that what you do not know cannot harm you, that nothingness cannot be bad, and so on. But ask them what else would be true, if it were true that death is not bad for those who die. There would be no proper justification for our grief and distress at the death of others,[12] no reason to avoid runaway buses, intensive care units would have their funding cut, murder would be a lesser crime than assault and battery. Those who recover from a coma would be worse off – aware of, and regretting time lost – than those who do not. Abortion, euthanasia and capital punishment debates would lose much of their urgency. Seemingly, at least, there are many counterintuitive consequences of falling for the Epicurean view. Here is one more. If death cannot be bad, it surely cannot be good either. But for many of us, even if it is never an altogether good thing, there are many circumstances in which death can be clearly preferable to life. So those who, because life is no longer worth living, judge that they would be better off dead, seem also to be making some sort of mistake.[13]

It appears, then, as if the Epicurean view, at least as standardly interpreted, is strongly counterintuitive. We mostly think it false.[14] It would be reassuring to be able to show that it is false. I do not promise to do that. But what I want to do here is to consider three issues concerning, respectively, the subject, the timing and the manner of the supposed evil of death. See that the importance of these puzzles is inflated, see as well the extent of their overlap, and you will see, or so I believe, that death's supposed badness is less curious, less anomalous than it might otherwise appear. This is not to say that its badness can be easily understood, or even in the end that it is bad. There are a number of difficulties in explaining, generally, how and when something can be bad for us. These general difficulties bear on what should be said about death. And I consider some of them in Chapter 5.

For whom?

The problem here is often referred to as the problem of the subject. My death can be bad for friends and relatives who grieve. But can it be bad for me? Most say yes, but the Epicureans deny it. They say the dead do not exist. And then they say that nothing can be bad for someone who, or something that, does not exist. Are these claims true?

The first claim is very widely accepted.[15] But, as I have argued, it is not clear that it deserves to be. We might say there are millions of dead people who do exist. Cemeteries and mortuaries are full of them. Of course, there are billions who do not exist, and probably billions more about whom, because of their state of decay, it is hard to decide whether or not they exist still. Nevertheless, ceasing to exist at the moment of death is extremely rare. And it is implausible to suppose that between those who do, and those who do not exist there are differences that bear on death's badness. Epicureans are not going to hold to their view about the vaporized, but abandon it for the intact. So this claim is often false, and never relevant. And the problem of the subject disappears.

Not for long. The Epicureans can appeal to a familiar distinction. Bodies, or organisms, may exist after death, but persons do not. And we are persons. So, as thinking, consciousness and our ability to experience pleasure and pain all come to an end with death, so personhood disappears and we cease to be. But this, of course, is not quite right. For our mental lives can come to an end before death, as in an irreversible coma, or PVS. So if the emphasis rests on personhood then the Epicureans will want to claim that the irreversible coma, like death, is also not bad for us. But there are problems here. It is not easy to see how the Epicureans, avowedly materialists, can hold, as the person view seems to imply, that we are some sort of mental substance, and so the sort of thing that might cease to exist when consciousness disappears. So suppose they hold only that what matters to us, what is important, ceases when consciousness ceases. They might in the end still be able to claim that neither death nor coma harms us, but this will not now be linked to a non-existence claim. There is a third way. Epicureans might ally themselves to those animalists who insist that we cease to exist precisely with death, independently of both the prior collapse of consciousness and the subsequent fate of the corpse. But there is still a tension. For the "privation of sentience" can still precede non-existence. So non-existence, on the one hand, and immunity from harm, on the other, are still failing to line up.

There is more to say about comas. Believers in persons hold that we can survive a temporary loss of consciousness. We can survive sleep, a general anaesthetic, a short-term coma. The emphasis is on the capacity for consciousness. But consider someone who passes, without recovery, from a reversible to an irreversible coma, and thence to death. If there is some difficulty in holding that ceasing occurs just when death occurs, there is more in locating the critical division at the moment the coma becomes irreversible.

There are difficulties, then, with the non-existence claim. And it would be unfortunate if the Epicureans had to rest their case on such contentious views right at the outset. But it would be similarly unfortunate if counters to the Epicurean view needed to insist that with death our existence is not normally ended. So I shall just suppose, at least for purposes of argument, that the widespread claim is true: when dead, we do not exist. Why should this be thought to generate a problem for those who believe that death is bad?

Different issues perhaps get conflated here. There is, first, that of identifying and properly referring to the subject of the alleged evil of death, then, second, that of attributing certain appropriate properties to this subject and finally, that of explaining how having such properties can be bad for that subject. Yet it is not at all clear that any of these is particularly puzzling. And nor is it clear that all of these should be lumped under the subject problem.

Consider the first. Some people think there are serious difficulties in referring to nonexistent things. So there are difficulties here for Hamlet, and unicorns, and the sister I never had. But whatever these problems are, those, if any, for the dead are different. The dead were living, and did exist, even if they exist no longer. And there does not appear to be any problem in identifying the subjects of our conversations about the dead. Who is Napoleon's death bad for? Arguably, it is bad for – among others – Napoleon. Imagine we talk about him at different times. We say, in 1805, that his death will be bad for him, and then we say, in 1905, that his death was bad for him. Both claims may be false. But it is not that one makes sense, while the other does not. So, just as we can refer to the living, we can refer as well to the dead.

It will be objected that this misses the point. The question is not whether I can refer, at a time he no longer exists, to someone who earlier did exist; that manner of referring to the dead is uncontentious. It is, rather, whether I can successfully refer, at any time, to a time when he no longer exists, and pick out, or identify him at such a time. And in connection with the difference here a number of writers have wanted to distinguish between ante-mortem and post-mortem persons, allowing of the former that they can be identified, described, benefited and harmed in familiar and straightforward ways, but then finding it difficult to similarly treat of the latter.[16] Yet it would surely be a mistake to overplay this distinction and think there are actually two persons to consider here: Napoleon 1, who won some, lost some, married Josephine, fell ill and – presumably – died; and Napoleon 2, of whom none of these things are true. And contrast Napoleon with Macbeth. Perhaps we should here distinguish two individuals: an authentic Scottish king and the Shakespearean character loosely based on him. You might well be asked if you are talking about the real or the fictional Macbeth, the one who once existed or the one who never did. But questions about Napoleon require no such distinction. Talk is always about the same person, one who was alive but who is now dead. And even if we allow, with the Epicureans, that the dead do not exist, still there is just the one Napoleon, who once existed but who exists no longer.[17]

Perhaps, then, this subject problem is one of not reference but attribution, with the difficulty that of meaningfully saying anything about the current state of those who no longer exist. Certainly, I can talk about the past. And I might well enough say, of someone who does not now exist, that he made, apparently, a happy marriage, and yet messed up at Waterloo. But what of the present? Napoleon is not now small, or irascible, or empire-hungry, or in pain. We might add, he is not now dying. But surely he is now dead. Nor is this all. A dead person, someone who allegedly no longer exists, might still be famous, or remembered, or spoken of well or badly. Suppose again someone presses me here. Who, exactly, is famous? I shall say that it is Napoleon, who was alive, but is now dead.[18] And it is hard to see that this is not exact enough, or that any puzzle remains. It is hard to see too how our position on the contested claim makes any difference here. Our confidence in, or commitment to, the claim that Napoleon is now dead does not, surely, depend on whether or not we think the dead exist.

Perhaps it makes a difference somewhere close, however. Napoleon might be famous after he is dead. He might, further, then become more or less famous. So his being dead allows that he can have certain properties, and also that some of these properties can change with time. But now it will be objected that these are only so-called Cambridge changes: becoming more or less famous does not represent or involve any real change in Napoleon himself, but only in his relation to things or people elsewhere. And the thought here is that when dead, and so – as allowed – no longer in existence, a thing can no longer undergo any real or intrinsic change. But harm a thing and you change it. And so when dead it can no longer be harmed.

Now this may be right. But, as I said there can be a conflation of issues. And it is one thing to ask whether the dead can be harmed, and quite another to consider whether the living can be harmed by death. Similarly, we should distinguish the questions as to whether being dead one can be harmed, one's situation changed for the worse, and whether being dead one is now, already, in a bad situation. There is a related conflation in lumping together the subject question "Who is dead?" with the value question "Is it bad to be dead?" Here is an example: "So long as the person exists, he has not yet died, and once he has died, he no longer exists; so there seems to be no time when death, if it is a misfortune, can be ascribed to its unfortunate subject" (Nagel 1979: 4). If there seems to be a puzzle here it may well be because Nagel twice muddies the waters: first in running together the issue of misfortune with that of death; and second in failing to separate out different death-related properties that might be attributed to their subject at different times. We might say a little about the first blurring, and more about the second.

Certainly, "when death, if it is a misfortune" is a slippery turn of phrase. Perhaps there is a difficulty in saying just when it is that the dead suffer a misfortune, but no difficulty at all in saying either when they are dead, or, indeed, who is dead. But then the misfortune problem is not one of identifying its alleged subject, but of establishing that the alleged misfortune is genuine.

Nagel's wording suggests, I think misleadingly, that if death is bad then it will be hard to pick out the dead, but otherwise not.[19]

The second muddying is harder to spot, but more important. Consider again that threefold distinction between dying – a process, death – an event, and being dead – a state. Dying is a property of living, and existing people. Being dead, in contrast, attaches to dead, and, let us say, non-existing people. Now think about the intermediate category: the momentary or near-momentary event of death. That too affects the living. Just as only existing people can be dying, so too only existing people can die, suffer the moment of death, pass – perhaps in an instant – from being alive to being dead. And death is at least one of the major causes of our ceasing to exist. Epicurus works with just a twofold distinction, contrasting life and existence on the one hand, with death and non-existence on the other. Perhaps, in the sentences I quoted above, Nagel does the same. But the threefold distinction has merit. We might agree that once a person is dead he no longer exists without agreeing that he similarly does not exist at the moment of death. So even if you thought there was a subject problem concerning the state, you would be wrong to think there was a similar problem over the event.

The threefold distinction deserves further comment. First, my account is more or less standard except in one key respect. I have claimed that death – the event – clearly affects the living. Only the living die. But a number of writers, surprisingly, seem to want to deny this, implying that when death occurs we no longer exist.[20] It is as if, having insisted on three categories, they slip back into thinking there are just two. Second, even if dying is distinctive, the divide between death – an event, and being dead – a state, is less sharp. Being dead is not simply the state of not existing. Hamlet, unicorns and the population of Britain in the twenty-second century are all in this state. Roughly, being dead is no longer existing, having previously been alive. And death is not to be characterized simply by looking to the content of a moment. Roughly, it is the moment that introduces subsequent and endless non-existence. Third, there is room, given this, for important harm-related distinctions. So we can consider here the further interpretation of the subject problem, concerning neither identification nor attribution, but evaluation.

We can pick out the dead, and say various things about them. Perhaps, though, what we cannot truly say is that there is anything good or bad about being dead. But the distinctions above suggest certain refinements. We might want to say that nothing bad can happen to someone who does not exist – and so rule out posthumous harms – while still allowing that both death and being dead – the onset and the persistence of non-existence – are bad for a person. And because the event and the state are so intimately related, there is a reply to those who say that neither can be bad. The moment of death is not bad just in itself, it is not intrinsically bad; rather, it is bad just because it introduces endless non-existence. Nor is endless non-existence bad just in itself; it is bad when it is the alternative to the continuation of a good life, and thus when it is brought about by death. Who is harmed by death? Someone who, at the time of death, exists and who, were it not for death, would continue to exist, living a good life. Who suffers from being dead? The same person: someone who did exist and who, were they not now dead, would exist still. These are, at least, seemingly plausible views.

When?

When is death bad? I am asking here the timing question. It cannot be bad when you are alive. For when you are alive you are not yet dead. And it cannot be bad when you are dead, for then you do not exist. And it is tempting to think that post existence you are beyond benefit and harm. So the time at which death is bad is hard to pin down. Or, as Nagel puts it, "If death is a disadvantage, it is not easy to say when a man suffers it" (1979: 3). The Epicureans, of course, are untroubled by this. They insist that as there is no time when death is bad, so death is not bad. Others, thinking that death is bad, need a solution to the timing problem. I shall first sketch what I think is straightforwardly the right answer here, and then consider certain further, and rather more elaborate, answers that have been given.[21] Then I shall return to my answer, and fill in some details.

The question might be put slightly differently. When does someone suffer the evils of death? Remember, I have some reservations about the death–being dead distinction. They cannot often be usefully prised apart. And so a respectable, even if far from final answer here is, at the time they die, and for the time that they are dead; that is, thereafter.[22]

This answer makes the badness of death somewhat like that of a headache, or a coma. Both are normally bad from when they start until (at least) they end. So they are bad for (at least) as long as they last. Their badness has a temporal dimension. Some people have wanted to give a quite different account of death's badness, suggesting that it is timelessly or eternally bad. One part of their motivation here concerns the subject problem. Another part may be the thought that although while when alive we are in time, death takes us into a different, timeless and also spaceless realm. And so it may be not altogether unsurprising that the properties of death, and here its badness in particular, have similarly a dimension of timelessness. So imagine the death of a girl. Feldman, after acknowledging that "in one sense" dating the misfortune of death is straightforward – look in obituary columns, for example – settling when it is a misfortune for her is less so.

> If Lindsay is the girl, and d is the state of affairs of *Lindsay dying on December 7, 1987*, then the question is this: "Precisely when is d bad for Lindsay?" I have proposed an account of death. According to that account, when we say that d is bad for Lindsay, we mean that the value for her of the nearest world where d occurs is lower than the value for her of the nearest in which d does not occur. So our question comes to this: "Precisely when is it the case that the value for Lindsay of the nearest world in which d occurs is lower than the value for her of the nearest world in which d does not occur?
>
> It seems clear to me that the answer to this question must be "eternally". (Feldman 1993: 321)[23]

There is not much wrong with this except that it misses the point. It does not address the allegedly distinctive timing puzzle about death. For what Feldman says here is perfectly general, in that we can say of any misfortune that it is always or timelessly bad. When is toothache bad? Always. When is it bad to have toothache on Tuesday? Again, always.[24] And nothing is changed if we agree that we are not considering here the misfortune of death, but the relation between two lives. When was Tolstoy's life longer than Keats's? Again we might say, always. What may remain at issue, though, is an ordinary dating problem as to when someone suffers from or is harmed by a particular misfortune.[25] We might need to discover when the toothache began, and when it ended. And in relation to lives, we might care to know, for example, when the first started to outlast the second, how long the outlasting lasted and so on. There may be further questions. In the coma case, for example, it may be that there are coma-related harms that continue after recovery. Hence my "at least". And if there are timing problems relating to death then, as I shall explain, they will be of this kind.

Harry Silverstein picks up on these shortcomings in Feldman's account. But his approach to the timing puzzle is simply bizarre. The problem, as the Epicureans see it, is that we are not aware of, and have within us no bad experiences or feeling generated by, being dead. So how, then, can being dead be a bad thing? Silverstein wants to retain the hedonism (hence his assumption that values connect with feeling [VCF]) and still account for death's badness. He adopts, as he thinks controversially, a four-dimensional framework ("à la Quine"), which then:

allows, indeed requires us to view posthumous objects and events, as existing – in Quine's words, it views objects, events, etc. from all places and times (or better, from all place-times) "as coexisting in an eternal or timeless sense of the word." Thus, we seem to have solved our problem. By adopting the four-dimensional framework we can say … that posthumous events exist; … that posthumous events can therefore be objects of appropriate feeling in the sense required by VCF; … and, hence, … that the Epicurean view can justifiably be rejected. In brief, A's death coexists with A ("in an eternal or timeless sense of the word"), and is therefore a possible object of A's suffering, and is therefore an intelligible A-relative evil.[26]   (2000: 117–18)

Again, there are no egregious mistakes here. In particular, Silverstein acknowledges that he is not suggesting that future events can *cause* present suffering. The claim is only that to the question "What's upsetting you?" the answer "My future non-existence", might, just like "My future visit to the dentist", be the appropriate answer. So the badness of death is, as hedonism evidently requires, linked to feeling. Someone might disagree, arguing that it is the thought of the future that lies behind, and indeed straightforwardly causes, the pain. But let us just allow that we can both think about and be upset by future events. This does not explain the badness of death. I shall make just two points. First, death is supposed to be bad whether or not we think about it, and whether it is announced or catches us unawares. Second, just as spiders are not evil simply because we fear them, so too the Epicurean will insist that our bad feelings about death are wholly irrational. To take issue with that, as most will, requires us to point to something about death that legitimates our current concerns. Silverstein just does not engage with this problem.

Feinberg is not much troubled by the problem of the subject. But the timing problem occupies him more. If it occupies him more than it should, this is in part because he wants to tie together the death problem with that of posthumous harms. For "Death and developments after death are alike in coming into existence during a period when there is no longer a subject … both death and posthumous events are post-personal. Either death and posthumous harms both alike can be harms or neither can" (Feinberg 1984: 82). Feinberg does not draw on the death–being dead distinction. So what he says here is particularly curious. We do not, in most cases, first cease to exist and then die. So while posthumous events are post-personal, death – the event – is not. And even if being dead – the state – is post-personal it, unlike posthumous events, does not in any clear way "come into existence" after the subject has ceased to be.

Having, as I think, caused himself difficulties by lumping these two concerns together, how does Feinberg address the death problem?

> We should now say that it is the living person antemortem who is (usually) harmed directly by his own death. When then did his harmed condition begin? Presumably not at the moment of death itself, because that is when he ceased to be. Let us say then, still following the model of harmful posthumous events, that the harmed condition began at the moment he first acquired the interests that death defeats …
>
> … Almost everyone will die with some interest that will be defeated by death. And because of the inevitability of death, all of us are, while alive, in at least a partially harmed condition in that *those* interests are doomed, and thus generative of harm, from the time they are first acquired. (*Ibid.*: 92–3)

Much of this is right. Living people are typically, although not invariably, harmed by death. Whether and to what degree they are harmed depends on how their life is going, and would continue to go were they not to die. And how it is going depends in part both on what interests they have and the chances of their fulfilment. But other things are wrong. It is one thing to say that a necessary condition of being harmed by death is that we have certain future directed interests that death will thwart, and another that we are harmed by having, and at the time that we acquire, those interests. Something might be inevitable even while it has not yet occurred. So we might now be doomed – with a bad future ahead of us – without now being harmed. And this unconvincing account[27] is not needed. For it is hard to see just what could be wrong with the more obviously appealing view: being harmed by death begins at the time that you die. And again a coma analogy might be made. It is Tuesday. A man knocks you on the head and takes your money. Even if your having the money and wanting to keep it led to the coma, we surely want to say that the harm began on Tuesday, and that this man caused it, rather than that it began months or years ago, and that you caused it. Being harmed by a coma begins when you lose consciousness.

So return to my more straightforward account. The badness of death, assuming it is bad, begins when you die. In this, it is like toothache, or coma. And, like these, it remains bad for as long as it continues. Nagel finds this objectionable, and insists here on an asymmetry between life and death:

> If it is good to be alive, that advantage can be attributed to a person at each point of his life. It is a good of which Bach had more than

Schubert, simply because he lived longer. Death, however, is not an evil of which Shakespeare has so far received a larger portion than Proust.[28]   (1979: 3)

There is right and wrong here also. First, distinguish now between toothache and coma. Toothache is painful. It feels bad. We can say that it is intrinsically bad. And this is why it is bad, in at least one important way, when it starts, and for as long as it continues. But it might not be overall bad; say, because of the toothache you meet a particularly fetching dentist and fall in love. Coma does not feel bad and is not painful; it is not intrinsically bad. But it is normally bad, nevertheless, just because it keeps us from doing good things, having good experiences and living the good life. Often, it keeps us from these things from when it starts until it ends, just because, were we not comatose, we would throughout that period be living the good life. We might say that coma is extrinsically, and conditionally, bad. And so we might offer a deprivation account of its badness. A coma is bad just when it prevents us from enjoying the good. Unsurprisingly, very many writers, Nagel among them, have suggested that death's badness needs to be seen in similar terms: it is bad, when it is bad, not because of its intrinsic features, but because of what it takes away.[29] This is surely at least in large part right. But it means, of course, that my initial suggestion needs to be amended. Death is not bad simply from the time it starts, and then thereafter; rather, it is bad, or bad for us, when it deprives us of a good life.

In this respect, then, there is an important asymmetry here. Life is good, when it is good, in virtue of its contents. It has a character, and a value, of its own. It may now be tempting to say simply that death, like coma, is bad, when it is bad, because of the life it deprives us of. Its character, and its value, are derivative. But this is not quite right. Death, or being dead, is in itself characterless and value neutral. Even if it is not for these reasons bad to be dead, still it is not good. So there is in this sense a starting-point from which comparisons with life, and ensuing deprivations, are made or measured. And this, I think, is why we can say that death is often bad, and not merely worse than life, and, when better than life, still not good. There is a second asymmetry. Life is finite. So, of day-by-day equally good lives, we can say longer is better. Death, unlike coma, lasts forever, so thoroughly analogous comparisons in terms of length are impossible. But there is no reason to believe in a third asymmetry. There is no reason to think that things that are intrinsically bad, such as toothache, have a temporal dimension and can be dated, while things that are extrinsically bad somehow slip through the calendar. Shakespeare has been dead for longer than Proust. Assume their lives were, and would have continued to be, good.[30] Because he has been dead for longer, Shakespeare has missed out on more than Proust. So in this sense he has, thus far, received a larger portion of death's evil. Nagel offers no reason to think otherwise.

There is a confusion to guard against here, and an objection to consider. The confusion is about different ways of ranking badness against time. Consider coma. Bob has been in a coma for a month, Betty for a week. He has, at this time, missed out on more of life, and so has, thus far, lost more. But all comas last six months. So they are equally destined to lose six months of their lives. Even so, it remains true that Bob has, at this time, lost more than Betty. Similarly for death. Even though it lasts forever, and even though in the end we might all lose infinite amounts of good, still Shakespeare has, so far, missed out on more than Proust. And as death is endless this will always be so.

The objection is this. If death is bad so long as the alternative is a good life then it is bad, for all of us, for a relatively short time. Forget infinite amounts. There is no possibility of our living the good life for much more than around eighty years. Shakespeare and Proust both died in early middle age. They both lost thirty or forty years from dying when they did. So Nagel is right, and Shakespeare has not lost more, is not now worse off, than Proust.

Evidently there is merit in this objection. But it does not challenge my revised claim that death is bad when it deprives us of a good life, nor the underlying claim that death has a temporal dimension. Rather, it simply insists that for anyone who died more than a century ago, there is just no possibility of their leading a good life now. Their time is up. And so for all those people death, or their being dead, is no longer bad. This may be right, but it is not obviously right. Even if, currently, it just is not possible for someone to live for more than around a hundred years, it is not clear that we need other than technological developments in order significantly to extend our life span.[31] And even if it is not physically possible for someone to live for, say, a thousand years, this is surely logically possible. On the face of it, at least, it is logically possible for someone to live forever. If an immortal life would be good, then dying when we do, at around eighty or ninety, is bad even if dying earlier, prematurely, is worse. So if there is any sense in which Shakespeare could be living a good life now, then he has missed out on more of this good life than has Proust.

The issue here is whether we should think of the life you would have lived, had you not died, as ending at best, at around eighty or ninety, or whether that life might better be thought of as ending much later. The underlying issue is that of determining how relevant comparisons between our actual lives and some possible life are to be made. I return to these issues in Chapter 5.

A different issue can be further pursued here. A coma is bad, often and perhaps typically, when it starts and as long as it lasts. For often, perhaps typically, were we not in a coma we would be living a good life. But, of course, there are countless exceptions. Suppose that while in the coma your condition deteriorates. If you came round now you would be living a very bad life. Then the coma, which was bad, is in this way bad no longer. It is now better than consciousness. Similarly for death. Someone dies at thirty. If they had not died, then they would have been living a good life. But had they lived to fifty they would have been caught in a nuclear war. Their life would not have been good. Plausibly, death is bad, as it is worse than life, for twenty years, and thereafter good. Consider a different example. You are held by terrorists and subject to daily torture. They plan to keep this up for months but, fortunately, you die of a heart attack after the first week. How fortunate is this? Neither you nor the torturers knew this, but had you survived then you would, after only a couple of months, have been rescued. Plausibly, death, or being dead, is not bad for you at those times when, had you lived, you would have been tortured, but is bad for you later when, post-rescue, you would have been living a good life.

We contrast, even in our everyday language, entering a coma and being in a coma. But talk of death blurs the distinction between the event and the state. Bring that to the surface and situations can be better described. We can say that being dead is good at some times because it is better than life, while bad at others because it is worse than life. Yet we need a different view about the event of death. But what view? There appear to be three possibilities. First, death at some time t is bad if being dead is for the first ensuing moment or period bad. Second, death at t is bad if being dead is overall bad. Third, there is no such straightforward answer. In order to help decide, think about a different case. You accidentally drink some substance on Tuesday. It has no effect on Wednesday, certain overall bad effects on Thursday and Friday, but then overall good effects on Saturday. Was it bad for you to drink this substance? We should not say it was neither good nor bad, just because it had no effects on Wednesday. Nor, I think, should we simply say it was bad, just in the case that the bad effects outweigh the good. If we say it was in some ways good, some ways bad, or if we say that it was overall bad, without implying it was unqualifiedly bad, or uniformly bad, then we have given a truthful, not misleading, but still not complete answer to the question being asked. And we can offer a similarly elaborated answer in the case of death. There is no good reason to think that unmodulated yes/no answers are always available, nor that when we are disinclined to provide them then something is amiss.

I know that many people will remain dissatisfied with the answer given here to the timing question. But it is hard to pin down just where their reservations come in. On my view we can make a series of claims. Jane died on Tuesday.

If she had not died, she would have been at the party on Thursday, having a good time. Death prevented her from being at the party, and deprived her of certain pleasures. So even though she was not in an intrinsically bad state, being dead on Thursday was worse for her than being alive. Nor was it merely worse; there was nothing good about her situation on Thursday. Being in an intrinsically neutral state is worse than being in an intrinsically good state. When, had you not been in the neutral state you would have been in the good state, being in the neutral state is bad. Hence the badness of death.

What is objectionable? Certainly people die. And, surely, various counterfactuals are then true of them. Of course, the longer things go on the less clear it will be which counterfactuals obtain. But as we can say, if Jim had not been arrested for drunk driving he would have been at the party, and if Jess had not fallen into a temporary coma she too would have been there, so similarly for Jane, alas now dead. In all these cases we can be equally confident we are describing a life that would, were it not for a regrettable change in circumstances, have been lived.

But are these changes regrettable? Are they all changes for the worse? Some people insist that as the dead do not exist then they can be ascribed no level of welfare, they are in no situation, or state. Therefore they are not deprived of anything by being dead, and are not worse off than they would be, were they alive. So much, then, for death's badness. But the objection here is not forceful. There are, I suggest, different ways of being in a neutral state. You might be undergoing pleasures and pains that happen to cancel each other out, as on a rather disappointing holiday. Or your experiences might each of them be of neutral value. You might be subject to no experience – nothing good, nothing bad – at all, as when in a temporary coma. Or you might be either in a permanent coma or dead, and so, as I have allowed, no longer in existence. In all these cases you have an overall zero level of welfare: you are in a neutral state. I intend this talk about states to carry no more weight than this.

A further objection is that if you are in such a state when dead, then you are similarly in a neutral state before birth. And if it is bad to be dead then it is similarly bad to be not yet alive. That is an odd view. So too, then, is the view that it can be bad to be dead. Unsurprisingly this is an issue I shall need to consider at greater length. But in anticipation of that longer discussion I can say here that although the first point might be accepted, the second should not be. Before I was born nothing good or bad was happening to me. I was – and I shall say this just because it has, as I see it, no suspect implications – in a neutral state. But being dead is bad only when, were I not dead, I would have been in some better state. And it is far from clear that there were similarly alternative good states to my being not yet alive.

A final objection here, again made by someone who is doubtful of the suggestion that the dead are in any state, is that death is bad just when it occurs, when it puts an end to life, and not, as I have claimed, both when and after it occurs. But there seems here to be a reversion to the ambiguity surrounding the "When?" question that I noted earlier. We might say that death – the event – is bad when it deprives us of a good life, meaning here that it is bad in those circumstances, or under those conditions; but it is in this way bad only if there really are times, and stretches of time, subsequent to this event when, had we not died, we would be living a good life. Death *qua* event is bad only in virtue of these post-mortem datable contrasts between our current condition, that of not now existing, and the life we would otherwise have been leading. And it is hard to see how the timing question can be answered without reference to these times.

How?

Perhaps we can, as I have suggested, say who, if anyone, death is bad for. Perhaps we can, as well, say when, if at all, death is bad for that person. But is it bad? As Nagel noted:

> doubt may be raised whether *anything* can be bad for a man without being positively unpleasant to him: specifically, it may be doubted that there are any evils that consist merely in the deprivation or absence of possible goods, and that do not depend on someone's *minding* that deprivation.   (1979: 4)

Nagel thinks he can settle these doubts. I think that they might be settled, but that Nagel's way with them is unconvincing and unnecessary. I hope to explain. But first we need to understand more of the problem.

Many of us will think of extreme pain as paradigmatically bad: this is something that is positively unpleasant. So the Epicureans are right, and genuinely consoling, in so far as they insist death is not in this way, is not intrinsically, bad. Because it is not in this way bad, because, further, it is an experiential blank, then perhaps they are right too to insist that there is in death nothing to fear. Thus far there is something in their hedonism. But it could be bad in other ways. And it could be something to regret and to avoid.

How could something be bad without being painful, or positively unpleasant: without itself being experienced as bad? Surely, first, the causes of bad sensations are, usually, bad.[32] In a restaurant, an enemy secretly injects you with a radioactive drug. Three days later the headaches begin. Headaches are bad for you, but it was bad for you too to be given this drug, even though it did not feel bad. Secret injections are, usually, things to regret and avoid. This does not help with death, however. As we mostly agree, it is not as if you die and then some days you are assigned your place in hell. But now, second, the causes of your being deprived of good sensation are also bad, as too are those deprivations themselves. Someone steals your winning lottery ticket, and you never experience the joy that vast quantities of money can bring. You arrive late for the cinema and have to make do with a poor seat, behind a man with a big head. Or the hotel you wanted is fully booked and you can only get in to a humdrum bed and breakfast. There are many such examples. Here is another. You unwittingly drink the potion and fall into a coma for seven years. When you wake up, the princess is gone. So as well as pains, and things that are positively unpleasant, we might count reductions or obliterations of pleasures as among the bad things that can befall us.

Yet we need further distinctions here. It may be that in these cases you are aware of your situation, and aware too of what it might have been. You know, with the cinema or hotel, that you are making do with second best. You know, on waking from the coma, that much has been lost. There is some frustration, disappointment or regret. Perhaps this is not positively unpleasant, but you would have preferred things otherwise, and mind that they are not. Contrast these cases with others where frustration, disappointment or regret are absent. You never discover this, but a crook swaps your first-prize lottery ticket for third-prize one. Or you choose philosophy over physics at college, live a good life, but would have lived better had you chosen differently.[33] Or, as in one of Nagel's cases, you suffer brain damage and your life changes from that of a successful scientist to one of a contented infant.[34] Or the coma is one from which you never wake. Is it bad to regret how things turn out? Perhaps it is not as clearly bad as feeling pain but still it is bad, it feels bad, when you spend time wishing things had gone otherwise. Is it bad to have things to regret, even if, because you are unaware of the situation, you feel no regret? Even if it is less clearly bad, many of us will think this is bad too. And we will think, of some of the lives of others, that they are, in various ways, going badly, and significantly less well than they might have gone, even though they are neither painful nor unpleasant.

In these four cases there is a clear difference between the actual life and the life that would have been lived had some event not occurred. There is too the reasonably resilient thought that this actual life is in some important respects worse. But it might be worse than what might have been even while better than what was, as with lottery tickets. Or it might be worse than what might have been, even while clearly good, as with the career move. Or there might be a situation where things are both worse than they were and worse than they would otherwise have been, but only marginally so: Bill Gates loses a dime. Or, finally, the possibility of the better life might be remote. Had evolution taken a particular turn eons ago we would all have had wings. Had you been a lottery-ticket-buying type and splashed out when last in the supermarket you would have been considerably richer today. In all such cases, and no doubt there are others, we might hesitate to think that anything bad has occurred, or that one is genuinely in a bad situation now. But there will not be this hesitation, surely, in the brain damage and the coma cases. Our victims are: (i) not in a good situation, not living good lives; (ii) living lives that are much worse than they were; and (iii) living lives that are much worse than they might, in some non-remote possibility, have been. It was bad that certain events occurred.

Similarly with death. In large numbers of cases, and in particular the prime of life cases, death – the event – is bad, and is so just because the resulting state, our being dead, is worse for us, and considerably so, than the life we would otherwise, and might easily, have lived. Further, being dead has few redeeming features. And it is bad to be in an intrinsically neutral situation when one's situation would otherwise have been good. Again, there will be the objection that the dead, perhaps unlike the comatose, are not in a situation at all. But I have nothing further to say about that.

There is a need now to explore another distinction, made earlier, between something's being bad in itself, or from the point of view of the universe, and its being bad for you. The hedonist thinks that pleasure is good and pain is bad. He should think too, as I have wanted to claim, that decreases in pleasure are bad, while decreases in pain are good. But here we need to be careful. Consider animals. Although most of us think that animal pain is bad, fewer suppose that it is bad for animals to undergo a sudden and painless death.[35] Still, if we think the more pleasure the better, then it will, other things equal, be a bad thing that some animal, one that would otherwise have continued to enjoy a pleasant life, should die prematurely. The concern here, however, is with the badness of death for one who dies. And the difference between much human and much animal death concerns the significantly more complex psychology that we possess. We might express this in terms of personhood, or in the difference between biographical and biological lives, or again between categorical and conditional desires.[36] But the point is the same: death is bad for us not simply by generating an overall loss of pleasure within the one life, but by cutting off a particular life, a biography, life story or narrative, that we were wanting to enjoy. And the difference here might warrant a moment's rethink about two cases sketched above. Brain damage, and thereafter the life of an infant, is bad in those cases where a life was unfolding, and is now suddenly curtailed. But even if choosing philosophy over physics results in a worse life from point of view of overall pleasure, it is rather less clear how such a choice can be worse for me. There is more about this in Chapter 7.[37]

A suggestion might be that what this amounts to is our dropping hedonism and focusing instead on future-directed desires. Death is bad for us as it prevents us from getting what we want. It is not bad for animals, as they lack such desires. But the problem here is that it is hard to see how getting what I want, having my desires or preferences satisfied, can be good for me if it makes no difference to what I think, or how I feel. And so it is similarly hard to see how, in such circumstances, their being thwarted can be bad for me. I discuss these matters in more detail in Chapter 6. But I shall suggest now that a better way forward is to marry these two accounts. As hedonists, the Epicureans think our mental states are what matters. But we can evaluate our mental states in various ways. We can look just to their intrinsic qualities, and how much pleasure or pain they contain. We can compare the states someone has with others she might have had. And we can consider the connections between them, and distinguish between mental lives that are complex, interesting or coherent and those that are disjointed, repetitive or tedious. Animal lives are arguably of the second kind. Most of us have longer-term interests and desires, memories of our earlier desires, awareness of what has gone right and what wrong, and an ability to reflect on and think about our lives as wholes. To varying degrees, then, our lives are of the first kind. There seems no reason to suppose that the hedonist must take a simple and atomistic view of what is good and bad, better and worse about our mental states. And so there is no reason to think that there is not, within a broadly hedonistic frame, the wherewithal to counter the Epicurean.[38]

Nagel tries a different tack, one that involves giving up on hedonism. And as is well known, and not unlike Feinberg,[39] he connects the badness of death to that of undiscovered betrayal and the breaking of deathbed promises. There are certainly similarities, in that all these examples pose challenges to the view that what you do not know cannot hurt you. But there are clearly significant differences here, such that someone may well think that death is bad while denying that there is any badness in these allegedly analogous cases. The difference, of course, concerns hedonism. For even if we do not experience being dead – and so it is neither painful nor frustrating – it does have a big effect on, and makes a big difference to, our experience. It ends it. Plausibly, this is what is bad about it. But undiscovered betrayal, and the whole range of so-called posthumous harms, leaves our experience untouched, so that it continues just as it would were we not betrayed in the former case, and remains equally nonexistent in the latter. I do not say here that undiscovered betrayal is not bad, and I do not insist that there are no posthumous harms, but it is more difficult to explain how the subject is harmed in these cases than it is with death. And because of the difference here, we can continue to think that death is bad while taking a somewhat sceptical stance on certain later comments. After discussing the case of the man reduced to the condition of a contented infant, Nagel insists that:

> it is arbitrary to restrict the goods and evils that can befall a man to nonrelational properties ascribable to him at particular times. As it stands, that restriction excludes not only such cases of gross degeneration but also a good deal of what is important about success and failure, and other features of a life that have the character of processes. I believe we can go further, however. There are goods and evils that are irreducibly relational; they are features of the relations between a person, with spatial and temporal boundaries of the usual sort, and circumstances that may not coincide with him either in space or in time. A man's life includes much that does not take place within the boundaries of his body and his mind, and what happens to him can include much that does not take place within the boundaries of his life.   (1979: 6)

Yet it is one thing to allow that we cannot fully describe or assess someone's condition by taking merely an internal and time-slice approach, and another to agree with the further claim that our lives extend beyond our bodies and minds. Certainly we have concerns for and interests in people, issues, events other than those involving ourselves, and the places and times in which we live. And things may not turn out as we would have liked: our posthumous reputations are tarnished, our grandchildren become wastrels, our pet projects founder. But when such things happen it is not easy to see how this is bad for us, or something by which we are harmed. This is discussed later; the main point here is that we need no such apparatus to account for the badness of death. Death affects us more straightforwardly, marking one of the boundaries of our lives, and altering, usually, both the body and the mind. At least in these respects its harm is unproblematic.

Two positions

Consider now two somewhat more formal presentations of certain key positions. Both are often identified and often discussed in the literature. Both contain, as I see it, errors worth noting. And their discussion here encourages clarification and reinforcement of points already made.

Stephen Rosenbaum offers, and then defends, the following version of the Epicurean argument:

(A) A state of affairs is bad for person P only if P can experience it at some time.

Therefore, (B) P's being dead is bad for P only if it is a state of affairs that P can experience at some time

(C) P can experience a state of affairs at some time only if it begins before P's death.

(D) P's being dead is not a state of affairs that begins before P's death.

Therefore, (E) P's being dead is not a state of affairs that P can experience at some time

Therefore, P's being dead is not bad for P.   (1993a: 121)

It looks as if the point here is to show that death lacks a necessary condition of something's being bad. But this is not quite right. Rosenbaum insists on the event–state distinction. So on his reading Epicurus is simply silent about death; it just gets no mention. And it seems that were we to want to mention it we would need a differently shaped argument. Someone may doubt whether momentary events have beginnings. But they have temporal locations. And even if it does not occur before, certainly my death does not occur after the end of my life. As I have said, death comes only to the living.

That is, I think, one shortcoming of the argument.[40] But what is particularly curious here is the first premise. As stated, it is surely false. Being irradiated is bad for me, as is spending seven years in a coma. Rosenbaum must mean to include experiencing a thing's effects here. The main puzzle about this premise, however, is why Rosenbaum wants *can* rather than *does*. Of course, given the traffic here in necessary conditions this might appear only to be cautious, with my being dead failing to meet even the weaker condition. But Rosenbaum needs the distinction, as he wants to allow that something can be bad for me even if in fact it does not affect experience, and wants, in particular, to concede to Nagel that undiscovered betrayal can be bad. For, "We can grant that what one *does not* consciously experience can hurt one without granting that what one *cannot* experience can hurt one" (1993a: 127).[41]

This is curious. And we need more detail about the modal terms. Suppose, as seems plausible, that it is logically and physically possible to discover, and so be affected by betrayal, but neither logically nor physically possible to experience being dead. Rosenbaum thinks undiscovered betrayal is bad, but death is not. What about a bad coma, or PVS? It is not clear what he will say. Suppose he thinks recovery needs only to be logically possible for this coma to be bad. It is not clear why you would think it is not bad to die, but it is bad to be in a coma from which there is in fact no possibility of recovery. Suppose he thinks it needs to be physically possible. Someone in a coma dies without recovering consciousness. It is not clear why their situation is bad if, but only if, in fact they might have recovered. Nor is it clear how our evaluation of their condition should wait on our understanding of neurophysiology.

Rosenbaum's is, then, an anomalous position. Perhaps we might understand why someone thinks either that both death and undiscovered betrayal are bad, or that neither is bad. Perhaps we might understand too, and as I have been urging here, that death is more clearly bad than is undiscovered betrayal. But it is hard to see why anyone should want the reverse of this last position.

McMahan very usefully distinguishes between three positions implicated in discussions of death's badness.

> *The Existence Requirement:* A person can be the subject of some misfortune only if he exists at the time the misfortune occurs.

> *The Narrow Experience Requirement:* An event can be bad for a person only if he experiences it as bad.

> *The Wide Experience Requirement:* An event can be bad for a person only if it in some way affects or makes a difference to his conscious experience. (1988: 33)

These experience requirements both preclude the badness of undiscovered betrayal. But then they differ in that the former rules out, the latter allows for, the badness of death. So we should, I think, be tempted to reject the former, and accept the latter. Should we succumb? The Wide Experience Requirement is, I think, almost right, but there is room for a clarification. Jane is in a coma. She would have recovered, but in order to inherit the nephews kill her. Jimmy, after a suicide attempt, is also in a coma. He wants to die, but the doctors intervene, restoring him to a miserable life. Both cases are covered by the requirement even though the person harmed by the intervention is not currently enjoying any experiences at all. The nephews make a difference by preventing experiences that would have occurred; the doctors make a difference by permitting experiences that would not have occurred. Neither of them affects or makes a difference to experiences already under way.

What about the Existence Requirement? This looks tempting, too. How can something that does not exist suffer any misfortune? And, further, it appears to be implied by the Wide Experience Requirement. For surely the only things whose experiences can be affected, either by making them worse or by ending them, or again by preventing or permitting their recurrence, are existing things. But there are some problems here. The bomb goes off ten years before you are born. As a consequence, you develop some genetic abnormality. Now certainly you did not exist at the time of the explosion. Equally certainly, the explosion is the cause of your current misfortune. So must we reject the requirement? Well, we might make two distinctions. Even if you are the subject or victim of a misfortune that happens before you are born, you are not subject to misfortune at that time. And even if a harming event can occur before birth, you cannot be harmed at that time.[42] So what I take to be the substance of the Existence Requirement remains intact. But consider a different case. I believe something can go out of existence, and then come back into existence. And I believe that even if it is not physically possible, still it is logically possible for the dead, even if death brings about non-existence, to come back to life. So death is not necessarily irreversible. Grant me all this. And now imagine that the nephews, in order to inherit, prevent your resurrection. Here you are subject to misfortune at a time when you do not exist. This constitutes one, and certainly a contentious, area of exception to the general rule. Setting this aside the Existence Requirement, or so I believe, remains intact.

But what does McMahan think of these various requirements? Unsurprisingly, he rejects the Narrow Experience Requirement. Rather more surprisingly he rejects the Wide Requirement and the Existence Requirement as well. Consider his holiday man, sunning himself on some desert island. On Friday his business collapses. On Monday, the news reaches the island. But on Sunday he is eaten by a shark. As McMahan notes, the Existence Requirement allows that he suffered a misfortune, while the Narrow Experience Requirement denies it.[43] But now:

> Suppose we agree that the fact that his life's work has come to
> nothing is a misfortune for him. On reflection, it seems hard to

believe that it makes a difference to the misfortune he suffers whether the collapse of his life's work occurs shortly before he is killed or shortly afterwards. Yet, according to the Existence Requirement, this difference in timing makes *all* the difference. If the collapse of his life's work occurs just before he dies, then, even though he never learns of it, he suffers a terrible misfortune. If on the other hand, it occurs just after he dies, he suffers no misfortune at all. If we find this hard to believe then we may be forced to reject the Existence Requirement.

Most of us, however, will be disposed to do this anyway. The example is probably superfluous, since most of us find death itself a sufficient counterexample. Apart from suffering great pain, it is hard to think of a clearer example than death of something that most people believe to be in most cases bad for the person to whom it happens. The Epicurean simply denies what most of us believe. Death, he claims, cannot be bad for us because when it occurs we will not exist at all. But that is precisely what we object to …   (1998: 38–9)

There are several oddities here. First, the difference in timing makes a difference, for the holiday man, only if we have already accepted that the loss of his business is a misfortune, whether or not he learns of it. But to accept that is by no means mandatory, and many will doubt that he is harmed by a loss of which he is unaware, and that has effects on neither his body nor his mind. Go with these doubts, and the Existence Requirement, offering only a necessary condition of badness, here implies nothing that is hard to believe. Second, as I said, the Wide Experience Requirement implies the Existence Requirement. If McMahan wants to reject the latter he will need to reject the former also. He is never explicit about doing so, but it is, of course, precisely the rejection of this claim that allows through the contention that holiday man is harmed when, although unknown, his business collapses. Third, this unstated rejection of the Wide Requirement is actually in place earlier. I said that McMahan, unsurprisingly, rejects the Narrow Requirement. But in fact he does this on surprising grounds. Rather than something like a bed and breakfast or coma case, where experience is worse, but painless, he appeals here to a variant of undiscovered betrayal.[44] That, if it works at all, counters the Narrow and Wide Requirements with equal effect. Fourth, the claim that death itself overturns the Existence Requirement is surely false. When death occurs we do exist. It could hardly end the existence of something that was already nonexistent. Nor could McMahan object that even though we exist the moment before, we do not exist at the moment of death. That is in any event an implausible claim. And as he allows that death ends experience, there seems no reason, here at least, to deny that it ends existence also. So both the Existence Requirement and the Wide Experience Requirement remain buoyant.

Summary

I have discussed, at some length, three well-known puzzles about the evil of death. I have tried to show how these puzzles are, as I see it, less pressing than is often claimed. We can identify the subject who is affected by, and perhaps also harmed by, death: it is just that person who died, who now allegedly exists no longer, and who, were it not for death, would be alive and in existence still. We can say when the alleged misfortune, or harm, or badness of death occurs. It happens in time. It happens, normally, when the person dies, and continues so long as, or for those periods when, were they not dead, the life they would have been living would have been good. And we can account for the nature of this supposed harm, claiming, as I think plausibly, that it is bad when things get much worse, and that, often at least, it is much worse when life is much shorter. So we might accept that death is not experienced as bad, and yet still hope to accommodate its badness within the general hedonist frame.

Does this clear things up for the evil of death? Far from it. I have not described in any detail the circumstances under which death is bad, or said how bad it is, or even that it is really bad at all. My concerns so far have been only to tackle claims that there is something highly distinctive, special or anomalous about the badness of death. I deny this. Death's badness is something like the badness of a headache, and even more like the badness of a coma. But when, and how, headaches or comas are bad, and whether they are really bad at all, are matters less straightforward than they might at first seem. Some of the more general issues about the badness of things need now to be considered.

5

Circumstances and degrees

Consider two questions. When is death bad? And, how bad is death? The first question is ambiguous, asking about the circumstances in which death is bad, or about the time or times at which the badness of a bad death hits home. I discussed that question in the previous chapter. The focus here is on the circumstances under which death is bad. Views are that it is always bad, bad in all circumstances, or that it is never bad, bad in no circumstances, or that it is sometimes bad, bad in some circumstances, but not in others.[1] The last is the prevailing view, and the one I explore here. How bad is death? Someone might think that death is not always bad, is not bad in all cases, or under all circumstances, but nevertheless think that when bad it is bad, always, to the same degree. But a more common, and more defensible, view is that just as it is bad in some circumstances and not others, so its badness varies from case to case. So, some deaths are worse than others. The main concerns here, then, are to discuss the circumstances under which death is bad, and to say something about how and why its badness might vary. But there is a third question. Is death really bad at all? It seems that it is bad in at least the prime of life case. But is that really so? Several of the Epicureans' concerns can be set aside. But can they all? Towards the end of the chapter I shall revisit this.

Deprivation and harm

Consider the deprivation account in more detail. Neither death – the event – nor being dead – the state – is intrinsically bad. Death is bad when it deprives us of a good life. Many are agreed on this. And many are agreed that Feldman's articulation of the deprivation account is on the right lines. He asks: how are we to understand the badness of a deprivation? Your life is going a certain way, and has a certain overall value. If some event intersects with your life it may alter its direction, and its value. If you do not win the lottery your life as a whole is good; if you do win it is even better. Take the tablets and you fall into a coma for a week; life without the coma is better than life with it. Catch the plane the terrorists have targeted and you will die within hours; the world in which you fail to catch the plane gives you a longer and better life than the world in which you do. Failing to win, falling into a coma and dying in each case deprives you of some good. How much? We can evaluate these different lives. The difference between them reveals the extent of your deprivation.

We can, in principle at least, introduce numerical values here. The value of a life is a function of its length and content. There will be many exceptions but, where possible I shall use from hereon a very simple model, assuming first that you live at most to 100, and second that when life goes very well you get 10 points per year. So let us say that without the win life has a value of 850, with it, a value of 900. Avoid the coma and your life as a whole scores 750, with it, it drops to 745. Finally, if you do not board the plane then you live to 90, with an overall value of 900, while if you do board you die now at 40, and thus live a life at 400. Focus on this last case. An overall value of 400 is considerably lower than 900. It appears that death has deprived you of a good deal. It has cost you 500 points. It was bad for you to die.

From worse to bad

Kai Draper sees considerable merit in this life–life comparison model.[2] Even so, he suggests that Feldman's account, as it stands, involves an important mistake. It is one thing to believe that one life is worse, or even much worse, than another, and another to think it bad for us, or a misfortune, that we do not live the better life. And it is one thing to think that some event offers us a much improved life, and another to hold that the event's non-occurrence harms us, or is in some way an evil. Suppose that yesterday you had found Aladdin's lamp. Your life would have been very much improved. But, intuitively, we do not think it is a misfortune that you failed to find it. And so Feldman's account needs some sort of amending. Draper suggests, for openers, the following:

> For any person S and event P, if (1) it is highly likely that S will
> receive a large benefit and, knowing this S hopes to receive it, but

(2) P prevents S from receiving it and, consequently, prevents S from leading a life that would have much more value for S than the life S does lead, then (3) *ceteris paribus* P is a misfortune for S, and severe disappointment on the part of S would be a fitting emotional response to this misfortune.[3]   (1999: 393)

One thing to note is that this formula is intended only as giving an overall sufficient condition for something's being a misfortune. I think it is fairly clear the components here cannot all be necessary; you can, for example, surely be unfortunate in not receiving some benefit even while never hoping to receive it. So a major task for Draper is in deciding how far these conditions can be relaxed, while still a misfortune occurs. And one thing to sideline, I suggest, is the emphasis on disappointment in particular, and emotional responses more generally, that features here and throughout the paper. The main concern is to distinguish *worse* and *bad*: death can be very bad, a genuine misfortune, an evil, without anyone feeling disappointment. But, of course, if it is an evil then disappointment, say at my imminent death, or at the death of another, would be appropriate or fitting. A third thing might be mentioned. You could suspect that to lose something, and for your life to get worse, is more evidently a misfortune, more clearly bad for you, than to fail to gain something, and so for your life not to get better. You could think you will notice if things get worse, but might not notice if they fail to get better. But none of this is obviously right. And Draper's formula is neutral between the two interpretations. Take one pair of cases. You are expecting promotion, but a management decision prevents this. Or, you are expecting to keep your job, but a management decision throws you out. Either way, their so deciding is a misfortune for you: you are deprived of some good and your life is worse with that decision than it would have been without it.

Is the formula, thus qualified, true? I think it is. It is a misfortune to fail to receive some substantial benefit that you were close to receiving, the loss of which has a serious negative effect on your life. And this view meshes well with what we would be inclined to say about a number of cases. You lose, or fail to acquire, a winning lottery ticket, or promotion, or a kidney transplant, or a girlfriend. Had you kept, or gained these things, all within reach, and all hoped for, then your life would have been substantially improved. These losses represent genuine misfortunes. The formula fits well too with coma and death. You expect, not unreasonably, to be alive and conscious next year, carrying on with your good life. But a road accident interferes, and you end up in hospital. Whether you are in a coma for a year, or whether you die, this accident prevents your making anticipated gains, and is certainly something to regret. So Draper is right to insist, first, that the life you live might be worse than some life you might have lived, even while it is in no way a misfortune, or evil, or bad thing that you do not live this second life. After all, it is not an evil that we do not all live the best possible life. And he is right, second, to suggest that when all the above conditions are in place, your living the first, and not the second, better, life, is a misfortune or bad thing for you. Take a prime of life case. You die prematurely, both wanting and expecting, quite reasonably, to live for another thirty or forty years. Had you lived, your life overall would have been considerably better. It is bad for you that you die young.[4]

A major concern of this chapter, then, is in considering whether, and to what extent, death is bad in cases that in some ways do, and in some ways fail to meet the conditions obtaining in the prime of life case. But first, some further points about Feldman's life–life comparison account.

Numbers and the zero level

We might hope to compare the goodness of ice cream with the badness of toothache.[5] But we cannot in that way compare the goodness of life with the badness of death. For death, construed either as an event or as a state, is not intrinsically bad. Hence part of the motivation for Feldman's approach. And the approach is further motivated by the thought that the dead do not exist, and so cannot be thought of as suffering when dead. Residual concerns about subject and timing issues are sidestepped by the seemingly uncontroversial move of comparing the overall values of two lives. But this misses something. Death brings our level of well-being down to zero. This is surely, in part, what is bad about it.[6] Compare two lives that have a value of 950 but that would, were it not for some event, have a value of 1,000. In the first the lowering event is some mild worsening of sight that lasts throughout the life. In the second it is the onset of a coma that lasts a few months. Intuitively, we might think of this coma as more obviously a misfortune than the impaired vision, even though the net negative effects are the same overall. For the result here is that there is a significant period of your life where there is just nothing good going on at all.

Similarly with death. Death at a certain time might make very little difference to the overall value of a life, say when someone dies in old age. But still we might think that their death is a serious misfortune. As I have noted, we sometimes think it a misfortune even when it might be overall better that you die. We think that with death you lose everything. And in an important sense that is true, and significant, even if you do not have much to lose.

Consider again Draper's criticism. Certainly he is right to say that one life might be worse than another, even while the second life is not bad. Further, it might not be bad that some event occurs, or fails to occur, as a result of which you live the second life. It is not bad that you fail to discover Aladdin's lamp. But now death might be a special case. Your life might be overall good, even though you die ahead of time. But death gives you a period at the zero level. There is just nothing intrinsically good about this. And consider again the point about losses versus failures to gain. As I said above, in either case a misfortune might occur. But we might say that it is always bad when things get worse, but only sometimes bad when they fail to get better. It is bad when things get worse, even if: (i) they get only marginally worse; (ii) your resulting situation is nevertheless good; and (iii) the decline is inevitable.[7] Conversely, it is good when things get better, when there is an incline, even if they get only marginally better, and your resulting situation is still, and regrettably, bad. But it is not always bad when they fail to get better (and so it is not obviously bad to fail to find the lamp, even if it is bad not to get promoted) and it is not always good that they fail to get worse (it would be odd to say it was good I did not get toothache yesterday – I was not at any clear risk of toothache, and there was not much hanging on my not getting it). And so, at least when life would otherwise have been good, death is bad both because things have got worse and because you end up at the zero level.

Closely connected with this is a further shortcoming in Feldman's account. Comparisons between whole lives overlook the obviously important point that lives have their ups and downs. And this temporal dimension might be taken into account. A week at the zero level, caused by a coma, makes a different sort of difference to your life than an ongoing mild impairment to sight. We might want to capture this temporal dimension in the following way. Just look at a period of time. Suppose, had you not died, you would have lived for ten more years at a very good level. So the difference between being dead and being alive is, for that period, 100 points. Thus we can give a value to that period of life lost because of death. This is what death costs you.

It is surely easy to accommodate this. Call the value of the longer of two lives A, the value of the shorter B. The value difference here is C. Thus $A - B = C$. Suppose John dies at sixty, rather than at eighty. All his years are good. So $A = 800$, $B = 600$. Compare the two lives and it is evident that dying early has cost him 200 points. But now it will seem that we can come at this from a different direction. Add to his actual and shorter life the total value of the period lost by his early death. Those twenty years would have been good. So they would have been worth 200 points. Hence we can assess how valuable his longer life would have been. And thus $A = B + C$. So then there are two

98

ways of assessing death's badness. It is bad either in so far as B is lower than A, or in proportion to the value of C, calculated directly. This might appear a distinction without a difference, with the value of C coming out the same, either way. We will, though, need to return to this.

Before going further, note a pair of important caveats about the position so far. I have said that death is bad when it deprives us of a good life. It so deprives us in, for example, the prime of life case. And it is bad to be in that way deprived. But I have not said it is bad only when it deprives us of a good life. On the contrary, I might have appeared to suggest that it is much more generally bad. For I might have appeared to suggest, above, that it is bad when it puts us at a zero level. In this case it will always be bad. But I did not say that. I suggested only that in locating us at the zero level, where there is nothing good going on, there is always something bad about death. Even when better than life, death is not unqualifiedly good.

Comparisons

We die. This is not, just in itself, bad for us. Whether it is bad depends on further factors. It seems that if it deprives us of a good life, then death is bad. It seems, further, that how bad it is depends, at least in part, on how much life, and how good a life, it deprives us of. Perhaps it depends too on our chances of living that longer life. How can we tell what life would be like, had we not died? There are puzzles here.

Imagine someone dies at a certain time. Plausibly, had they not died then, they would have died at some other time. At least part of what is needed, in order to assess the badness of their death, is a comparison between these two lives: the one they did live, dying at just this time, and the one they would have lived, dying at some other time. But there are two kinds of case here. In the first you actually die at eighty. We can ask: supposing you had instead died earlier, would that dying earlier have been bad for you? In the second you actually die at forty. We can ask, supposing instead you had died later, was that dying at forty bad for you? In the first case all the details relating to life–life comparisons might be clear. We know what happens in the longer life and, assuming we consider a case where death comes suddenly, from elsewhere, rather than, say, as a result of some chronic illness, then we know what would have happened in the shorter life also. Suppose we ask: would it have been bad to die, not at eighty but at forty? We have all we need to answer this question.[8] In the second case, although we know the full details of the shorter life, thereafter there are problems. For what we want to know is not, if you had not died at forty but had instead lived to eighty under such and such conditions, would your death have been bad? Rather, we want to know, if you had not died at forty which longer life would you have led, and, in light of that, would dying at forty have been bad? Comparing lives is easy. What is more difficult is knowing, in this sort of case, which possible life is the right one to compare with the actual life. And clearly, we need information both about its length, and about its content. Start with length, and think first about age.

Comparisons I: timing

In the simple prime of life case focused on so far, we have looked at a premature death, and contrasted that with death coming at the end of the normal human life span, say around eighty. And the thought is that this early death is bad because, had he not then died, this person would have continued his good life into old age. Certainly we often think this way, taking death at around eighty as the default position. But it might be complained that this is neither one thing nor the other. If he had not died at all, then he would have lived forever. For if there were no such thing as death then we would all live immortal lives. But if he had not died just when and how he did, had not suffered that particular death, then he would have died at some other time, of some different particular death. He might have died just hours later, or after some years, or at eighty, or ninety, or, supposing certain medical advances had taken place, at 110, or 150, or 400. Here, then, are two broad strategies for arriving at the relevant comparison, the appropriately longer life, in assessing the badness of death.

Immortality

Perhaps we should simply acknowledge that if people did not die they would live forever. And then, in assessing death's badness we need look only to the content of that much longer life. Perhaps this too is straightforward. An infinitely long life would be infinitely good. So in dying we all lose a great deal. Death is very, very bad.

Is it true that if we did not die we would be immortal? Perhaps this is true, but we considered earlier whether there might be deathless exits from life.

And one possibility here is that we could turn into someone else.[9] Notice that, in one sense, the converse is arguably not true. We could be immortal, in that it is biologically and technologically possible to keep us alive forever, such that we are either not subject to ordinary deterioration and decay, or there are means to repair damage and replace parts. But still we might be destroyed by buses or bombs, and so still able to end our lives. Assume, for now, that in at least one of these ways, the idea of our living forever is coherent.

Suppose it would be good to be immortal. Then we would understand one of the views mentioned earlier, about death's being always bad. It is always bad because it always deprives us of a good thing: an immortal life. Suppose an immortal life would not only be good, but would be supremely good. And this because it contains an infinity of goods. Then we would understand another of those earlier views, that death is, for each of us, the ultimate evil. For, the claim goes, in enjoying a merely mortal existence we are deprived of this infinity of goods, the sum value of which is infinitely high. Nothing could be worse than to lose so much as this. Nagel expresses a view somewhat along these lines: "death, no matter how inevitable, is an abrupt cancellation of indefinitely extensive possible goods … If there is no limit to the amount of life that it would be good to have, then it may be that a bad end is in store for us all" (1979: 10).[10] But the suppositions here should be challenged. Someone might think that, if we are immortal, then the enjoyment of an infinity of goods is inevitable. They might think, with infinite time, everything possible is actual. I see no reason to believe this, nor, even, that it makes much sense. It would seem to be possible for the one thing – reading and rereading Hamlet – to continue forever. And it is surely possible to visit Italy before Greece, and, as well, to visit the latter country first. But only one of these possibilities can be actual, no matter how long you live. Further, it seems on the face of it possible for someone to exist forever in hell, and thus in a place notorious for its absence of goods. But suppose that whether or not it is inevitable, you do in fact enjoy an infinity of goods. That would be good. But it does not follow that it would be supremely good, or even that it would be overall good to be immortal. We would still need to know that the infinity of goods is not counterbalanced, either wholly or in part, by an infinity of bads.

My suggestion here is only that there is no reason to think an immortal life would be a good life, and so no reason to think it is bad for us not to enjoy that life. As is well known, some have argued, more strongly, that there is reason to think the immortal life would inevitably, for creatures like us, be a bad life.[11] I am sympathetic to these arguments, but cannot address them here.[12] Let us assume the immortal life could be and, further, would be, very good. Is death, or the termination at around eighty of what seems to be our naturally allotted span, bad, or indeed very bad, in depriving us of such a life? A rudimentary life–life comparison suggests it is. If the longer life is better, then death at some earlier time is bad. But there are grounds for doubt.

Think realistically. Someone dies at thirty, in a car crash. Perhaps we have good reason to think that if she had not died she would have lived another fifty years. But no one can believe she would have lived forever, even if it is conceivable, or imaginable, or in some sense possible she would have done so. Plausibly, and as already suggested, in making life–life comparisons, we need to contrast the actual death with what would otherwise have happened, not what, in some remote possible world, could have happened. So the immortal life is merely a distant fantasy, and in bringing it into the fold we are making "the wrong comparison" (McMahan 2002: 104), just as we are making the wrong comparison by ranking our everyday so-so lives against the one in which we find Aladdin's lamp. So even if an immortal life would be good, and better than a shorter life, still it is not bad, is not an evil, that we do not live it.

Yet it is not clear that the suggestion can be so easily dismissed. What does realism involve? It is not clearly logically impossible that we should live forever. And even if it were, the immortal life still might be desirable. Perhaps it would not be if anything logically impossible was out and out incoherent. But many think time travel is logically impossible but, as it is not evidently so, still desirable. Nor is it obvious that immortality is physically impossible, at least for those who take care of themselves. Again, even if it were it might still be desirable, and still bad that we die so soon. Perhaps natural childbirth is inevitably painful. That does not stop the pain from being bad.[13] Might it nevertheless be technologically impossible that we should live so long, not ruled out by the laws of physics, but still something we will never be able to initiate, or control? Who can say? But move the goalposts a little. It does seem as if superlongevity, at least, is both physically possible and something that may be actual within a few generations.[14] Scientists are working on techniques that promise to keep, if not us, then at least the guinea pigs among our grand-children, alive for 150, 300, maybe 400 years. It is easy to see how living just to eighty is, other things equal, much worse than living to 150, or 400. But is it bad that we do not enjoy these longer lives?

There is no quick answer. But certain observations appear relevant. Few of us, at the moment, spend too long thinking about this. When old people die we might regret their deaths. But we do not, I suggest, have in mind their living on for extra centuries. That is not a comparison we make. Suppose we meet Martians, who have lives somewhat like ours, but who live for centuries, or forever. Or suppose we discover that the scientists are getting very close to making the superlongevity pill, or even that they thought they were close, but were disappointed. Then, inevitably, we would think more about the longer life, and compare it favourably with ours. We would think it bad that even the longest of our lives are so short. And there is a difference, as Draper notes,[15] between this case and that of the lamp. Not finding the lamp stands in the way of an incline. But our happy enough lives carry on as well, and for as long, as before. Not finding the elixir stands in the way of preventing a decline. When we die we go to the zero level. Even if both possibilities are remote, there is reason to think the latter is worse. Is it, then, bad, that we are not much longer-lived, or immortal? It is not clear there can be much to add here. Nevertheless, I shall say a little more at the end of this chapter.

Mortality

We need to go back to the problem of establishing just which longer life someone would enjoy, were they not to die when they do. For that seems to be needed, in order to find out just how bad their actual death is. One easy way – comparing death with immortality – fails. We know that if he had not died at all he would have lived forever. But this does not normally figure in our thoughts about the badness of someone's death. Another way, similarly easy, also fails. McMahan wants to link the contrast between death in general and some particular death with the type–token distinction. And he suggests that we think of any particular death as "death at this time and of this cause". But then "What would have happened had this particular death not occurred?" is easily answered. The victim would, in almost every case, have died milli-seconds earlier or later. So any particular death is, at worst, minimally bad. That too seems not to be the right result. We need something less blunt. That there are a number of difficulties in making these life–life comparisons is a point insisted on by several writers. McMahan has, on a number of occasions, usefully investigated several of them. I shall first reprise some of his earlier discussion.[16]

Counterfactual conditionals and the problem of specifying the antecedent

Mort suffers from cancer. And he dies at thirty. A haemorrhage, caused by the cancer, is the immediate cause. In assessing the badness of his death we aim to consider what would have happened, what life he would have led, had he not then died. But this can be fleshed out in several ways: if he had not

103

died on just the day he did; if he had had cancer but had been cured; if he had never contracted the disease and so on. And for each of these ways, some answer to when he would have died and, in light of that, how bad his actual death is, suggests itself. So, "his death today was perhaps a good thing relative to living on a few days in agony, but it was bad relative to continued life free from cancer" (McMahan 1988: 43). Is this satisfactory? McMahan thinks not. He wants a "single, most general, context-independent way of understanding the idea that he might not have died" (*ibid.*).[17] He wants, then, some sort of decision procedure that gives the right construal of such antecedent clauses.

The problem of causal overdetermination

Contrast two cases. In the first Joe is killed by a bus just short of thirty. Had he not died then, he would have died, at thirty, from some disease. Before we learn of the disease we think it very bad that the bus hit him. When we learn of the disease we revise our view, thinking it less bad. But now McMahan asks, "if death at so early an age from the disease would have been tragic, how can it be *less* bad when he is killed today by a bus at an even earlier age?" (1988: 45).

The second case is that of a curiously unnamed cavalry office killed in the Crimean War. Volleys are fired. Had he not been killed by Ivan he would have been killed, seconds later, by Boris. If you think Joe lost relatively little in being hit by the bus, should you not also think this officer lost even less in being hit by Ivan? Both victims would have died the second death had they not died the first. But, says McMahan, "Obviously we cannot accept this" (*ibid.*).

A proposal

He thinks the two cases are different. Identification of that difference points the way to solving the problem of specifying the antecedent.

Go back to the issue of immortality. Those who think that in considering this we are making the wrong comparison say this is too remote a possibility to be relevant. What we should do, in assessing the badness of death, is consider not such distant possible worlds but those that, metaphorically at least, are close at hand. Roughly, what would have happened had he not died, rather than what could have happened. But McMahan sees a problem here. The closest possible world, for the Ivan-slain officer, is one in which Boris kills him. Hence his death is not bad. Hence we need some amendment to close-ness. And a hint as to what this is comes from comparing these two cases. Joe seems to be threatened from two different directions – the bus and the disease – while for the officer it is just the one – being in that battle. So:

> What this suggests is that we can secure the intuitively correct counterfactual claims in these cases if our formula for specifying the antecedent is to subtract the entire causal sequence of which the immediate cause of death is a part. Thus, if the entire causal sequence leading to the officer's being shot by Ivan had not occurred, then he would presumably have gone on to lead a long and prosperous life; whereas if the entire causal sequence leading to Joe's being hit by the bus had not occurred, he would still have died within two months of the condition. Because of this, we may regard Joe's death as less tragic than that of the officer.   (McMahan 1988: 47)

There's some "tightening up" to add, but the upshot is clear: McMahan is offering here a procedure for uncovering a general, overall, context-independent procedure for identifying the appropriate alternative time of death and thus, in virtue of that, an assessment of the badness of the death that does occur. Was his death a tragedy? Imagine away the causal sequence leading to his death. If he lives a good life, for a longish time, then it was; if a bad life, for a shortish time, then it was not.

Now I think there is something in this, but perhaps not quite as much as McMahan believes. For there seem to be problems, about both the detail and the general strategy. When does a causal sequence start? Either with the Big Bang, or with some subsequent uncaused event. And whether there are any of those is moot. So although it is right to say that the causal sequence leading to the officer's death includes the whole of the war, it hardly begins there. And it is not at all easy to see what we are supposed to imagine, or indeed what is left to imagine, when we imagine the world with some entire causal sequence removed. Take Joe's case. Suppose the disease that kills him if the bus does not is caused by industrial pollution. But imagine away the causal sequence: not only the crash, but the bus, bus factories and the disease might not occur. So although, intuitively, we think of these causes as distinct the causal sequence route might well link them, and fairly soon.

So unravelling a causal sequence does not clearly help with the problem here. We need to rethink. Is this search for an objective or context-independent measure of just how bad some death really well conceived? There are reasons for doubt. And there are reasons for doubt too as to whether there is here any distinctive problem about death. The general issue is one of determining the identity conditions for some event, and in establishing what would have happened had that event not occurred. So we can ask what would have happened had Mort not died, had the planes not hit the twin towers, had Krakatoa not erupted and so on. In each case there is a myriad of possible answers. And in each case, the more thoroughly some hypothetical situation is described – Mort never got cancer at all, the planes missed because the passengers jumped the terrorists – the more certain of these answers need to be ruled out. I think McMahan would agree thus far. But then he seems to think that there is one scenario – one way of rolling back actual events and plotting its consequent alterations – that takes precedence over others. But this just is not true. I have commented already on one aspect of his attempt to pin down a particular death, one occurring at a particular time and of a particular cause. I shall comment now on the other. What is the cause of some event? Even though we might, in principle, identify all the antecedent events, and as well plot the various causal and other connections between them, there does not seem to be the least hope of identifying any one of these as, uniquely and objectively, the cause. Rather, picking out a cause is context- or interest-relative. Why did the twin towers collapse? Some will point to the design technology, others to the mendacity of the terrorists, others to American foreign policy, and so on. What caused the officer's death? Some will suggest the bullet, others the war, others his folly, still others the unstoppable flow of blood from one of the body's chambers as the cause of his death. There just is no context- or interest-neutral right answer here. So there is no best understanding of what is involved in a particular death. And so, in turn, there is no optimal way of assessing what would have happened had he lived on, and thus of assessing just how bad it was that he died. But what we can do, at least in principle, is describe any death-containing world in detail, imagine some death-preventing change, and then plot the different outcomes. So the world where he does not die in the battle is one where he lives a long and happy life, where he is not shot by Ivan he lives a few second more and is shot by Boris, where the blood does not flow this way, it flows that, with equally bad results, and so on.

This must not result in an overly sceptical position. We do not want to lose our grip of the ordinary thoughts both that some alternatives are realistic, others outlandish, and that some deaths just are worse than others, and that many are simply bad. And even if several construals of a death are possible, certain of these are clearly more plausible and more natural than others, both in general, and given our particular background and relation to the victim. Take Mort's case. The family think about the entire history of the disease, the doctor or hospice staff the final days.[18] Or consider death at seventy-nine. We do not think it is particularly bad. We might think differently if the super-longevity drugs were seemingly close. Nor, then, should we be tempted to follow Broome who, at least on one reading, denies that there is any way to rank the different evaluations of the badness of a death. He insists that "all the significant facts have been fully stated once we have said what dying at 82 is better than, and what it is worse than. There is no further significant fact about whether or not dying at 82 is an absolutely bad thing" (Broome 1999: 171). Broome can push his line about nothing being absolutely good or bad if he wants, but he appears to have missed something here. There are surely significant facts to be noted about attendant circumstances, and the alternatives they suggest. For someone in good health, hit by a bus, death at eighty-two is considerably worse than it is for someone who is already terminally ill. And this is true whether or not it is in some sense absolutely bad.

McMahan is happy to concede some of this, and to allow that context-dependent evaluations have their point, and "need not be wrong" (1988: 49). Even so, he suggests that their point, and that of these supposed context-independent evaluations, are distinct. The former "can help guide our action in relevant circumstances, but they do not tell us, for example, to what extent it is appropriate to feel pity for someone because he has died" (*ibid.*). But take Mort's case. Imagine away the causal sequence here and, presumably, he does not get cancer. So his death is uambiguously bad. But that does not seem right. Getting cancer is bad, but a haemorrhage rather than a few days pain is not so bad. So should we pity him (and to some precise extent) because he underwent some particular death, or because he contracted a terminal disease? The ambiguity wants, in some way, to remain. More recently, McMahan appears to be less ambitious, no longer committed to the view that "there is always, or ever, a single, uniquely correct evaluation of any particular death" (2002: 112). Of course, I think this is better, but there is room for a quibble. Specify any death-related situation in great detail, imagine some particular change, and there is always one situation, one longer life, that would have happened had the death not occurred. What is also true, and more germane, is that for any vaguely indicated death there are many alternatives. Talk to someone wondering or worrying about someone's death, and you will be able to discover what they have in mind.

Some premature deaths

We might clarify this by considering some further cases, including one that might at first be thought particularly troubling. So contrast five deaths occurring at thirty. And bring to bear, on these deaths, our everyday thinking about alternative possibilities. Jane is hit by a bus. We have every reason to think, had she not been hit, she would have lived to eighty. Jess dies from anaphylactic shock after a bee sting. Had she not died then, she would have died at thirty-five, or so we believe, from an incurable liver complaint from which she has suffered for the past ten years. Jo succumbs to an overdose. Had she not died she would have lived for a year, in extreme agony. Jill dies while mountaineering. It is a notoriously dangerous sport, and she might well have died within a few years anyway. Jude dies of Huntington's disease. There is no cure. And she was born with the genetic predisposition to develop the disease. Let us assume, further, that the condition is identity-determining, such that anyone without the condition would not have been her. In some sense, her death at thirty was inevitable.[19] How should we think about the badness of these deaths?

Jane's death is bad. If she had not died at thirty she would have lived a good life for fifty more years. Jess's death is, apparently, less bad. If she had not died at thirty she would have lived only a further five years. Jo's death appears not to be bad; at least, it is better than living on, in agony. Jill's death, in contrast, surely is bad. Jude's death is not bad at all. She could not, given the illness, have lived any longer. And she could not have avoided the illness. But now this does not seem right. No matter how inevitable, it seems bad that someone should die at thirty rather than, as is standard, live on into old age. Should we then say that all premature deaths are equally bad? This does not seem right, either. Jess's death does seem considerably less bad than Jane's.

Given certain comparisons, we can rank the deaths. It is, other things equal, much worse to die at thirty-five than at eighty. And it is much worse to die at thirty-five, thereby losing good years, than to die at thirty-one, losing only bad. Similarly, it is worse to die at thirty, of a congenital disease, than to live to eighty and die of old age. But in Jude's case this seems to involve the wrong comparison; living on was not, for her, an option. Still, surely her death at thirty, ahead of time, is bad.

McMahan offers an explanation. He wants a threefold distinction, contrasting the badness of death with, first, that of having no more possibilities for good, and second, that of someone's overall loss.[20] Jude's misfortune is not that she dies when she does, but that she has no more good in prospect: that it just is not possible for her to live a good life. But then, as McMahan acknowledges, we need to explain why her situation, dying unavoidably at thirty, is any worse than that of someone who dies, similarly unavoidably, at eighty with, similarly, no more good in prospect. And he points to the *Previous Gain Account*:

This suggests a radically different approach to understanding the badness of death. Rather than attempting to measure a person's losses in dying, perhaps we should evaluate how bad it is that life is over by looking back to see what it has contained. The fuller and more complete it has been, the less bad it is that it has ended. One might even claim, more precisely, that the badness of death is inversely proportional to the extent to which the life it ends was good overall. (McMahan 2002: 136)

There is right and wrong here. We do think, other things equal, that the earlier death is worse. One way in which other things might be equal is that in both deaths there are the same number of years remaining. But it is one thing to insist that the deprivation account – assessing badness in terms of quality years lost – is not the only game in town, and another to suggest that we ditch this account wholesale and replace it with one equally narrow in scope. McMahan toys with the Previous Gain Account before eventually jettisoning it in favour of something more complex. But is it not obvious that there are a number of factors bearing on how bad it is to die?[21]

And there is, I think, a better approach. Considering Jill's case may help. Is it bad that she dies on this mountain? The answer at least in part depends on identifying the relevant alternative. But perhaps all we can say here is that death within a few years, in similar circumstances, on a similar mountain, was highly likely. And now it seems her situation is somewhat similar to that of the cavalry officer. We might very much regret that she has taken up this peculiarly challenging sport, given that it makes a premature death much more likely than dying of old age. But given the sport, and her commitment to it, this particular death is unlikely to have cost her much. We should take this into account in reacting to her death. Contrast this case with that of someone who tries rock climbing just for a day. Here the death is tragic as, had it not happened, the alternative of a long life was highly likely.[22]

Now the difference between Jill's case and that of Jude is one not in kind but rather in degree. Her early death, a result of fortune rather than choice, is not so much likely as inevitable. Still the appropriate comparison is with someone who lives to eighty, because that is what we could have predicted if, *per impossible* and most regrettably, she had not had this disease.

The way forward is to appeal to a softer-edged version of McMahan's suggestion about imagining away a causal sequence. And this is softer-edged because the distinction we need to work with here involves only a loose and intuitive notion of cause. Jane's death is bad because had she not died she would have lived for a further fifty years. Jess, in contrast, would have lived only for five years. Her death is less bad. But Jude's death is bad because had she not died she too would have lived for a further fifty years.[23] Jill's death is much less bad, for she is likely to have died prematurely in any event. And Jo's death? We think this is not bad, as the alternative with which we naturally compared it is that in which she survives a further year, with a life not worth living. But the case is scantily described. Taking the drugs either is or is not linked with the cause of her death a year later. If it is linked then we shall think of her death now as bad. The more clearly it is linked the more we shall think this. So the way forward here involves, as well, a looser handling of the type–token distinction. As those terms suggest something of a precise application, I have in the main avoided them, preferring instead to refer to particular deaths, and to death in general, and hoping that these more ordinary terms will not have me committed to anything infelicitous. The problem with the others is this: we can talk of death as a type, but also of premature deaths, or mountaineering deaths, or deaths on Saturday, and so on, also as types. And suppose we refer to token deaths as McMahan suggests: death at this time. Then for any token death, if it had not occurred, by far the likeliest alternative is that some other token death, a second or less later, should occur in its place. Consider Jill's death again. If she had not suffered one type of death, dying on this day, on this mountain, she would probably have died on some other day, not too far off, on another and not dissimilar mountain. That she succumbs to this type of mountain death is not so bad. But that she succumbs to some mountain death or other – the type *mountain death* more broadly construed – is bad. For if she could avoid mountain deaths she would probably live into old age. Jude's token death, like all others, is not so bad. Nor are the types of death "dying from this complication" or "dying on this day". But the broader type, "dying from this disease", is bad as, without the diease, she would live into old age. Which type should we focus on? There is no straightforward decision procedure. It is a matter of judgement, and judgement sensitive to interests, as to how we should understand the cause of someone's death, and the situation that will obtain should that cause fail to operate. And, as I said, confusions and complications can always be resolved.

Comparisons II: timing and content

Assessing the badness of a death via life–life comparisons requires that we weigh the shorter, actual life against the longer, possible life: the one that would have been lived had the earlier death not occurred. So we need to know when the later death would have occurred. That was the major focus in the discussion above. We need to know also, what the longer life would have been like. Roughly, if it would have been good then death was bad, and vice versa. So there are issues about both timing and content. And now a relatively simple model for thinking things through suggests itself. Unfortunately, this simple model is deeply flawed.

Death is bad when it deprives you of a good life. And now we might think that the more good life it deprives you of, then the worse your death is. Compare two deaths. Assume the content is good, and year on year the levels are the same; then the person who loses more years suffers the worse death. Assume the number of years lost is the same; then he who loses more good content per year suffers the worse death. If two people lose the same number of years, with, within that period, the same level of good content, their deaths are equally bad. Put another way, the badness of a death is inversely proportional to the intrinsic value of the life that would otherwise have been lived.[24]

Yet, as I have already noted, there is an ambiguity here. For "the life that would otherwise have been lived" might refer to either of two victims of your death; to an entire alternative life, or just to an additional period. Go back to the model, where the value of the longer life, A, is summed from the shorter actual life B, and the period lost, C. We can make some independent assessment of A and, given B, derive C from this. Or we can independently establish a value for C, add it to B, and so discover the value of A. One assumption might be that either way the values will be the same. A second assumption has it that where the values for C are the same, two deaths are equally bad. But both assumptions are under threat. That this is so will already have been noted, in relation to some of the discussions above. First, the concern is with death's badness for the one who dies. Suppose, had you not died, ten years of extra good life would have been lived. This is not bad for you unless that life would have been your life. No matter how high its intrinsic value, it has to relate to your life in the appropriate way. We might say, more strongly, that it has to represent an extension of your life. I shall need to say more about this below. Second, as noted above, there are issues relating to premature deaths. We can start here.

Proportion

Jack and Jill both die prematurely. Jack is sixty. Had he not died he would have lived to eighty and died of old age. Jill is twenty. Had she not died she would have lived to forty and died, then, of a genetic condition. Suppose that the content is such that the extra twenty years would have been of the same overall intrinsic value in both cases. So, in one sense, the earlier deaths bring about equal losses. But suppose they live. For Jack this represents a twenty-five per cent increase on his life so far, while for Jill it offers a fifty per cent increase. In dying when she does she loses a greater proportion of those years otherwise available to her. Suppose you think that for this reason hers is the worse death. Then, although in both cases the longer life is better, it is better by unequal amounts.

Shape

Hamm and Clov both die at fifty. Had they not died then they would have lived to eighty. As it has a similar content, the intrinsic value of this extra life is the same in both cases. But whereas Hamm's life to fifty was overall better than this extra life, Clov's was worse. So Clov was about to enjoy an incline, while for Hamm death prevented a decline. We might think, for that reason, that Clov's death is worse.[25]

Structure

In the cases discussed so far it has been assumed both that the longer life is better, and that the extra life, stopped by death, is good. What has been denied is that the degree of betterness, in each case, corresponds precisely to the degree of goodness. Might it be possible for this correspondence to fail more markedly? I think it might.

At sixty your great novel is still incomplete. Die now and your life will have been mostly a failure. Live on, finish it, and it will be considered a great success. But those later years will not be, in themselves, particularly enjoyable. Their value is in contributing to the whole.[26] In the second case a considerable rift takes place at sixty. Several projects are completed, others are cut short. You move to a new country, and make a new beginning. The last twenty years go well, but they are not fully integrated with the years that went before. These years are well worth living, but not because of their contribution to your life as a whole. And there might be more extreme cases. You can complete your projects only at considerable personal cost. Considered just on its own this extra period of your life would not be worth living. Still, you might choose to live this extra life in order to give shape to your life as a whole. In another case, living on, although rightly considered worthwhile in itself, might detract from the value of your life as a whole, bringing about a loss of meaning or coherence. Some might say it would have been better, and better for you, had you died at the earlier time.[27]

The concern here is with what is often referred to as narrative structure.[28] We want our lives to have an internal coherence, to make sense. But this point should not be confused with one made earlier. A minimal requirement on its being bad for you to be deprived of extra life is that this extra life is yours, a life lived by the same person. That requirement might be satisfied even while the desire for narrative unity is not. For a disjointed life might still be one person's life. And now a further point emerges from this.[29]

Desert

Some think that desert plays a factor in the badness of death. There are two versions of this view: on one, the better your previous life the worse the death; on the other, the worse the previous life the worse the death. Both views surface in everyday discourse. So, you might hear people say that it was particularly tragic that he should die, having achieved so much, or having had such a wonderful life. Or they might suggest that her death was especially bad, given that she had for so long been dealt such a poor hand. One view seems to suggest that good fortune should continue, the other that overall our lots should be roughly equal.[30]

Such views are, I think, somewhat puzzling. And they should not be confused with another altogether less puzzling view. Someone might think that a particularly bad person deserves to die. But they do not think this person's death will not be bad for him. Indeed, it is precisely because it is bad for him, because he has desires relating to and interests in staying alive, that death can be suggested as a punishment. That may be a callous view, but it is not puzzling. We well enough understand the idea of moral desert, and with it the notions of praise or blame. But what seems to be suggested here is that someone might deserve, or not, more life just in virtue of past fortune. That is less well understood. Can someone's death really be more, or less, bad for them just because their lives so far have been in certain respects better or worse than they might have been? Anyone tempted to think this might have fallen victim to one of a number of mistakes.

Suppose you think someone having had a good life deserves more. But the past is often a guide to the future. So someone who is good, happy, successful, creative is likely to continue to be so. One of the blessed dies in an accident. We may well have reason to think that had they not died their good fortune would have continued. But then their death is bad because life would have been, rather than because it was, good. Desert is not playing a role. Or suppose you think the badly off are more deserving. But you also think there is some sort of natural justice, or cosmic harmony, that tends to ensure our overall lots are roughly equal. So someone living a bad life is more likely to have a good life in the future. Death is bad because life would have been good, rather than because it was bad. A second mistake connects with narrative structure. Suppose you think someone who has had a good life is less deserving of still more life. But it may be that the good life is, in some sense, already rounded off. It is not that they want or need more life but deserve it less; rather, their want or need is reduced. A third mistake involves premature deaths. Suppose you think a younger person is more deserving of more life than an older person. If they will both live to eighty then the younger person loses more in death. So it is not that he is more deserving of a given good than an older person; rather, he loses out on more good. That is why his death is worse. In all these cases, then, the decision is driven not by the thought that someone has a greater claim to a given good, irrespective of benefit, but rather that they will make more, benefit more, from receiving this good than will the rival claimant. So although we are supposed to be looking backwards, we are actually looking forwards.

But there are other cases. Link two discussions of premature deaths: the one just above and the one that ended an earlier section. Joe is thirty, Mo sixty. A transplant will give each of them ten years of quality life. Some will say we should toss a coin. Others will give the transplant to Joe, as he has had less life so far. His, they may say, is the more deserving case. And they may say this even if it is insisted that Mo will get as much out of the extra years as Joe. Suppose her overall life value increases from 600 to 700, and Joe's from 300 to 400. Still, as he happens to be younger, Joe is the more deserving. There are two points to be made here. First, I believe that we are all familiar, and many of us comfortable, with such reasoning. That a health service, for example, might distribute resources on the basis of age, even when the added years are the same, whether or not we agree with it, is hardly surprising. Second, as the figures above will help make clear, this example, cast here in terms of desert, is just the earlier point about proportion repackaged.

Consider a different case. Cal and Sal, both forty, will each get an extra ten years from a transplant. And these will be years of roughly equal quality. We might toss a coin. But suppose that Cal's life so far has been considerably better than average, while Sal's has been considerably worse. Fortune has simply dealt with them differently. Some will say that we should still toss. But if it is legitimate to give to Joe rather than Mo, simply because he has the worse life in terms of length, then it is equally legitimate to give to Sal as she has had the worse life in terms of content. If quantity makes a difference, so too does quality. But I suspect fewer people will want to discriminate in this case. And a health service that favours the poor and disadvantaged over the better off will come in for criticism. But perhaps this can be explained. The sorts of mistakes catalogued earlier may well resurface here. It might be hard to believe that Sal's fortune will suddenly change. So we might think she will, in fact, benefit less from the extra years than will Cal. Or we might think the difference in their lives is to some extent down to them, and the efforts they have, or have not, made. But if that were true, then it would be considerably more difficult to justify discriminating against Cal. He would, in the moral sense, be the more deserving.

In sum, then, it does seem not unreasonable to think that how bad it is to die, and to be deprived of some future good, is in part a function of the value of your life so far. The worse your life so far, in terms of either quality or quantity, the worse it is to die. We might cast this either in terms of proportion or, even though the moral overtones to the notion can muddy the waters, in terms of desert.

Desires

Most of us want to go on living. How does this connect death's badness? Having a desire for life is, as I shall argue, necessary but not sufficient for our death's being bad.

It is not a sufficient condition of death's being bad that you want more life. It may be that the extra life available to you is one that is not worth living. If this life is intrinsically bad then, providing it does not contribute to your life as a whole, it is not good for you to live this life. Even if this life is intrinsically good it still might not be good for you. You are told that extra life will consist in a series of good experiences. You want this life. But you have failed to understand that these experiences will not connect, either with your life now, or with each other. It is not bad to miss out on such a life. Often, we talk of interests. So the point here might be put differently. Although there is a desire, it might not be in your interests to live on.

Someone might think that, conversely, it can be in your interests to remain alive, even though the desire is absent. But I want to deny this. A desire for life is necessary if death is to be bad. Perhaps this is too restrictive. Someone might not consciously have a desire for life as such, but nevertheless have other future-directed desires, the frustration of which, by death, is enough to make for death's badness. We can usefully distinguish between categorical and conditional desires.[31] Viv and Tom both want a new bicycle. Tom wants one because, assuming he remains alive and in work, this is the best form of transport available. Viv wants to tour Scotland; she gets a great kick out of cycling. Tom's desire is conditional on his being still alive: if he is alive, he will have need for a bicycle. Viv's desire is categorical: it gives her a reason to go on living. Death is bad, other things equal, for those having such categorical desires, even if they do not consciously have a desire for life as such. But for those having only conditional desires, death is not bad.

There will be objections. Consider a depressed person. Beth, a teenager, is moping about the house. Some boyfriend has dumped her. She hates school. Her parents are so misunderstanding. She wants to die. But death is bad for Beth. Is there here, then, a counter to my claim that death is bad only if one desires to live? I say no. For I did not say that death is bad only if one desires to live at the time of death. Beth has had desires to live, and to live beyond her teenage years. That she has had such desires is a part of the reason for thinking her mood now a temporary aberration. And it is because this mood is temporary, because when she gets through it she will again want to live, and because further (as we can assume) her life will be good, that Beth's death now would be bad for her. There must be a place, somewhat like this, for non-occurrent desires. For it is normally bad to die in your sleep, or during a temporary coma. Now Beth's desires may be absent on a longer-term basis than this. Still, were it not correct to say that this is just a phase she is going through, the badness of her death now would, I claim, be far less evident. There is a further, and more contentious point to make here. I have denied that having a desire for life is sufficient for death's being bad. So I am not going to say that it is bad for Beth if ever she had a desire to live into adulthood. Suppose we doubt this is just a phase. She last had such a desire when she was seven, and since then she has been clinically depressed. With treatment this might be cured by her mid-thirties, after which she will again have desires for life. I need to return to this point below, but I am not sure that death, now, would be bad for her.[32]

What I claim is that without, now or in the future, future-directed desires, death is not bad. What I now want to add is that the degree of badness depends in part on the number and strength of such desires. Harry and Richard both want to see Venice. For Richard this has long been his life's ambition. He has read all the books and thinks of little else. For Harry it is something of a whim. Other things being equal, it is worse if Richard dies.

All of this is seemingly at odds with McMahan's position on the relation between desires and death's badness. He states, bluntly:

The idea that the badness of death can be fully explained by reference to the frustration of categorical desires is, I think, decisively undermined by two considerations …. One is that this idea cannot recognize that death can be bad for fetuses, infants and animals. The other is that it seems clear that the loss of future goods that are undesired at the time of death can contribute to the badness of death. (2002: 182)

But "fully explained" is odd. I doubt if anyone thinks there is nothing to say about any of the various other matters discussed here. And I claim only that having such desires is a necessary condition of death's being bad. Setting that aside, there is not as much disagreement here as there might seem. There is some. Although I need to return to this later, I do not think death is bad for animals, any more than it is bad for trees. Animals, unlike trees, can have good experiences. Some hedonists will think that if an animal death reduces the total of good experiences then that death is bad. But it can be bad for us, or for the world, or impersonally bad, without being bad for the animal. I do not think it is bad for the animal if a string of disconnected good experiences is cut off. And, possibly excepting a few handfuls of species, that, I suspect, is what animal life is like. Nor do I think that death is bad for foetuses. But there are important differences between animals and (human) foetuses. So I shall say more about that, and about infants, below. But the second consideration is one that I will not quarrel with, as my above remarks about coma and depression should suggest. Not only can undesired future goods contribute to death's badness – suppose, say, they are adjuncts to other future goods that are now desired – but the loss of such goods might be sufficient for death's being bad, at least when extra life would be overall good, and some future goods are desired either now or recently.

Reviewing the model

How do these various remarks bear on life–life comparisons? The basics remain in place. Death is bad for you if it deprives you of a good life. Recall the model from earlier. A is the value of the longer of two lives, B the value of the shorter, and C the difference between them. If A is greater than B and C is positive then, assuming the longer life is suitably integrated into the shorter, death is bad. But A might be greater than B even while C is negative, and vice versa. For there might be a mismatch between the good, and the good for you, in an extra period, and the contribution of this period to your life as a whole. Here it will be hard to say, simply, whether death is bad. In less extreme cases the value of *C*, even while positive, will not correspond to the difference between *A* and *B*. So, even though it is bad, it will be difficult to say how bad death is. And we need to look further at *B*. Even if there are two cases where *C* is positive, and *A* is greater than *B* by this value *C*, the deaths may be unequally bad. It is, other things being equal, worse to die early than late. As this suggests, factors other than deprivation bear on the badness of death. So it may be bad to die even if a longer life is not possible, and *B* is the only value in town.

From bad to worse

It is, other things equal, worse to die early than late. So death at fifty is worse than death at seventy, death at thirty worse again, and so on. But how far can we take this? Is death at three worse still? And is death at three months, or three days, or at three months prior to birth each of them correspondingly even worse? Consider the three-day-old baby. Suppose we can save his life or that of his thirty-year-old cousin. Which should it be? Some will say the man. He has fifty years ahead of him. There is every reason to think they will be good years, and they are years in relation to which he already has long-term desires, plans and projects. Others will say the baby. Although he has few concerns beyond his next meal, he has about eighty years still to go. So his is the greater loss.[33] If you think that earlier is worse, you probably think that if the man and the baby are trapped in a burning car, you should save the baby.

Both views, that the baby's death is worse and that the man's death is worse, have considerable intuitive appeal. People are roughly equally divided on this.[34] So which is right? I think the man's is the worse death. Moreover, I am not sure that the baby's death is, for the baby, bad at all. Contrast his death with that of his three-year-old sister. Her death is bad. Her case, and the man's case, both conform to the life–life comparison model. Both deaths are bad, as the longer life is of more value to the one who dies than is the shorter life. Thus in both cases there is reason to prevent the death, and for the victim's sake. But I claim that in dying now the man loses more than does the girl. And the baby loses nothing at all. Unsurprisingly, what I said above about desires figures in here. The man loses more in large part because he has more, stronger and further-reaching desires for more life than does the baby. The girl has fewer and shorter-term desires, and for this reason loses less. The baby has no desires, of the relevant kind, at all. (I say "in large part" because this is not all that matters here. As I said above, the desires-based and the time-based models can be at odds with one another, with neither always taking precedence. Were this man seventy-nine he would still have more and stronger desires. But it would be far less clear then that his is the worse death).

Ben Bradley (2008) disagrees. He argues that there is no reason here to abandon the otherwise attractive view that, other things equal, the earlier death is worse. More of a worthwhile life is lost when the baby dies. It is his life. So he loses more. Imagine a close correspondence between the two lives. The man has a certain history behind him, a certain future still to come. Should the baby not die now, his life will take a shape parallel to that of the man's. So at thirty he will have the same future ahead of him, the same desires, plans and projects wanting to be fulfilled. If he dies now, he loses everything the man loses, plus the initial thirty years that the man has already lived. Perhaps it is not easy to see how this can be a less bad death.

Bradley can, then, get at least partially on board with my insistence on the importance of categorical desires. We agree that desires matter. The man has such desires now. The baby will acquire them in the future. So it is at least in part in virtue of impacting negatively on the formation and fulfilment of categorical desires that death is bad. We agree also that, for death to be bad, it is not necessary that you have such desires at the time of death. The depressed teenager has no such desires. But, as I have conceded, death can be bad for her nevertheless. Perhaps we can agree on a further point. Death is bad at some time only if you would have categorical desires either then, or at some later time. But we disagree on two points. I think that the number, strength, reach and resilience of such desires, occurrent or dispositional, at the time of death, bears on the badness of that death. So the sister's death is considerably less bad than the man's. And I think that absenting all such desires, death is not bad at all. So it is not bad, at least for the baby, that the baby dies.[35]

Our agreement, and our disagreement, might be couched in terms of personhood. We agree that death is bad for persons and are, for present purposes, somewhat agnostic on whether it might be bad for non-persons also.[36] And we agree that identity is an issue here; death is bad for me in so far as it deprives me, rather than some other person, of future life. But whereas I think you need to be a person at (or before) and after a given point, for death to be bad at that point, Bradley thinks it enough that you are a person later. And whereas I think your being the same person is a necessary condition of death's being bad, Bradley seems to think that, assuming the future life will be overall good, it is also sufficient. Consider this point first, in relation to what Bradley has to say about one of McMahan's examples:

> *The Cure.* Imagine that you are twenty years old and are diagnosed with a disease that, if untreated, invariably causes death … within five years. There is a treatment that reliably cures the disease but also, as a side effect, causes total retrograde amnesia and radical personality change. Long-term studies of others who have had the treatment show that they almost always go on to have long and happy lives, though these lives are informed by desires and values that differ profoundly from those that the person had prior to treatment. (McMahan 2002: 77)

I agree with McMahan that it is altogether reasonable to refuse this cure. Your personality, memory and character could survive another five years. But they go out like a light, replaced by others altogether unknown to you. Why choose that? Bradley disagrees: "The decision to refuse treatment is short-sighted and irrational. It seems in many ways similar to the decision of a child to ignore the consequences of his behaviour on his adult self, since he does not currently care about the things his adult self will care about" (2008: 293). Suppose we believe the treatment is identity affecting: take the medicine and you cease to exist, being then replaced by someone else. Here Bradley thinks that refusal is appropriate. But the effects are not that radical, affecting personality rather than personhood. Even so, Bradley's complaint seems harsh, and his analogy ill judged. The child's entry to adulthood is seamless, even if it is not foreseeable. And there is not a choice. But the patient here will undergo psychological rupture. He prefers five years of the life to which he is already committed, and which he can hope to pull into shape, rather than fifty years of something about which he knows little and cares less. I cannot see that his refusal is irrational.

I think it may be better to save the man than the three-year-old girl. But she is a person. And her death is bad for her. Even so, her interest in and commitment to the future is, right now, considerably less than his. But the baby is not a person at all. So there are relevant differences between him and the girl. What about a foetus? There are problems with a pregnancy, and the doctors can save either the mother or the second trimester foetus. Most of us, including, I imagine, Bradley, will save the mother. But this may be for reputable, although here strictly extraneous reasons concerning probabilities of success, duties, extant affections and so on. Sideline all this, imagine other things are equal, and it seems that anyone committed to saving the baby rather than the man from the burning car will here save the foetus rather than the mother. The foetus has more years ahead. Now someone might urge this, on the grounds that this is the way to maximize overall utility or welfare. It is, they will say, good for the world if more, better and longer lives are lived. Whatever the merits of that view, it is not to the point here. Bradley wants us to save the baby as it is bad, and very bad, for the baby to die. I think he must hold that death is similarly bad, and similarly very bad, for the foetus. A question to be asked, although not pursued here, is whether anyone holding to this can avoid holding also that we should prevent the destruction of embryos, eschew contraception and so on. For if it is good that very early lives be saved, perhaps its good also that lives be started.

Broome is another friend of the "earlier is worse" view. Both he and Bradley have most clearly in their sights a position that McMahan advances in connection with his arguments for putting the man first. This *Time Relative Interest Account* says that in assessing death's badness we need to consider not only years lost and their content, but also the degree of, commitment to and interest in those years at the time of death.[37] Both writers find considerable fault with this account. Perhaps it has faults, but I am not sure that they need to surface in relation to the earlier is worse view. Broome, for example, charges McMahan with adopting here a "relativist teleology [that] leads us into incoherence" (2004: 250). After considering a case where a doctor has to choose between a baby and an adult we might:

> Suppose the doctor has a different choice. As before, one of her patients is a new-born baby and another is a young adult. But in this example, neither is threatened by immediate death. Instead, each has a disease that will kill her in thirty years' time unless it is treated now. (In the intervening period she will live in good health.) The doctor has resources to treat one of her patients, thereby saving that patient's life in thirty years' time, but she cannot treat both. Which should she treat? (*Ibid.*: 251)

Broome thinks a friend of McMahan's view will treat the adult, as she "is more strongly linked to her life thirty years ahead than the baby is". But if she does that, then in thirty years the young adult will be older, and in good health, while the baby will be a young adult, and on point of death. So at that time it will seem that the baby/young adult is the one who should have been saved. Relativist teleology has us in a mess (*ibid.*: 250–51).

Certainly there is a mess here, and it may be that McMahan's view gets us there. Bradley makes similar charges against him. But I do not at all see how we get in this mess, just by putting the adult over the baby. Nor do I see what is pernicious about elements of relativism *tout court*. Broome and Bradley both think that the badness of death varies in relation to the number and quality of years it takes from us. McMahan says that it varies too in relation to our desires for and interests in those years. I want to insist that we consider those desires and interests at the time of death. So, at least on my view, the doctor in the second case should straightforwardly choose to treat the baby. She does not have future-directed desires now, so if death were hovering now, she would be the one selected against. But death will be an issue only in thirty years. And both patients will be around then, with one of them facing her demise. Why is it not clear that it is their life expectancies and desires then that need to be taken into account? There is no puzzle or problem to be solved.[38]

Epicureanism revisited

Is it bad to die? I have claimed that it is, at least in the prime of life case. The Epicurean denies this. But is it really clear what these contrary positions amount to? A sceptic might have doubts, even though he will have little option but to agree with much that has been said. We have what appear to be vitally important future-directed desires: wanting to live on in order to do certain things, complete certain projects, give shape and structure to this unfolding life. Having such desires is, for creatures like us, first natural and, second, hardly irrational. Death will cost us, both in thwarting these desires and more generally in terms of future pleasures. Yet, and as we know, a sudden and painless death will both catch us unawares and put an end to all awareness. And this, the sceptic suspects, leaves us in something of a quandary. Death's badness is not yet transparent. It seems to be bad, but is it really so? Or, we say it is bad, but is it true that it is? Or, again, we often act as if it is bad, but are we right so to act? What do such questions amount to? They amount, I think, to something. For to many of us there does seem to be something residually right about the Epicurean position, and something unsatisfactory about its thoroughgoing rejection.

In this section I want to explore some of this. The strong Epicurean claim – death is not bad for us at all – does not, as I still say, seem plausible. But we can consider a strategy under which death's badness, although in one way real, makes no demands on us. This, I suggest, fails. A further strategy, accounting for death as more thoroughly, although still limitedly, bad, has more chance of success.

Bad for, and Bad that

This distinction can be further considered. So too can the relation between badness and limitations on a thing's flourishing. Think about trees. Just as we might say that an absence of mice is bad for owls – for mice have instrumental value as food, and make the birds' lives go better – so too might we say that drought is bad for trees. Trees under drought conditions fail to do what it is natural for healthy trees to do: they fail to flourish. The life of this tree, and thus of future trees, is under threat. Even those who find this a little brisk will be happier about suggesting that drought is bad for trees than, for example, that rust is bad for cars. This latter claim seems more evidently to be merely an underhand way of saying that rust is bad for us. Cars are of value only in so far as we value them.

But now if drought is bad for trees, if it is bad for trees to exist in a less than healthy condition, surely it is also bad for them to die. So hurricanes, cattle ranches and chainsaws are also bad for trees. Is this right? Although, as I suspect, the first claim is more widely supported than the second, it is not easy to see how, once granting the first, the second can be resisted. But this need not lead us into difficulties, or land us with a network of obligations regarding plant life. For what might be suggested here is that although drought is bad for trees, this need not be something that we should concern ourselves about. Of course, we should often be concerned about the health of trees because of their impact, direct and indirect, both on ourselves and on other animals, but it is far from clear that we need to be concerned about them for their sakes. We do not have to water them. Similarly with death. It may be bad for trees that they die, but it does not follow from this that we ought to intervene to prevent or stave off their death. Thus there is a contrast with certain of the harms that can befall animals. We think both that it is bad for animals to suffer pain and that we should take some steps to alleviate their suffering. How might we best articulate this point? We might say that drought, and death, is bad for trees while yet denying that it is bad that they wither and bad that they die. But not only is it bad for animals to be in pain, it is bad that they suffer; their being in pain is a bad thing.

The suggestion here, then, is that there may be an attenuated sense in which death is bad for those who die: attenuated in that it will not follow that we should pay a price to prevent these deaths. It might be bad for us that we die, while not bad that we die. And so there is significant content to the Epicurean view after all.[39]

But this is not going to work. For there is still an important difference between human death on the one hand, and most animal and all plant deaths on the other. Many of us either desire to live or desire certain things that requires that we live. Given these desires, we have reason to do those things that will help preserve our lives and to avoid those things that will tend to shorten it. Do others similarly have such reasons, finding themselves obligated on our behalf? I think that they do, and that there is a limit to the Epicureans' pretensions. When living on is good for us, and also what we desire, then not only is dying bad for us, but it is, further, bad that we die. We, and others, have reason to prevent this death. And, in light of the points made above about non-human species, the suspicion that this is hopelessly circular can be rebutted. By "good for us" I mean simply that our living on is the persistence of a healthy and flourishing human being.

The price to pay

Still there might remain something, and something not insubstantial, in the Epicurean position. This derives from two critical features of any badness pertaining to death.

First, there seems to many to be an important pleasure–pain asymmetry, with pain's being more clearly bad than pleasure good. Death, if it is bad, is so in cutting down on our pleasure rather than in adding to our pain. And death *qua* annihilation is, I think most agree, less clearly bad than death as the unending fires of hell.[40] If this is right then, even granting that a reduction in pleasure is bad, it will be an important and difficult question as to how much pain ought to be suffered in order to prevent such a reduction from taking place. Second, while it seems clear that given a life of a certain length, an increase in good content is good, it is less clearly good to increase the length of a life. And this remains so even when categorical desires are in the offing. Someone might appeal to a familiar distinction here, holding that while there is reason to improve extant lives there is no reason to start new lives.[41] And then, if we distinguish between the two ways of improving a life, relating respectively to content and length, this distinction might be refined: as there is no reason to start new lives so there is no reason to extend them. This is too blunt a move, and I am not making it. Even so, the solidity of the intuition about starting lives, allied to the rough connection between starting and extending, does, I suggest, give us some reason to pause over death's badness.

Death is bad, in so far as it is bad, in preventing there being more pleasure-containing future life. It does not, like catching a disease, promise us future pain, and nor does it, like some ongoing chronic condition, deplete our pleasures now. Even granting that it is bad when life is curtailed, we can ask: how bad is it? Of course, the answer to this question is not going to fall along the lines of, say, bad to degree 7. But, just as it might be useful even roughly to order symphonies in terms of merit, so what we might hope to do, in assessing death's badness, is rank it against some other bads. My suspicion, however, is that this will be hard.

Contrast two sorts of case. In the first we ask which of two deaths would be worse. A doctor might ask which of two lives should be saved. There is, at least often, a reasonable hope of answering such questions. Derek and Clive are both thirty, with good years both behind and ahead. But Derek might live for fifty years more, Clive only for ten. Derek's would be the worse death. In the other case we ask how to rank death's badness, the absence of some good, against a different but widespread bad, the presence of pain. Here are two examples.

Suppose an extra period of life is both in itself overall good, and contributes to the value of life as a whole. But it is not uniformly good. Either I die at sixty or I undergo a series of operations that will cause me considerable pain for two years. For those two years, life will not be worth living. But thereafter times will be good again. Should I accept the operation? It is not clear that there can be a definitive answer to this. Some people find pain intolerable; others can bear it. Suppose the period of intense pain is shorter: the operation and its bad aftermath will last only a week. Still it is not obviously irrational, if I hate pain, to decline this operation.[42]

Suppose you can save my life by inflicting some degree of pain on a third person. On several defensible views this is a permissible strategy. A utilitarian will say we should inflict some small pain on Buster to save Charlie from some severe pain. In such a case we simply assess, so far as is possible, the different pains involved, and aim at minimal impact overall. But it is not at all clear how we should weigh pain in one against death in another. Frank is in a coma; Bing is suffering some debilitating disease. If a doctor can either save Frank's life, giving him ten more years, or cure Bing's disease, improving the quality of a decade he will live anyway, it is not at all clear, I think, what he should do.[43]

That it will be difficult to reach a firm position on these matters is evident. But some writers are optimistic. McMahan considers the sorts of case discussed earlier, where an extra period of life, good in itself, may fail to contribute to life as a whole. As he continues, "the badness of the year in this respect may outweigh the fact that it is subjectively experienced as good. There is, of course, a serious question about how the two dimensions of well-being can be combined on a single scale. I will not pursue this matter here" (2002: 175).[44] Even so, the implication, in the text and the notes, is that we can hope to find this single scale. It is not simply that I have doubts about this, as if there might be a solution, but it remains elusive; rather, I cannot now imagine how we would rank the two categories of evil against each other.[45]

Summary

Jenny, still in her thirties, dies suddenly, painlessly in her sleep. Had she not died she would have lived a good life for a further fifty years. Does anything bad happen to her? Let us assume that we can say many things, answer many questions, about this case: she did not want to die, had much to live for; the later period would have been good in itself, and helped make sense of her life as a whole; large numbers of rational preferences go unsatisfied because of her death. But her death brings no pain, no knowledge of her altered experience and no awareness of her preferences being now unsatisfied. Most of us will think her death bad.

Other cases deviate from this prime of life model. Death comes later, or the life it deprives you of is less clearly good, or your desires for life are fewer. Is death bad in these further cases? Often it is. But we will not be able to uncover the boundary between the case where death is bad and those where it is not. Nor will we be able to say, in any of the cases, exactly how bad it is.

What do I mean, in saying we will not be able to uncover the boundary? Certain views here run in parallel to those presented in Chapters 1–3. I do not think we can sort all organisms into the living and the dead. Even so, some of us are clearly alive, others clearly dead. Take a disputed case, in the middle ground. Perhaps the argument is about certain empirical facts relating to the case. But these might be settled, even while we continue to be unclear as to what to say. In these circumstances there is nothing we should say, no substantive issue still to resolve. Similarly with death's badness. Jenny's case may be easy, but others will be less so. Suppose we cannot decide, knowing all the facts, whether it is good or bad, for the better or for the worse, that someone died. Then there is nothing to decide.

Is Jenny's case really easy? Someone says, "I agree with all you say. But I'm still not sure it's really bad that she should die". Is it? Suppose Jenny's friends are considering paying some price to stave off her death. Suppose someone is considering putting up with a week's pain. Would that be irrational? I have suggested that even if we do not think it is rationally required, still this would not be irrational. Pain is bad. If it is worth putting up with pain to prevent death, then death is bad. But is it worth putting up with pain? Naturally we think it is. But once doubts are raised, it is hard to see how they can be settled.

6

Posthumous harms

We will die. Before we die, good and bad things can happen to us. What about afterwards? Can we be benefited, or harmed, after we die? I shall focus just on the bad. Are there posthumous harms? Unsurprisingly, many people seem to think there are. They think that speaking ill of the dead, abusing or using their bodies or body parts, overturning their projects, ignoring their not unreasonable wishes or breaking our death-bed promises are all wrongs inflicted on dead people, evils done to them, causes of harms they then incur. Surprisingly, many philosophers believe that puzzles about the harm of death and about posthumous harms stand or fall together – if death can harm us then we can be harmed after death – while if the Epicureans are right and death is not bad, then the period after death poses no threat. Whether there are, or can be, posthumous harms is a question of some complexity, and will take us some time. A good part of its complexity comes about because the notion of a harm is, itself, in need of unpacking. This is not the place to attempt a full account of that notion but, along the way, some progress in this direction will have to take place.[1] Whether this harm question can be detached from that of death's badness is, I think, considerably easier. So I shall start there.

Death is bad, often, because it puts an end to both existence and experience. Assume that evil lies only in suffering, or bad experiences, and death's badness is hard to explain. But allow that there can be evil also in putting an end to good experiences, and understanding death's badness is seemingly straightforward. Not so with later events. How can anything bad happen to me, how can my existence be threatened, or my experience in any way take a turn for the worse at a time when I do not exist, and cannot thereafter have,

127

or cease to have, experiences? At least on the face of it, defending the idea of posthumous harms presents rather more of a challenge than showing that death is bad. Why should anyone think otherwise?

The motivation for such a view comes from buying into considerable parts of the Epicurean picture. If you think that where death is there we are not, then you either think that death cannot harm us, or you think our non-existing does not preclude our being harmed. If death does not harm us, then, fairly clearly, nor do posthumous events. But if we can be harmed by death, even when we do not exist, then plausibly we can similarly be harmed after death. As Feinberg puts it, "Death and developments after death are alike in coming into existence during a period when there is no longer a subject" (1984: 82).[2] But, as I have already urged, this central claim of the Epicureans does not seem right. Typically, we do not first cease to exist and then later die; rather, death is the event that always puts an end to life, often puts an end to experience, and sometimes also puts an end to existence. It is a big deal. And seeing what is bad about it is not too difficult. But then, in contrast, events that occur after death will appear to be much less potent. It may look as if we are now immune to change, and that the harm has already been done. Yet, according to many, this is at best a mere appearance, and we are indeed susceptible to posthumous harm. My point here is that this topic effectively stands alone.

Harming the dead

Consider first a series of positions that hold that although death harms us, its harm is not total. There is something of us that remains after death, and so we might be harmed posthumously.

The afterlife

Many of those who think we can harm the dead think, also, that in some sense the dead are still around, either ghostly, in this world, or more substantially in the next, and are in some way aware of, and affected by, what we do and say. Were this true then the notion of posthumous harms would be relatively unproblematic. But I am going to assume, as before, that it is not true.

Existence

I said above that death puts an end to our existence. But, of course, as I insisted earlier, that is not obviously true. Our bodies typically survive our deaths. If, as many people think, we are animals that are normally and for substantial periods conscious then, while death may put an end to consciousness, to life, and to a variety of bodily processes, it will not normally, setting certain animalist claims to one side, put an end to our existence. So long as our bodies survive we survive. Can we then be harmed?

Consider trees. Trees are living things. But they are not sentient, conscious or capable of experience. Can a tree be harmed? It can certainly be damaged or destroyed, but it does not follow from that that it can be harmed. It cannot be hurt, or made to suffer, but it does not follow from that that it cannot be harmed. So the question does not have an easy answer. Does a tree have interests that can be countered, and that are countered when it is damaged? I want to suggest, against those who resolutely connect interests with sentience,[3] that it does – that it has interests in surviving and flourishing as a tree – and that this is often why certain sorts of interventions count as damage, others not. And so I shall suggest that we can at least intelligibly and defensibly talk of harming a tree when we act contrary to its interests so understood. The point here can be put in different ways. A tree might be said to have some state of well-being, or a welfare, or a good if its own. It might be among the things having a degree of moral status. Someone might contend, also, that it has a measure of intrinsic value.

What this might suggest, then, is that the only things that can be harmed, in contrast to the many things that can be damaged or destroyed, are those things that have interests, or moral status, or a good of their own, or intrinsic value.[4] And I think that is right. So surely, then, a dead tree, or a dead human being, or a corpse, cannot be harmed. Even if I exist when dead, it is not at all clear that I continue to have a good of my own, status, intrinsic value or any positive level of well-being in that condition. It does not seem to be in my interests that I continue to exist. As with the tree, this does not mean only that I am not interested in continued existence, that I do not want or desire this; it means as well that it is not something, independently of my mental states, that is good for me.[5] The point is not that when dead I lack all value. A dead body might be of sentimental value to relatives. Or it might be of instrumental value to doctors, and those in need of organ transplants. The body might be damaged. This might harm, indirectly, someone else. So certainly it can matter what we do with, how we treat, a dead body. And if I continue to exist, as that body, it can matter what happens to me. But we should not assume that as long as I exist I can be harmed.[6]

129

Fictions

Bodies can be frozen, just before, or just after death, and stored for years. Unfortunately they cannot as yet be thawed, and brought back to life. Perhaps we shall never have the technology to do this. But imagine that the technology is developed. How should we describe these frozen bodies? I suggested earlier that it may well be right to say of at least some that they are neither dead nor alive. But suppose we should, instead, say that these people are dead. Then there can be posthumous harms. For we could do things to these dead bodies, or their attendant machinery, that either prevents them from being revived, or causes them to be revived in an impaired condition.

In these cases the body exists throughout, even though there are questions as to how it should be described. But, as I suggested earlier, I think that one and the same thing can go out and come back into existence. A watch could do this, so too could an animal, and so too could a person. Suppose this is right. Then it seems someone might be harmed when they are not only dead, but also nonexistent. A good person, or fairy, could want to bring you back into existence. A bad person, or fairy, could prevent this. It seems they would harm you.

These cases do not, I think, present much of a challenge to those who deny there are posthumous harms. For the central claim of those issuing such a denial is that, as things stand, the dead cannot be harmed, after death, either by human activity or by the play of events in the natural world. Perhaps some of these deniers will concede that in the future some of the dead, those whose bodies are more or less intact, might be harmed by incompetent technicians. And perhaps some will allow that even now the dead might be harmed by devils or fairies. But whatever the upshot of these disputes, on actual and current harms the deniers will stand their ground.

Harm: some generalities

The cases considered above might suggest, and are certainly consonant with, certain general claims about harm. But it should be noted that in what follows I mean only to identify certain of the major claims most of us will be inclined to make when talking about or thinking about what is involved in harming someone or some thing. That is all. I am not here hoping to say what harm really is, or to uncover its nature or essence. Again, our business is with a fairly familiar and fairly ordinary English word.[7]

We have already noted one such claim – only things having interests can be harmed – and there are others. If someone or something is harmed then they are made either worse off than they were, or worse off than they would otherwise be. Either way a comparison can be made between two states the person is, or might be, in.[8] So if there is an afterlife and the dead there are harmed, then, plausibly, they are made worse off: their level of welfare or well-being suffers a downturn. If we harm a nonexistent person by preventing them from coming back into existence then, plausibly, their situation is worse, not than it was a moment before, but than it would have been had we not prevented this. Similarly for non-death cases. A person is harmed – made worse off than they were – if a thief steals their lottery winnings. And they are also harmed – prevented from becoming better off – if a postal strike stops news of the win from getting through.

There is a second point. Talk of someone's situation or state is imprecise. On the face of it your situation might be worse in one of two ways. There might be a relational difference, as when you stand nearer to and further from a big bomb. Or there might be an intrinsic difference, as when you suffer a milder or more severe headache. Now plausibly, if someone is harmed they either undergo or are prevented from undergoing some internal change. Standing closer to the bomb does not harm you unless it brings about, or will bring about, a change of this kind. And you are not harmed just because the rich are getting richer. This fits with the examples above. Those in the afterlife feel distress when they pick up what we say about them. And the non-existent are prevented from regaining their material form.[9]

These two points suggest a third. We should contrast harms and misfortunes. Flim and Flam are both blind from birth. Flim is blind because the doctors made a mistake; he could have been sighted. Flam is blind because of an inherited condition; he could not have been sighted. I think Flim has been harmed, Flam not. Someone can be in a bad condition without being in a harmed condition. And harms have a location, and an onset, in time.

Two further points. Clearly, someone can be harmed even though no one and nothing intends to harm them. And, following from that, someone can harm and benefit you at the same time. A doctor breaks your leg in order to reset it. There is a short-term harm and a long-term benefit in what he does.

My suggestion here is just that these are plausible general claims about harm. I am not fully committing to any of these points. They need to be considered further. But it may be suspected that these points, taken together, suggest another; namely, that I am here putting forward an account that construes harm in terms of a loss in pleasure and a gain in pain. My account, then, is at least covertly hedonistic. But this cannot be right, even if there is a fair bit in it. It cannot be right for, as I have already said, trees can be harmed. They can be harmed in virtue of having interests, and in spite of lacking feeling. Even so, it may be plausible to suppose that human beings are different here, are particularly sensitive to interference with their interests, and cannot be harmed failing adverse effects on their experience. Either experience gets worse, or it fails to get better. And so, given that death puts an end to experience, it also puts an end to alterations in experience. And so, setting special circumstances apart, there cannot be posthumous harms.

Harming the living

Whatever their shortcomings, one of the advantages of all the views sketched above is that they encounter no timing problem. Some event takes place after death. When it occurs, then we are harmed. But there is no heaven, or freezing, or a set of good or bad fairies. And so the problem is that we actually seem to be, in that post-mortem state, beyond harm. We lack interests, experience and the possibility of experience when in that state. So consider now another view, wherein posthumous events harm not the dead body but the previously living person. Support for such a view is common, with most believers in posthumous harms thinking it clear that it is this ante-mortem someone, rather than the cadaver, that is the subject of harm.[10] Certainly it is clear that such a person, when alive, was indeed the sort of thing that could be harmed. But those harms were presumably brought about by events occurring when the person was alive. The problem here is that it is unclear how someone who was alive but is now dead could have been harmed, when alive, by events occurring now, after death. For this seems to be what is implied. Is this a big problem? Can we be harmed, at some time, by some event happening at some quite different time and, moreover, a time when we do not exist? It may seem clear that we can.

Prenatal harms

Your mother's drinking and smoking before you were born were both bad for you. Because of her activities then your life now is worse than it would otherwise have been. She did not have to drink and smoke. And so you were harmed, even before you began to exist. It might be objected here that had her child not been affected by such things then it would have been a different child. Roughly, your physical and mental condition, at the time of birth, is essential to you. This is far from clearly correct but it can in any event be fairly easily sidestepped. Another objection is that there is confusion here between existence and birth: you are harmed in the womb after conception even if before birth. This is more clearly correct, but can also be sidestepped. Sidestep twice with a different case. Your parents are exposed to radiation long before you are conceived. For the first twenty years of your life this has no discernible effect on you, or your life, but then as a result of this exposure some tumour begins to develop. Ten years later you begin to feel some pain. As the first twenty years would have been the same with or without the radiation there is no question but that we are here considering two versions of the one life. And because of the time interval, there is no question as to your non-existence when the exposure occurred. Here is a simpler case. Long before you are conceived someone drops some glass in a forest. When you are twenty-five you step on the glass. The bleeding begins.[11]

Should we say, of any of these cases, that you were harmed when you did not exist? No. In the glass case this seems clear. You are harmed when you step on the glass, not when the glass is dropped. Perhaps this is less clear in the radiation case. It might not seem right to say the harm begins only when you feel pain, or only when a tumour starts to grow. And so we might be tempted to date the harm earlier. But it does not seem right, either, to say you were harmed at the moment of birth, or conception. Hence the pressure to think you were harmed when the exposure took place, before you began to exist. But what needs to be resisted here is the uncritical assumption that the seemingly simple question "When were you harmed?" is clear and well formed, and has a straightforward answer. If it is, and does, then the best answer points to when the pain begins. Consider two further responses. We might instead prefer to say precisely when the pain first started, when (perhaps before this) you became terminally ill, when (although then undetectable) the first abnormalities occurred, and when (long before you were born) the event that caused all this occurred. And then the question of when you were harmed falls between the cracks. But we might be unwilling to write out, in this way, all the language of harm. And so we might distinguish between the harming event, or the cause of the harm, on the one hand, and the harmed condition, the effect of the harming, on the other. Harming events can occur when you do not exist, but the harmed condition occurs within your lifetime, either at its beginning or some way in.[12]

This twofold distinction should be augmented. Before you are born someone drops a glass. When you are twenty-five you step on this glass. From twenty-five to twenty-seven you have problems with your foot. The harming event occurs at one time, the onset of harm at another. And the harmed condition persists through an interval of time, starting with the onset and ending later. But here now is my last general point. In all this, the existence of a harmed condition is critical. Absenting such a condition, the harming event is, at worst, one that threatens to cause harm. And what begins, has an onset, is a condition that only in other circumstances would be harmful. Take blindness. This is normally a harm. For a period, at least, your life goes worse. But before you go blind the lights go out anyway. There is nothing to see. In these circumstances blindness does not harm you. Take a radiation case. Suppose you die, of some unrelated cause, before the pain begins. We discover the tumour in a post-mortem. We might say that you were in one way lucky, in that you died before it caused you any harm.

So, are there any prenatal harms? It depends what we mean. You cannot be harmed before you begin to exist. But you can be harmed when, or after, you begin to exist, by events occurring before that time.

The living, harm and time

The argument is supposed to run thus: there are prenatal harms. So you can be harmed when you do not exist. And then the way is at least open to allow that there are, as well, posthumous harms. But we needed to clarify this. A harming event occurs when you do not exist. But the harm – both its onset and its persisting state – occurs when you do. Can we understand posthumous harms similarly, distinguishing between a harming event that occurs after death, and the harm itself, situated somewhere within a life? There is a difficulty here. Where so-called prenatal harms are concerned ordinary causation is in play. The condition is an effect of the event, and occurs at later time. This cannot feature in the posthumous case. Events that occur after death might have long-term consequences but, failing backward causation, they are surely unable to make our mental or physical condition, during our lives, worse than it was, or would otherwise be. If, as seems plausible, that is what harm involves, then we would seem, after death, to be safe.

Harm: a broader view

It might be suspected that the discussion so far is set too squarely within a hedonistic frame. Being harmed is seen as causing pain, or as reducing pleasure. Unsurprisingly this allows for death as a harm, but makes for difficulties where posthumous harms are concerned. But perhaps hedonism should be dropped. Steven Luper offers two cases that allegedly bring it under threat. Plausibly, we are harmed "if we contract a disease that painlessly destroys our mental capacities and leaves us in the condition of a contented infant", and again "if we are betrayed by a friend whether or not we ever find out as a result" (2004: 66).[13] The first case can be set aside. Hedonism needs to countenance reductions in pleasure as well as increases in pain as bad. Hence we can, against the Epicureans, think of death as bad. It needs too to allow for the unwilled replacement of one set of mental states by another, even if, intrinsically, these second states are not worse than the first. We shall all think something bad happens to you if you wake up thinking and acting like Napoleon, no matter how great he was. Nothing here challenges the view that harm involves a change in our internal condition. The second case is more interesting. Although it was mentioned earlier, it, its relatives and the issues here raised need to be considered at some length.

Often things do not go as we want. Some of our wants are fleeting, frivolous or ill judged. Others are not so. We care, not unreasonably, about our own success in life, about the fate of our well-chosen plans and projects, about our relationships with our partners, friends and children. We desire that things go well, have hopes for the future and are interested in certain outcomes being achieved or sustained. Often, it is good for us, contributive to our well-being, in our interests, that in such areas things go as we would like. Often too we have made a considerable investment in time, money and energy in pursuit of certain outcomes, and have sacrificed other things, and perhaps in some ways also other people, to their success.

When things do not go as we want, is this bad for us? When we are betrayed, slandered, predeceased by our children, somehow denied the realization of our plans and projects, are we in any way harmed? Often we are. For often we are aware of things having gone amiss; we feel the dissatisfaction, regret, disappointment, frustration. Our internal condition is changed for the worse. There is no challenge here to the thus far suggested model of harm. But what about the situation where that is not the case? Are we harmed, is it bad for us, when, although betrayed, our life, our experience carries on just as it would otherwise be; or when our children die in another country, we never hear of it, and not long after die ourselves; or when the novel we have spent so many years writing, and with good reason expected to do well, falls victim to a sudden change of fashion after our deaths?

Many people think that we are indeed harmed by such turns of events. So many think we are harmed not only by normal betrayal, where we find out what has been going on, but also by undiscovered betrayal. But a further distinction is needed. In a pair of cases you never find out about the betrayal, but in one your partner now treats you less well than previously, while in another, doing everything possible to cover his tracks, he treats you just as he would have done had the betrayal not taken place. In the first of these cases, as when the betrayal is discovered, your experience is affected, presumably for the worse. Uncontroversially you can be harmed by this. In the second your experience, your mental states, your internal condition are untouched, and continue as they did, and as they would, had the betrayal not occurred. But many think that we are, in spite of this, harmed by such a betrayal. And many think we can in a similar way be harmed by posthumous events. Here experience is untouched in a different way. It is already ended, so it does not carry on as before. But whatever its shape, it has that shape whether or not these posthumous events occur. Still, as with the betrayal, things have not gone the way you hoped or cared about, or in the way that mattered to you. And, allegedly, you are harmed by this. One seeming virtue of this approach should be noted. Undiscovered betrayal does not generate a change in your internal condition, and so does not cause within you any physical or psychological harm, even if it harms you. Posthumous events, similarly, can allegedly harm you even without initiating any change in your condition. So here there is no threat of backward causation.

A considerable number of writers buy into posthumous harms so understood. Thus George Pitcher devises a case where a philosopher develops and writes up some systematic account of reality which in World I is suitably acclaimed but in World II is destroyed the day after his death by some disgruntled neighbour:

> We would all, I think, judge that the philosopher's life in World I is better than his life in World II, and that the neighbour's vicious action in World II really harms the philosopher …. The labour of a lifetime, that for which he sacrificed everything, all reduced to a heap of ashes! Poor man! (1993: 163)

Luper imagines we are working on something worthwhile, such as a cure for lung cancer: "it would be good for us if the undertaking were successful, and bad if it were not … Even if we are deprived of existence subsequent events might bring it about that lung cancer is cured, or that it is not cured" (2004: 69). And, he maintains, we are benefited or harmed accordingly. McMahan (1988) insists that his holiday man is harmed by the failure of his business whether that happens before or after his death. Feinberg (1984), rather abstractly, considers a woman who devotes thirty years to some worthwhile institution that then collapses without her ever knowing. John O'Neill (1993) constructs a number of elaborate cases in which, on his view, posthumous events alternatively benefit and harm those already deceased. And of course there is more. But I am unconvinced. We can look at this under three headings.

Bads and wrongs

One of my remarks above will be found unsatisfactory. It seems not to be right to suggest that you are harmed in so far as you suffer from certain bad feelings. As is often said, this gets things the wrong way round.[14] Those feelings come about as a result of your discovering that something bad – the betrayal, the slander, the death – has occurred. This bad thing precedes, and stands independently of, your negative response. Fair enough, but the question is not whether bad things can happen independently of your reacting a certain way, but whether you can be harmed independently of some such reaction. Contrast two cases. Your children die before you but you never discover this. There is no question, let us suppose, that their deaths are bad for them. So certainly something bad has happened. And this bad thing is something that you very much wanted not to happen. But is it bad for you, are you harmed, when this bad thing that you wanted not to happen happens? It is not clear to me that you are. You are secretly poisoned. This is bad for you as in a matter of weeks pain will begin and death will follow. To discover the poisoning is to discover that a harming event had occurred. You will feel bad. And so you will be further harmed. Now consider again the undiscovered betrayal. If you find out about this you will feel bad and will be harmed. But, in contrast to the poison case, you have not here clearly discovered that a harming event has occurred. Certainly you have not discovered that, independent of this discovery, your condition was about to change for the worse. Does this mean that your feeling bad, in light of the discovery, is irrational? Hardly. You have discovered that your partner acted wrongly. As he cannot be sure you will not find out, at the very least he risks seriously harming you, and others. But it is not clear, I think, that he harms you.

Pitcher makes much of the link between harms and wrongs: a son breaks a deathbed promise to his father; a panel of corrupt judges cheats a now dead runner of his Olympic victory; Mrs Tisdale's widower deliberately wrecks her good reputation.[15] These people all do wrong. They wrong the dead. Plausibly, to wrong someone is to harm them. But is any of this as straight-

forward as is made out? Some will say that in the absence of bad consequences it is unclear that any wrong occurs. We might easily disagree and
think of all these perpetrators as, in varying degrees, bad people, bearers
of bad characters, subject to vice. And, acting viciously, they do wrong. But
even if we agree that they act wrongly, from base motives, it is less clear that
there is a victim of their wrong. And even if we think some linguistic nicety
suggests there is, and that we should say who was targeted, whose legitimate
victory was overturned, who falsely believed a promise would be kept, and
want for that reason to identify just these people as those who were wronged,
still it is unclear that they were harmed by being wronged in this way. If you
are harmed, it seems that things go worse for you. And it is unclear how they
can be worse for you if your internal condition is just as it would be if you
were not harmed.[16]

In any event, it needs to be recognized that a route in via wrongs can
only work in a subset of cases. Most putative examples of posthumous harms
involve accidental misfortune rather than malicious, thoughtless or selfish
human agency. We need at least to be prepared to focus on those.

Success and sacrifice

We have, as did Aristotle, the notion of a successful life. And this notion, in
contrast to a defensible position on the pleasant life, makes appeal to situations beyond your body and mind. A successful doctor is one who saves lives,
rather than attempts to, or believes he saves them. A successful judge puts
away the guilty and sets free the innocent. A successful novelist writes books
that deserve and enjoy a lasting fame with readers and critics. So whether or
not your life is successful often depends – and it matters here what sorts of
projects you elect to pursue – on circumstances beyond your control. And if
your projects are sufficiently long term, as many are, then whether to count
them successes or failures can depend on events occurring at some time after
your death.

Pursuit of these projects often involves us in making some not inconsider-
able investment in, or sacrifice towards, them. If the sacrifice is made towards
some utterly hopeless project – you labour in vain to teach the flowers to
sing[17] – it reveals an error of judgement. If it is made towards some worthwhile project that you might reasonably expect to see through, then the judgement is fine. But things can nevertheless go wrong. This can happen in your
life, or afterwards, when you are dead. Posthumous events can, apparently,
render your sacrifice pointless, and your life a failure.[18]

Are you harmed by failure? Often you are. The doctor who loses his patients, like the judge sitting over a number of mistrials, will suffer as a result. There is little point in sacrificing years of your life to a long training for outcomes like these. You will note the failure, experience the regret and suffer the disappointment when, whether through your own shortcomings or the hand of fate, things do not go well in the end. You will be harmed. But is it the same when failure is determined only by posthumous events, and you never learn of it? The novelist has had some middling success within his life. Expectations of something rather special are not without foundation. The manuscript is finished before he dies. But computers crash, the editor failed to make back ups, and nothing is retrievable. His life is a failure. But is this bad for him? Is he harmed by the loss?

We might be determinists, and think that failure here, although of course quite unexpected, is inevitable. His life was always going to be a failure. Or we might think that it was undetermined just how things would turn out until, or very shortly before, the crash occurred. Either way, no one knows beforehand whether the sacrifice has point, whether the project will be a success, whether the investment will be repaid. We might say, in cases like this, that no one really knows how their life went. But that is a little misleading. You can know what happened on a day to day basis, chart the flow of events, note the shift in levels of welfare and well-being. But you cannot know whether your long-term desires will be satisfied and whether, in light of this, to count your life a success.

Desires and interests

Should we say that you are harmed either when your desires go unsatisfied, or when your interests are defeated? First it is worth clarifying the terminology here.

Desires, I take it, are in some sense mental states. But they have a content: we desire that the world, or something in the world, be a certain way. Suppose we talk of a desire being defeated. This might mean either that the mental state ceases to exist, or that what we desire fails to obtain, or it becomes impossible for it to obtain. The difference here might be usefully marked with a distinction in terms. So we might talk, as does Feinberg, of desires being fulfilled or thwarted when the object of our desire obtains or fails to obtain. And, in part following Luper, we might talk of a desire's being formed or removed when the mental state begins or ceases to be.[19] Suppose a desire is formed, persists and is then either fulfilled or thwarted.

These outcomes generally produce in us feelings of satisfaction on the one hand, or frustration and disappointment on the other. But the correlation is only general; the illusion of fulfilment might cause satisfaction, and genuine fulfilment might leave us cold. That distinction, between what happens in the world, and states or feelings in us, is real, but it is not always marked in just this way. Others talk of the satisfaction or frustration of desires just where Feinberg talks of fulfilment and thwarting. As this use is widespread, I am happy to follow it.

Is it good if my desires are fulfilled, or satisfied? It depends what I desire. It might be bad for others, and it might be bad for me too. But suppose my desire is satisfied and I am aware of it. It is likely to be good for me in some respect, even if not overall good for me, and even if not overall good. For I shall enjoy some feelings of satisfaction, in knowing that what I wanted has obtained. Although such feelings are sufficient for there being some good for me in the satisfaction of my desires, they are not necessary. I desire that my health is good. It is, and this is good for me, even though, hypochondria-cally, I never know that it is, and so never feel good about the satisfaction of my desire. In this case, whether my desire is satisfied or frustrated makes for a difference in my internal condition. Its being a certain way is what is here good for me. What about cases where this is not so? Suppose I have some desire that involves only some relational change. I desire that I be the best pianist in town. All the better pianists die, thus satisfying my desire. It is hard to see how this is good for me, or how it can then be bad for me if some mediocre pianist starts to practise, takes lessons and massively improves. I do not know anything about the competition, so feel neither good nor bad about these shifting patterns.[20] Here is a related, although importantly different, case. You meet someone on a train, pass the time by talking and find that she is ill. She gets off in Lichfield, and you stay on to Reading. You hope she will recover. But, although of course you never discover this, she dies. Her death is not bad for you, it does not harm you, nor, had she recovered, would this benefit you or be good for you.[21]

The important difference is this. In the piano example I desire that something be true of me, while with the train it is that something be true of someone else. We can talk of self-directed and other-directed desires. Desires *qua* mental states can be removed. All such desires are removed with death. Still, it may be that the object of the desire might nevertheless be fulfilled or thwarted. I get off the train and am hit and killed by a bus on leaving the station. What I wanted, that this woman recover, either happens or does not. Now most self-directed desires cannot be fulfilled or thwarted after death, simply because one of the component objects no longer exists. Death removes the desire along with the possibility of its fulfilment.[22] But this is not so with other-directed desires. The desire will not survive your death, but the possibility of its fulfilment will.

Are there any desires such that it is bad for you, or causes you harm, if those desires are thwarted at some time after your death? Suppose you have some frivolous desire, such as hoping that the restaurant where you ate last week gets a second Michelin star. It is not bad for you that they fail to achieve this after your death. Similarly with non-frivolous but passing desires, as with the woman on the train. And similarly too with non-frivolous, non-passing but unrealistic desires. You want Venice to be saved, not for the next two or three centuries, but for ten thousand years. Nine thousand years on it is destroyed. It is hard to believe that this can be bad for you.

Does it make a difference if the desire is sustained, more fully embedded in your life, realistic, and has involved investment and sacrifice? Look again at Luper's example:

> Suppose that what we want is that some project, say that of curing lung cancer within ten years, *be* completed (whether or not we are responsible for its coming to fruition). This might be an endeavour in which we personally have a great deal at state; perhaps we initiated it, and have invested in it a great deal of time and energy. So it would be good for us if the undertaking were successful, and bad if it were not. Even if we are deprived of existence subsequent events might bring it about that lung cancer is cured, or that it is not cured. We will not be responsible for the success that is good for us, or for the failure that is bad: that will be out of our hands. Instead, the good success or bad failure will be brought about *for* us.
>
> (2004: 69)

But although it is bad for the living, and the suffering, if the cure is not found, it is not at all evident that it is bad for the dead. Luper says it is, but he provides no reasons.

Perhaps though, the reasons are to do with interests. Some desires are such that their satisfaction is not in my interests. Many other-directed desires are like this, including the three examples preceding this cancer case. So too are many self-directed desires. It is not in my interests that, wholly unknown to me, other pianists die off. Nor is it in my interests to continue smoking, even though this does provide some short-term satisfaction. Arguably it is in my interests that the cancer cure be found. And this might explain why I benefit from its being found, even if the discovery occurs posthumously.

Again, we need more detail. Feinberg:

> would like to suggest we can think of some of a person's interests as surviving his death, just as some of the debts and claims of his estate do, and that in virtue of the defeat of these interests, either by death itself or by subsequent events, we can think of the person who was, as harmed. (1984: 83)

This represents, he says, a modification of an earlier position, one that seemed to imply a "bizarre ontological reification" in which each interest was "a little person in its own right" and itself the subject of harm (*ibid.*).[23] But I am not sure how much the modification helps.

As with desires, there is some sense in which interests are removed with death. I no longer find interesting many of the things that once interested me, and confidently predict that once I die I shall find nothing interesting at all. But, of course, having an interest in something is standardly contrasted with the things that are in my interests. I might be very interested in where my next fix is coming from, but it is not in my interests to do drugs. The difficulty, though, is that this sharp contrast is blurred when considering the sorts of examples that best support the case for posthumous harms. For those other-directed long-term projects – curing cancer, saving the tiger, developing some viable reality scheme – are both things one is interested in and, plausibly (and here in contrast with the frivolous), contributors to well-being, and so in one's interests.

Feinberg says that my interests can survive my death, as can debts, and claims on my estate, and that the posthumous thwarting of these interests can harm me. The analogy is not helpful. My debts, my assets, my children, my paintings survive in a non-controversial way. My interests do not survive non-controversially as these things do. And just what can survive needs to be considered more carefully. My being interested in something – saving the tiger – cannot survive my death. The possibility of the tiger's being saved – that which I am interested in – can survive. And perhaps fifty years later the tiger will either be extinct or safe. Can the saving of the tiger's being something that is in my interests, supposing this is true now, continue to be true later? Can its being in my interests survive my death? That it can is what needs to be made plausible in furthering a case for posthumous harm.

Beliefs

Go back to betrayal. It is somewhat misleading to say that you desire that your partner is faithful. This relationship is the backbone of your life. There has never been any reason to question it. Not at all in a complacent way you take for granted, assume, believe that he is faithful. But here you have a false belief. Clearly it is not always bad for us if certain of our beliefs are false. But often it is good if our beliefs are true. Often, having true beliefs is, for us, of instrumental value. It is good to have true beliefs about what is edible and what is not. But is it good for us to have true beliefs when this is not the case? Someone might think that having true beliefs is intrinsically valuable. But that is not the issue here. The question is whether it can be good for you to have true, rather than false, beliefs when their being true makes no difference to how your life goes, or at least makes no difference to your mental and physical states throughout your life.[24] Betrayal offers one case. Here are two more. You need to cross a rope bridge in the Himalayas. You believe, with reason, that it is safe and cross without any difficulty. But it was not safe, and you could easily have fallen to your death. And, you believe your doctor is competent, attentive and has your best interests at heart. But he fears his wife is betraying him and, although he disguises it well, is only half listening to what you tell him. It is just by chance that he prescribes the right medicine. Are you harmed by having false beliefs in these cases? You were in situations where there was certainly a risk of harm, or where harm was close. But being almost harmed and being harmed are different.

Consider two somewhat extreme cases where apparently key beliefs are false. We believe that our reputations, our lifeworks, our grandchildren and our country will all survive. Fifty years after our deaths an asteroid hits the earth. This harms many people. But does it harm us? A scientist pops you in an experience machine, unannounced, while you sleep. The experiences he feeds you are just those you would have had were you awake. While you are in this machine, and coincidentally, an asteroid hits the earth. So many of your beliefs through the last months of your life were false. But are you harmed by this? And contrast a pair of cases. Bad people capture you and plan to kill you. But this is not bad enough for them, and they very much want to harm you further before you die. One group suggests they capture and kill your wife and children, but tell you nothing of this. The other group thinks they should pretend to do such things, feed you fake pictures, screams and stage blood. I think the second group certainly does harm you. To be persuaded of all this makes your life, and your death, even worse. But does the first group, in secretly killing your family, harm you even more, or less, or not at all?

There might be an objection to much of this, deriving from a point about comparisons. Suppose you are being betrayed, but never discover this, and your experience carries on as before. My point has been that it is hard to see that you are harmed in such a case. For in the alternative world where you are not betrayed, your experience is just the same. But someone might object that this is not the comparison to make, or the alternative to consider. We should think instead about the world where you are betrayed, but then do discover this. Here your experience is different. Plausibly too your experience is better. Although it causes you considerable distress, the discovery of the betrayal leads, in time, to an overall better life. Your partner makes amends, or you find a new one. If betrayal occurs then failing to discover it can be bad for you, can harm you, in keeping from you this better life. Similarly with the bridge. You cross, falsely believing it is safe. One contrast is where that belief is true, another where you truly believe it is dangerous. Believe this, and your experience is different. Suppose you find a better route. Arguably, your experience is better.

Consider death, posthumous harms, and the pointless sacrifice. You spend years on the book, but tastes change and it falls stillborn. Suppose it had done well. Either way, your experience is the same. Hence there is some difficulty in seeing how the book's posthumous failure harms you. But had you been able to know of its fate you would have made different sacrifices, led a different life. And it may well have been considerably better. So ignorance is not bliss. You are harmed by this lack of knowledge.

This objection does not, I think, altogether hit home. The first comparison seems the right one to make. As the issue concerns the value of truth, and contrasts true and false beliefs, we need to consider cases where what obtains is the same either way. Normally betrayal harms you, provides you with bad experiences and makes your life worse. The question is, is harm incurred when the betrayal is undiscovered, and experience unaffected? We can, if we choose, consider instead a case where betrayal, assuming it is discovered, is overall beneficial. Assessing this world against the one where betrayal is undiscovered is relatively straightforward. For now different experiences are involved. And even more clearly, the objection fails to hit home where posthumous harms are concerned. You have worked hard all your life on what turns out to be failed cure for cancer. Had you known it would fail, you would have made different choices, different sacrifices, and overall lived a better life. But you did not and could not have known this. The knowledge was not available. And you are not harmed by not living this better life. Suppose the knowledge was available. A better scientist knows all along that your cure is illusory, and knows in time that this will become evident. But he says nothing.

Arguably you are harmed here. Yet you are harmed not posthumously, when the community sees the errors in your research, but rather while alive, when this rival scientist comes to his conclusions, withholds the information and prevents you from taking a different course.

Timing

I have wanted to deny that there is a timing problem for death's badness. Typically death harms us when it occurs and at those later times when, were we not dead, we would be living a good life. Exceptionally, as when it prevents us from being tortured, it may be bad only at the later times. The harmed condition comes into being along with, or later than, the harming event. But, as is generally acknowledged, there is a problem with the timing of supposedly posthumous harms. The harming event – the slander, the loss of the book, the sinking of Venice, the asteroid hit – occurs after your death, at a time when you may well not exist. So when are you harmed? As Luper nicely notes, there appear to be three possibilities. You are harmed before death, at death or after death. But *before* and *at* seem to invoke backwards causation, and *after* refers to times when you do not exist. So there is a difficulty here. And that difficulty remains even if we are persuaded that harms need not affect your experience.

Could the harmed condition occur alongside or after the harming event? Most people say no.[25] You may not even exist then. And even if you do, although you might be damaged you cannot, as I suggested earlier, be harmed. If anyone is harmed it would seem to be you in an earlier situation, before death, or ante mortem, when you are the sort of thing, with the sort of life and sorts of interests that make you susceptible to harm. But that earlier situation obtained at an earlier time. And so backwards causation now looms.

Is there a way round this? Pitcher thinks so. And Luper agrees:

> On Pitcher's view, posthumous events can only be indirect harms. The corresponding direct harms are certain facts about us that come to hold by virtue of the posthumous events that occur much later. If, for instance, Sarah's final wishes are ignored, the proposition "her will is to be ignored" is true of Sarah while she has these wishes; indirectly, she is harmed by the activities of those who set aside her will, but the corresponding direct harm is its being true of her that her will is to be ignored. She incurs this harm *while*

she has her final wishes. In sum, posthumous events that harm us do so indirectly. Partly because of these events, "certain desires of ours will be thwarted, certain goods unattained" is true of us, and its being true of us is the direct harm for which the posthumous events are responsible. We incur this direct harm precisely when "certain desires of ours will be thwarted, certain goods unattained" is true of us.   (2004: 70)

Pitcher offers his own example: "If the world should be blasted to smithereens during the next presidency after Ronald Reagan's this would make it true (be responsible for the fact) that even now, during Reagan's term, he is the penultimate president of the United States" (1993: 168).[26] And both examples succeed in avoiding any threat from backward causation. Things can be true at earlier times in virtue of different things becoming true at later times. But this by no means solves all the problems. First, it has been objected that Pitcher's example is something of a special case. For, "the description of the antecedent event essentially involves a temporal reference; it is the *penultimacy* of the ... [Reagan] presidency that is accounted for by the world's destruction" (Bernstein 1998: 61). How telling is this objection? As has been observed, it can appear that there are plenty of examples where this feature is absent. Posthumous events can make it true that Sarah's will is to be ignored, or that some sacrifice is not meaningful, but rather pointless. There is no temporal reference here. But this leads to a second difficulty. Suppose determinism is true. Then it is always, timelessly, true that Reagan's is the penultimate presidency, that the sacrifice is pointless and so on, even though none of this is always known to be true. Suppose determinism is false; then the number of his presidency, the nature of the sacrifice, hangs in the balance until events unfold one way rather than the other. Either way, what is being lost sight of here is the supposed harm that in many of these cases is said to occur. Even if it is always true that her will is to be ignored, we can, it seems, still ask just when Sarah is harmed by this? Luper is not altogether clear about the answer, suggesting, in the above, both that she is harmed so long as her wishes will be ignored, and that she is harmed so long as she has these wishes. One answer suggests she is always, or timelessly, harmed, the other that this harming has a more or less precise temporal location. Feinberg is more consistent, and prefers the second response. He thinks we are harmed by posthumous events at or from the time that we acquire those interests, or make those investments that such events will later defeat. From then on we are "playing a losing game" (1984: 91).

146

This provides an admirably clear answer to the timing problem, but hardly a satisfactory one. As he goes on to put it:

> Almost everyone will die with some interests that will be defeated by his death. And because of the inevitability of death, all of us are, while alive, in at least a partially harmed condition in that *those* interests are doomed, and thus generative of harm, from the time they are first acquired. (*Ibid.*: 93)

But this near-collapsing of distinct terms is surely unwarranted. Consider an unproblematic example. You leave home with a pocket full of money in the morning, intending to buy a used car. In the early afternoon a mugger mugs you, knocks you to the ground, steals the money and runs away. He initiates harming events. When does he harm you? The obvious answer here is when he mugs you, in the afternoon. And when he harms you is when you are harmed. You are harmed by the mugger. He is responsible. It is odd to say that you are harmed in the morning, when you leave the house with the money. And it is odd to say that you harmed yourself by acquiring this interest in a car, or that you are responsible. Similarly in a more problematic case. Suppose you do think that you are harmed in undiscovered betrayal, even though this has no effect on your internal condition. When are you harmed? Plausibly, when the betrayal takes place, and not earlier, when you enter into this relationship and so acquire an interest in not being betrayed. But certainly we can say of both cases that you were at that earlier time bound, or destined, to be harmed, or doomed, or marked by the hand of fate. And now surely it would be odd to preserve the distinction between doom and harm in these cases, but then to overlook it in a different case, where the harming event occurs later, after your death, and to insist there that your being harmed occurs much earlier, when certain interests of your first emerge. This smacks of desperation.

Is there a good solution to this timing problem? I do not think there is.

Last things

Clearly, there is substantial disagreement about the issues here. This disagreement: (i) needs to be explained; (ii) can perhaps be dissolved; and (iii) might still be settled in favour of posthumous harms. I shall start with this.

A last attempt

Perhaps this timing problem is not altogether as serious as it seems. For perhaps there are, in one way, posthumous harms after all. I may seem to have implied this above. I said that death normally harms us when it occurs, but might benefit us then, and harm us later, as the life we would otherwise be leading changes its character from bad to good. But if this is right, then it seems that we are harmed not at the time of death, but posthumously.

We can consider this in more detail. Suppose someone hits you on the head. This is a harming event. It might cause you pain, put you into a coma or kill you. Each of these is a harmed condition. Suppose you feel pain. How much pain you feel, how long it lasts and so on will depend on other aspects of your physical condition. Similarly for the coma. We might look to harm-related circumstances in order to understand how bad the coma is. If the coma causes you to miss important job interviews, a party, the Cup Final, it might be considered worse than if it robs you of a couple of groggy days in a hospital bed. And similarly, again, for death. Harm-related circumstances, many of them obtaining posthumously, bear on death's badness, varying its badness from time to time.

There are several things to note here. First, unlike the cases where you are prevented from regaining life, this sort of case actually occurs. There are people who, for a short time, are better off dead, but then, at a later time, worse off dead. Second, the harming event occurs not posthumously but at the life–death divide. And notice that this one event – the death – both benefits and harms the person. That is only superficially puzzling. A doctor might benefit and harm a patient by some drugs that relieve the pain but shorten her life. Third, the harmed condition, and many of the harm-related circumstances, occurs later than the harming event. So there is no timing problem here. Is there still a problem about how we can be harmed at this later time, when we do not exist? This problem is illusory. You can be harmed by becoming worse off than you were, or by being worse off than you would otherwise have been. In the sort of case envisaged here you are first better off, later worse off for being dead. This comes about because of changes elsewhere; obviously your internal condition remains the same. But even if this represents a merely relational change it is one that is consistent with your being harmed. It is not that you are worse off than other people; you are worse off than you would have been, had you not died.[27]

This is tentative. But even supposing there are posthumous harms of the kind here sketched, they are quite distinctive. One obvious way is that in our ordinary understanding of posthumous harms, when things go badly it is bad for you. Yet on this understanding it is bad for you when things go well.[28] Harms like this have no bearing on the case for posthumous harms of the more familiar kind.

Explanations

If there are no posthumous harms why are we so strongly inclined to believe that there are? Why do we think it matters how we treat the dead, what we say about them: that we give them something like respect? Geoffrey Scarre suggests it may be linked with the persistence of the view that we somehow survive death. As I have said, I think this view is false. And Scarre refers to it as an illusion.[29] Still, one false belief can explain others. And if, as seems true, it is hard to jettison all tendencies to believe in an afterlife, then it may be that we cannot but think that we, and others, will in some way be sensitive to post-mortem events. Then, of course, we can be harmed, posthumously, in a more-or-less straightforward manner.

There is a closely related tendency. And that is one not to make, and not to want to make, fine distinctions even when we know, or are able to know, that they can be made. It may be better that we teach children, cultivate in them, a disposition neither to set fire to cats nor to pull the wings off butterflies, even if there is room for a question about whether butterflies, as well as cats, can feel pain. Perhaps we should not make promises to the dying about what we will do once they are dead. But given the promise, it may be better that we are about as disposed to keep it as we would be were the parties still alive. Perhaps, though, we should make such promises. For perhaps it is good for us not to be disposed to distinguish so abruptly between the dead and the living, just as it is good for us not to betray one another, even when that betrayal will not be discovered. Similarly, it is perhaps good for us to regret the world's instability, that manuscripts are lost, woodlands flattened, cities sunk beneath the sea. And it is good to link, and to be disposed to link, such regret to the wishes, projects and investments of those now dead, even if there is in fact no good reason to think the dead can be harmed.[30]

Dissolution

Someone might still insist, against me, that there are posthumous harms. Someone else might suspect that, once again, the issues here are merely verbal. No one, living or dead, is hurt, or caused pain or distress, by events occurring after their death. But the living can be hurt by learning of events that will occur after death. It is not obviously irrational to care about posthumous events, when they impinge on either people or projects we care about. Nor is it obviously mistaken to construe the phrase "a successful life" in relation to the success of one's projects. But their success need not impinge on levels or patterns of welfare or well-being, construed in terms of mental and physical states, achieved within a life. And so on. Certainly, large measures of agreement between antagonists can, and should, be uncovered by any dispassionate attempt to find the middle ground. We might then think that whether to talk of benefiting or harming the dead is a matter of choice, or taste. There is no disagreement in substance. And nothing hangs on what we say.

But is this altogether right? It is worth thinking again about sacrifice. Other things being equal, it is better if harms do not occur. And we should be prepared to pay some price to prevent their occurrence. Should we, then, incur some cost to stave off an alleged posthumous harm? Consider some small-scale domestic example. Julia, in her later middle years, plants an orchard: apples, cherries, a few plums. She tends it and cares about it, investing both time and money in its success. And she wants it to remain after she is gone: some gesture to permanence in a changing world. Mary, knowing all this, buys the house. She has children. They would prefer a tennis court. What should Mary do? Wanting a tennis court, let us suppose, is not a frivolous thing. There would be no objection if the orchard, hardly a great success, was not there. And no agreements were signed or promises made. Is there any reason to deny her children the tennis court? If Julia can be harmed, then there is reason. The benefits to the children might be significant, and that reason easily outweighed, but it counts for something, and itself outweighs some reason on the other side.

Consider a more extreme example. We learn of aliens living on a distant planet. They are somewhat like us, and we understand their lives. Like us, they have projects, art and architecture. Suppose an asteroid threatens their planet. I think we fairly clearly have some reason to help, and should incur some cost to prevent the asteroid strike. But suppose that because of a prior radiation outbreak, they are already all dead. Yet their paintings and buildings, things they cared about, survive. Their art is not ours, and we have no direct interest in its survival, but we know well enough how much it mattered to them. Should we again pay some price to deflect the asteroid? Will they be harmed if we do not? There were millions of these aliens, so presumably even if harm to any one of them is slight it will, in total, amount to something fairly significant. Should we suffer a cut in our standard of living, or risk a few human lives, on their behalf? If we do not think we should make sacrifices to preserve their planet then, it seems to me, we do not think they can be harmed.

There is a further important question that has not been addressed. Suppose we do think, in this case, that we should pay some price to preserve this planet. What price? We might decide that there are posthumous harms, but that they are of vanishingly low importance.

I think we cannot harm the dead. Do I then think that no sacrifice should be paid to prevent the occurrence of alleged posthumous harms? I need not think this. My view, again, may be that there are social benefits from a broad structure of intergenerational, and perhaps also interplanetary, ties – we are somewhat inclined to respect the wishes, concerns and projects of past peoples, and hope that those in the future will be similarly disposed towards us – and for those reasons might think that it is worth paying some price for stability. But those who believe there are genuinely posthumous harms will need to explain why, often, that price should not be high: why our sacrifices should not be significant. Disagreement here is not merely verbal.

Summary

Are there posthumous harms? I have suggested that candidates for harm include only things with interests or a good of their own: things having a certain sort of value. Most living people can be harmed. Dead people cannot. But then the question is, can living people be harmed by events that occur after they are dead? The timing problem presents obstacles here.

Even so, we have to agree that people can, while alive, have desires for, investments in, projects concerning situations and events taking place or reaching completion only after their deaths. Or not. If something you care about, and not unreasonably, goes wrong – the deathbed novel is not published after all – are you in any way harmed by this? Because the notion of harm seems to point to some description of your internal condition – it is not as good as it was, or not as good as it would otherwise have been – I want to deny this.

We can ask another, closely related, question. Is it a pity, or sad, or unfortunate, that your novel is not published? I think it is. When someone fastens on and invests in some perfectly respectable project it is, generally, unfortunate when things do not work out. That is how, subject to and in sympathy with the human condition, we properly speak. And we should not be tempted to deny this because we are sceptical about posthumous harms, and think that if it is unfortunate the novel is not published, then it must be unfortunate for someone, and a good candidate is you, and that means you are harmed. Misfortunes need not cause suffering, and they need not cause harm.

7

An asymmetry

Life is never particularly long, and for some of us it is especially short. Could it be longer? It seems that it could: our lives are not necessarily of some precise length. Would it be good if it were longer? Assuming life is good, then it seems, at least to most of us, that it would. And so it seems that death is bad, in depriving us of this longer life. The Epicureans, of course, disagree.

Lucretius offers the following argument in support of the Epicurean view. Think of life as a brief flurry of activity, falling between two periods of non-existence. Life could be longer either by dying later or by being born earlier. If it is bad to die when we do, and not later, then surely it is in the same way bad to be born when we are, and not earlier. Our activity could be extended at either end. But we do not regret our non-existence before we are born. We do not think it is bad that we were not born earlier. So we should not regret our non-existence after we die. We should not think it bad that we do not die later.

The argument appeals, then, to an alleged symmetry between prenatal and post-mortem non-existence, and encourages us, in light of this, to be rid of our asymmetrical attitudes. It admits of three responses. We might acknowledge this symmetry and agree that neither state of non-existence is bad. This, evidently, is to play into the hands of the Epicureans. We might acknowledge the symmetry but now come to believe that as death is bad, so too is prenatal non-existence. The argument could backfire, causing us to think things are even worse than they seemed. Or we might reject the symmetry claim, arguing that our difference in attitude conforms to some genuine difference in these boundaries to our lives. I shall argue for a version of this third response.

153

Experience

First, though, an alternative account. Anthony Brueckner and John Fischer (1986) offer an ingenious explanation of our difference in attitude. Their work draws on Derek Parfit's (1984) discussion of a related asymmetry concerning our attitudes to pain, earlier identified by Nagel (1979) as throwing light on Lucretius' problem. Frances Kamm (1988, 1993) has, in various of her writings, shown herself sympathetic to this stance. And there are still other philosophers adopting a similar approach.[1] The strategy here needs to be taken seriously. But it is, I fear, altogether misguided. I shall start with Parfit.

Indifference

Imagine you had a month of severe pain ten years ago, which is now completely forgotten. Then you are reminded of the pain. Is this of concern? Parfit says he would "react to this reminder with *complete indifference*" (1984: 173). Nor is this mere biography. For he maintains that unless memories are themselves painful, most of us view our past suffering with "complete indifference" (*ibid*.: 173–4). This general claim is surely false. We are not indifferent to the past. And we are not indifferent, in particular, to our past pains. We look back to moments or periods of pain often with regret that they ever occurred, sometimes with distress, occasionally with fear for the future. How can the contrary claim, that we are indifferent, appear even plausible? Consider two cases:

> *The Surgery Case.* Imagine you are in hospital for an operation. It lasts an hour, and is so painful that the doctors induce amnesia, so that you forget both the surgery, and the pain. You wake up, and ask the nurse about your situation. But there is some confusion. She can at this stage only tell you that you either had the operation yesterday, in which case it is now forgotten, or you will have it tomorrow. (*Ibid*.: 165–6)[2]

Parfit contends that you will, in this situation, hope that your operation is over. Having pain behind us seems much better than having it still to come. Brueckner and Fischer alter the example slightly. They offer:

> *The Hospital Case.* Imagine you are in some hospital to test a drug. The drug induces intense pleasure for an hour followed by amnesia. You awaken and ask the nurse about your situation. She

> says that either you tried the drug yesterday (and had an hour of pleasure) or you will try the drug tomorrow (and will have an hour of pleasure). (Brueckner & Fischer 1986: 218–19)

And it is quite clear, they say, that you will prefer to have the pleasure tomorrow. Just as with pains, here too temporal location makes a difference. But of course pain is not pleasure. Whereas we prefer pain in the past, pleasure is better situated in the future.

There are two points, both important, to be made about these cases. They are extraordinary. And they are, with respect to a certain aim, ineffective. Both cases have quite special characteristics. Amnesia and drugs play salient roles. And the pleasures and pains involved are both short-term and unimportant. When in the past, the experience is now forgotten and makes for no discernible difference to the present. When in the future, the experience will be forgotten and will make no discernible difference to subsequent experience. Such experiences are, then, both inaccessible and, as I shall say, inefficacious.[3] When experiences, although you were aware of them at the time, have these characteristics, I shall refer to them as *blank*.

Are we indifferent to the past, even under these special circumstances? I want to use "indifferent" in its ordinary sense.[4] If we are indifferent to a certain event's occurring, we care neither one way nor the other that it occurs. This does not mean, of course, that we just do not care what occurs; indifference to one thing usually assumes that other things stay as is. If you are indifferent to the prowess of a football team then you do not care whether they win or lose. But you still might care if they are killed in a plane crash. If I am indifferent to past pain, I will not prefer a neutral state to pain, and will not prefer a smaller to larger pain. Similarly for pleasure. If indifferent, then I will not prefer pleasure to a neutral state. But I still might prefer pleasure to pain. If I am indifferent to past pleasure and pain alike, however, it would seem I do not care at all how things feel. What, then, of the surgery and hospital cases? If one is at all tempted by the indifference claim, it might at first be thought that these cases do lend it support. But that would be a mistake.[5] The surgery and hospital cases, although extraordinary, certainly do not show that we are, in this ordinary sense, indifferent. All they show, surely, is that with respect to such experiences we are more concerned about future than past occurrences. That I prefer past to future pain does not at all show that past pain is of no concern.

Does anyone claim that these cases do show indifference? Parfit does not. He gives the case, contends later that we are indifferent to past pain, but does not strongly suggest that the case supports the contention. Brueckner and

Fischer do, insisting that we are indifferent to past pleasures. Further, they believe Parfit takes the surgery case as revealing indifference to past pain.[6]

These cases do not support the indifference claim. Other cases, which again make a feature of blankness, might fare better. Imagine that the nurse says that you had either a one-hour, or a ten-hour operation yesterday. Either way, the memory is obliterated. If you are indifferent, you will not care how long the operation lasted. Less pain will not be preferred. In another case, you had either a painful operation, or you tested some pleasure drug, yesterday. If you are indifferent to past experience, you will not hope to have had pleasant times.

Would we be indifferent? As these cases are artificial, and depend on extraordinary circumstances, it may not be clear. But I doubt we would be indifferent. We prefer even blank pains not to have occurred. We prefer some pleasures, even if inaccessible, to have occurred. And if something has occurred, we much prefer it to be pleasure rather than pain. Irrespective of any derivative concern for the present, we would like our past lives to have gone well.

So even in these very special circumstances, figured by blankness, the claims that we are indifferent to our past experiences are less than cogent. But, more importantly, precisely because these cases are special, no inference can be made to the general case. What of that case? In general, past pleasures and pains are neither inaccessible nor inefficacious. Most past experiences are or can be remembered, affect us and help plot the shape of our future lives. And our interest in them is correspondingly greater. Some might still think the indifference claim in its restricted form is true. But given general form, the claim is certainly false.

Bias

There is a weaker position to be considered. For, and as I have suggested, both Parfit and also Brueckner and Fischer run together claims about indifference to the past with claims about a bias to the future. Bias occurs when, although from a temporally neutral point of view we would rank two experiences the same, our position in time causes us to rank them differently. Imagine we are biased to the future, where pain is concerned. Then, although we may be concerned about both, a future pain will worry us more than a past pain of equal intensity. Similarly, a future bias will lead us to prefer pleasures in front of us, rather than behind us.

Are we, in this way, biased to the future? Bias, if it exists, will at least on the face of it be puzzling. When all other things are equal, why should we care about the future more than the past? And bias will show most clearly where other things are equal, and so will show most clearly where inaccessible experiences are concerned. Otherwise effects of memory and physiological and psychological consequences can skew our choices. Someone worries about the future more than the past because they believe that what is yet to happen might, with care, be avoided. Or they worry more because they believe that as they get older their resistance to pain will decrease. The differences here should not be considered as evidence of bias, for it is not temporal location alone that generates the difference. To test for bias, factors like these need to be eliminated. Such factors are eliminated in the surgery and hospital cases. And yet these cases do suggest there is such bias: we prefer pain behind us and pleasure in front of us. But bias can be suggested even when blankness is no longer a factor. Another of Parfit's cases, in which the past is remembered, helps to make this clear:

> (*Case Two*). When I wake up, I do remember a long period of suffering yesterday. But I cannot remember how long the period was. I ask my nurse whether the operation is completed, or whether further surgery is still to be done. As before she knows the facts about two patients, but she cannot remember which I am. If I am the first patient, I had five hours of pain yesterday, and my operation is over. If I am the second patient, I had two hours of pain yesterday and I shall have another hour of pain later today.
>
> (1984: 167)

And Parfit hopes to be the first patient. He says, "I would prefer my life to contain more hours of pain, if that means none of this pain is still to come" (*ibid.*). Is this plausible? I think it may be. But notice that the bias claim is not overturned even if you suspect you would react differently to this particular case. Perhaps, for you, four hours of past pain is better than two hours in the past and one in the future. But beyond that you would not trade. Still you are biased. Whether future pain is slightly or immensely more distressing than past pain of an equal size, bias still exists.

Allow, then, that there is bias in cases like these. Does it spill over into ordinary cases? Is there, in general, a bias to the future? Indifference is all or nothing.[7] Because bias, unlike indifference, can hold to varying degrees, the claim that there is in many cases some element of bias is a modest claim. And thinking about ordinary cases may suggest there is, generally, some future bias. Consider the dentist yesterday, or the dentist tomorrow. Because the bias claims are modest, and because they seem to be supported by reflection, not only on fanciful cases, but on much of our everyday experience, I shall allow that these, unlike the indifference claims, are true.

Experience and existence

How are our attitudes to death and to pain connected? Many writers think there are important parallels. Brueckner and Fischer, for example, claim that we worry about future non-existence while remaining indifferent to its counterpart in the past.[8] And this, they say, is of a piece with our more general attitude. Death is bad when and because it deprives us of future pleasure: the sort of pleasure we want. Prenatal non-existence is not bad, because it deprives us only of the pleasure to which we are indifferent: past pleasure. Parfit believes that future bias does much to account for our attitudes to both pain and death. If we could rid ourselves of this bias, perhaps by reflection on our attitude to the past, then future non-existence might seem less terrible.[9]

But there are problems here. First, and as just explained, the requisite claims about our attitudes to experience are far from established. Although there does seem to be some bias to the future, there is no indifference to the past. Second, even supposing these claims do go through, their relevance to Lucretius' problem is, in a number of dimensions, far from evident. Consider Brueckner and Fischer's attempt at a parallel:

> *The Birthday Case*: It is now 1985 and you will live eighty years in any case. Suppose you are given the following choice. Either you were born in 1915 and will die in 1995, or you were born in 1925 and will die in 2005. In each case, we will suppose, your life contains the same amount of pleasure and pain, distributed evenly through time. It is quite clear that you would prefer the second option – you want your good experiences in the future.
>
> (1986: 219)

Is this clear? They say it is, but I deny it. Even if you prefer a pleasure drug ahead rather than behind, the same is unlikely to be true for decades of your life. There are too many disanalogies. I shall first make a general comment, and then look further at some detail.

The surgery and hospital cases focus on certain of our experiences. Pleasure and pain are, respectively, intrinsically good and bad. Non-existence, the concern in the birthday case, is, in contrast, intrinsically neutral. But it is bad, although extrinsically bad, when it deprives us of a good life. There are links here. The badness of death does, as I have granted, stem from its effects on experience. Suppose we are already in an irreversible coma. That is bad, but it is not obviously a further bad now to die. But although not unsympathetic, I have wanted to draw back from a straightforward or thoroughgoing hedonism. Even though it centres on experience, there is more to the good life than simple pleasure. The focus so far, however, has been on simple pains and simple pleasures. So we might anticipate a certain strain in shifting from the earlier cases to the birthday case. It should not be surprising if this last case fails immediately to convince. But we should look at key claims more closely.

Consider indifference, and take first the restricted claim, focusing on those rare cases where past experiences are inaccessible. And suppose that in fact we were indifferent to such experiences. Does this have much bearing on our attitude to non-existence? Presumably if we had been born earlier we would have a bigger fund of accessible memories to draw on. And presumably these would have made a considerable difference to our present and future lives. As I said, we cannot just assume our attitude to inaccessible past experiences will throw light on our attitude to accessible past experiences. Still less can we assume our attitude to inaccessible past experience will throw light on our attitude to past non-existence. An earlier start would make a discernible difference to our past and present lives. What happens in the ten years would not be blank. So this first claim, even if true, would be of no clear relevance to our attitude to non-existence.

Drop the restrictions. Suppose we were generally indifferent to past experiences. It would not strictly follow that we would be indifferent to prenatal non-existence, but it would, surely, be most likely. If we just did not care about previous experiences, even when they do affect our future, it seems unlikely we would care about when we were born. Being born at a different time would give us either more or fewer past experiences. Why care about that, if we do not care about the experiences themselves?[10] So this second and general claim would, if true, bear on our attitude to prenatal non-existence. But although the general claim is relevant, it is, I have wanted to say, simply false. We do, in general, care about past experiences. The problem here, then, is that the most plausible indifference claim – the one restricted to blank experiences – is irrelevant to our attitude to prenatal non-existence, while the version of the indifference claim that would be relevant – the non-restricted version – is pretty plainly false.

Now consider bias. Suppose I am right in thinking that, unlike the indifference claims, the bias claims are true. We are distressed by both past and future pain, but past pain counts for less. Similarly, pleasure pleases, but prospective pleasure pleases more. Is there a connection here with our attitudes to non-existence? Again, we might anticipate a link. If we are concerned more for future than past experience, we are, surely, likely to care more for future than past existence. But how far can we push the parallel? Are we likely, as with bias concerning experience, to regret non-existence whenever it occurs, but to regret future non-existence more? Shall we expect, that is, to find we have a modest wish that we had been born earlier?

There is a further problem with the strategy here. General indifference to past experience would make indifference to past existence likely. But this is not to the point. The question is not: what attitude to non-existence might we predict, funded with this knowledge of attitudes to experience? It is, rather: how is our actual attitude to non-existence to be explained?[11] And in order to explain, we need first to more precisely identify that attitude. It does not seem we are indifferent to our pasts. Perhaps we are biased to the future. Still, as I have just suggested, the fine print of our bias regarding non-existence may well differ from its counterpart regarding experience.

Existence

What, then, are our attitudes to non-existence? The birthday case is bizarre. How can we now choose when to be born? It is not easy to see how to make sense of this. How can we now choose whether to have tested a drug? But the hospital case centres on which situation we would prefer to be in. And the birthday case can be revised to improve the parallel.

> *The Amnesia Case*: You suffer from amnesia. The doctors know you are either Bill, who was born in 1925 and can be expected to live to 2005, or you are Ben, who was born in 1915 and can be expected to live to 1995.

Is it clear you will hope to be Bill? Suppose you believe your amnesia is incurable. As you will never again remember the past it may seem reasonable to be wholly forward looking. You will hope to have the longer of the two futures. But even though the past is inaccessible, it is not inefficacious. And it would be very strange to have no interest in, to be wholly indifferent to, the experiences you have had, and the life you have lived. Accessible or not, this past has shaped who you are today. And amnesiac or not, you presumably are

160

someone, with interests, dispositions and a character. It did not come from nowhere.

Suppose the amnesia is curable. You still hope to be younger, with the longer future. But then it is cured, you once again remember the past and discover that you are older than you had hoped. Will you be disappointed? Perhaps. But other factors will be even more clearly in play. Ben was a hero, Bill a villain. Even though older, you may prefer heroic memories.

Most of us are not amnesiac. Our attitudes to past non-existence are not going to be those of someone in such special circumstances. What are our attitudes? We are not indifferent to prenatal non-existence. It is just not true that we simply do not care either way when this period of non-existence came to an end.[12] What would such indifference involve? If we were indifferent, it would matter to us not at all when we were born. So it would not matter to us whether we had been born two or three hundred years earlier, or a dozen or so years later. It would not matter to us how old we were now, or what shape our lives had taken. But all of this plainly does matter. It matters both in that it has consequences and that we care deeply about them.

Nor are we, just as with pleasures and pains, biased to the future. We do not have a mild desire to have been born earlier, but a much stronger desire to die later. Most of us do not want to have been born earlier at all; we do not want, even to a modest degree, to be older than we are. The opposite is not infrequently the case. Older people sometimes say they would like to be younger. They want more experiences in front of them, and they want to have, now, younger and healthier bodies. But this desire is, I think, neither widespread nor resilient. Many older people are accepting of their lot. And although some do say they want to be younger, what this amounts to, in most cases, is a younger-seeming body, and a mind that is not succumbing to the ravages of time. Very few want that which, on reflection, they know must accompany genuine youthfulness: an obliteration or reduction of their pasts.

There is already a hint here at a further attitude. This attitude is more prevalent and more stable. It better captures the position that most of us, for the most part, appear to occupy. And it can be both described and explained. We want, most of us, for the past to be as it is, and so are neither indifferent to its shape, nor interested in amending it. Older people can, on occasion, express a wish to be younger. Historians, focused on research, sometimes, and unthinkingly, say they would like to be older than they are. The rest of us generally do not. We recognize that our being born at a certain time is, in large part, responsible for who we are today. My being who I am now – my being a person with certain interests, a certain character, plans, friends, commitments

– depends on the past, both its boundary and its contents having been a certain way. Someone born at a different time just would not, in an everyday sense, be me.[13] And so we are neither indifferent to prenatal non-existence nor, revealing bias, somewhat inclined to wish its period longer or shorter than it was. Rather, our concern is with *conservation*, with keeping the facts of prenatal non-existence just as they are. For many of us recognize, and many more can easily be brought to recognize, that a concern for the present to be as it is, and for us to be who we are, implies a concern that the past be as it was, and thus that we be born when in fact we were. Nor is this, I think, to misstate the matter, such that only being *as* rather than *who* we are, is threatened by a supposed altering here of the past. Indeed, the point can be put more dramatically: to want to be born at a different time is, in effect, to want not to exist, and for someone else to exist in your place. It is not surprising that this is something only a very few of us want. Contrast this with the future. Both who I am and what I am like now is independent of the future's being a certain way. Suppose I live on for forty rather than thirty good years. The later death gives me more of what I want, and represents a benefit for me, in a way that an earlier birth does not.[14]

We have, as Lucretius notes, an asymmetrical attitude to past and future non-existence. We want to die later but not to have been born earlier. But this is not puzzling. Given that we care about who we are, and what we are like, we have reasons to keep the past as it is, to want conservation. Given that we want more of life, more of the life we are living, we have reasons to prefer dying later, to want extension. Non-existence, in itself, is always the same. But the alternative to non-existence – more of life – differs critically in relation to our lives depending where it comes.

Two objections

I need to consider certain objections to the position as I have outlined it so far. I merely anticipate the first, while the second (which will here demand more time) has already been made. They are related, and both maintain that I have misconstrued the position that I have wanted to oppose, seeing it as broader and more general than in fact it is.

I have said that we do not want an earlier birth, in contrast to our wanting a later death, because we see well enough that the consequences of this would be, for us, wholly undesirable. A life that begins earlier might in many respects be better, but it will not, I have wanted to say, be mine. And so it is unsurprising that I do not wish for this better life.

It can be objected, however, that this is simply to conflate cause and effect. There is no obvious reason why we should not wish for something that will at least appear to be logically possible; namely, that we be born earlier, while yet not being significantly different today. It is indeed the consequences of an earlier birth that are repellent, not the earlier birth itself. But surely we can, at least where desires are concerned, simply detach these and set them aside. We might wish for the cause without wishing for its effects. Or we might wish for the cause and some among its effects, while not wishing for the others.

There are two components within the reply. First, our attitudes are, not unnaturally, typically sensitive to physical facts. I am wary of the Aids virus. Someone points out that it is not the virus, but its consequences that are so devastating. I am unimpressed. Explaining hostility to a cause by reference to its effects is, in most normal circumstances, perfectly proper. Second, if we were to divide up the objects of our desire along logically possible lines, there would no longer be any good reason to wish for an earlier birth. Other cases are different. I might want intoxication without the hangover, or to be in Hanoi without the tedium of airports. In such cases antipathy to the effects does not imply antipathy to the cause. But an earlier birth is, of course, not wanted for its own sake. Nor will it do to suggest we should wish for this as a means to our acquiring a selection among its effects. For once it is realized that some of its effects are undesirable, we might simply wish for the others directly, and not via this cause. I would do better, as an historian, to wish for a time machine rather than to have been born earlier. Similarly, I would do better, as an old person, to wish for longevity, looks and health rather than to be genuinely younger today.

A second objection will follow from the first. Consider an earlier birth in itself, and shorn of its consequences. This is not, I have argued, in any obvious way desirable. But then nor is it undesirable. It may seem that while we do care about its various implications we shall, to an earlier birth itself, be simply indifferent. Now the objection here is not that my argument leads to a contrary position; it is, after all, precisely on our attending to consequences that my conservation claim is based. It is rather that no stronger claim, no claim about indifference to an earlier birth more broadly construed, has yet been proposed.

Just such a line is taken by Brueckner and Fischer, who insist in a later paper that I misunderstood their original argument, seeing it as more general and wide ranging than in fact it was. I thought they had claimed that we were generally indifferent to the past whereas, or so they say,[15] only a restricted indifference claim was ever advanced. And in attempting to explain this they appeal to the distinction between accessible and inaccessible pleasures, insisting that "the asymmetry claim as regards inaccessible pleasures is the claim pertinent to the issue of death's badness" (1993a: 329).

But this is puzzling. Only a very few past pleasures (and very few past pains) are inaccessible in this way. How can indifference here, if such there be, explain an indifference to prenatal non-existence? If we had been born earlier, there would be more accessible pleasures: more to remember, more that had affected the present and would affect the future shape of our lives, and so on. What could show we are indifferent to all of that? Nothing could. The authors now accept that these consequences of past experience can be of present concern:

> Clearly the deprivation account of death's badness is quite compat-ible with our wishing to maximise our pleasures in the (present and) future and thus not being indifferent to past pleasures *insofar as they are connected favorably to (present and) future pleasures* ... [and] ... the deprivation thesis does *not* entail that it cannot be the case that being born earlier would be desirable insofar as it would issue in a more attractive total pattern of life experiences.
>
> (*Ibid.*: 330)[16]

But these various instrumental concerns are distinct from a concern with the past *as such*. To the past as such, or the past in so far as it is past, in so far as it is inaccessible and inefficacious, we are indifferent. The idea seems to be, then, that although genuinely inaccessible pleasures of the kind offered in the hospital case may be few and far between, we can consider all pleasures *as if* they were inaccessible, detaching the past pleasure itself from its several effects and consequences. And to past experiences so construed we are simply indifferent.

I do not, as I have said earlier, think this is true. And I do not think the authors offer any reason for suggesting it is true. But suppose it were. It does not at all explain our actual attitude to prenatal non-existence. Even if we were indifferent to the past *as such*, there would still remain the central ques-tion: why are we (purportedly) indifferent to being born earlier? If I had been born earlier, or so it appears, I would have more to look back on. If times had been good, looking back would give me greater pleasure now. Why do we not want this? Why do we not want an earlier birth when this (apparently) would connect favourably with present and future pleasures, and issue in a more attractive total pattern of life experience?

Brueckner and Fischer, in restricting the scope of their claim, fail to address this question. What I took to be the authors' original claim – we are generally indifferent to the past – would, had it been true, have explained why we are (purportedly) uninterested in an earlier birth. Their revised claim – we are indifferent to the past *as such* – will, even if true, explain nothing of the sort. The pursuit of truth has led to a neglect of relevance.

Thus both objections fail. There is no reason, first, to suppose that we should be interested in an earlier birth, detached from its normal consequences. We would be indifferent to a reduction in prenatal non-existence, if it were so acquired. And there is no reason, second, to suppose that indifference to past experience *as such* will throw light on our attitude to prenatal non-existence. Our actual attitude takes full note of the probable effects of an earlier birth.

Self and others

We have an asymmetrical attitude to pain, caring more about its future than its past occurrence. And we have an asymmetrical attitude towards non-existence, hoping to reduce its future but not its past occurrence. So should we allow that important parallels are, after all, sustained? And should we think that in both areas there is detectable a form of bias?

We should not. Bias to the future occurs when we distinguish between past and future experiences that, considered in themselves, seem to warrant the same reaction. Our different views are a function of our position in time. And I have allowed that there is such bias, at least where simple pleasures and pains are concerned. Not so with non-existence. Our different views are not simply a function of our position in time. Even supposing we occupied a temporally neutral position, our views would not change. The asymmetry is, in contrast, a perfectly proper reaction to a genuine difference between, if not the blanks themselves, at least their relation to the structure of our lives.

This point might better be seen by considering further ways in which the parallel between death and pain breaks down. And we can usefully explore differences, first, between ourselves and others, and second, between now and times other than now.

Imagine you have just discovered your mother was in great pain a month or two ago. You have discovered also that she is now fully recovered. The pain is past. Are you concerned? Parfit would be (1984: 181–3). He argues that where pain is concerned, indifference to the past is restricted to our own case. Concerning others alive now, there is no such indifference.[17] In their case, we recognize that pain is bad whenever it occurs. Parfit offers no explanation of this difference in attitude, claiming simply that it is a "striking asymmetry" (*ibid.*: 183). Brueckner and Fischer agree thus far. But they do offer an explanation. They emphasize the experiential quality of my present pains.

> Inevitably, such pains are of concern to me. My past pains are not now, and never again will be, experienced. But the pains of others do not, for me, differ in this important way. Their pains, whenever they occur, sit outside my experience. Thus temporal location makes no difference, where my attitude to the pains of others are concerned. (Brueckner & Fischer 1986: 218)

There is some virtue in this explanation. But the costs outweigh the gains. Suppose I am, as they claim, indifferent to my past pains. And suppose the explanation of this is that they are not, and will never again be, felt by me. You would expect the authors to claim that I am indifferent to the pains of others whenever they occur. Unsurprisingly, this is not their claim.[18]

Yet even if explanation is wanting, let us suppose Parfit is right here, and that the phenomenon obtains. I have a strikingly asymmetrical attitude to my own pains, but not to the pains of others. But then our attitude to pain is again unlike our attitude to non-existence. For here our attitudes are equally asymmetrical throughout. I hope I shall die later, but do not regret not having been born earlier. And I hope my friends will die later. But I do not regret their not having been born earlier. I have to them, concerning non-existence, just the same kinds of attitudes I have to myself.

Our attitude to the pain of others needs to be considered further. We are not indifferent to their past pain. But are we, in their case as in ours, biased to the future? Consider:

> *The Revelations.* You learn that someone, of whom you know nothing further, will suffer a month's pain at forty-nine, or a week's pain at fifty-one. You prefer for this person the later and shorter pain. Then their age is revealed. You learn the person is alive, and is fifty, now. Then their identity is revealed. You learn, further, that this person is you. You prefer, for yourself, the earlier, but longer pain.

There is, first, a focus on another person who perhaps exists at a different time. This person may be dead, or may not yet even be born. Towards the pains of both the dead, on the one hand, and the unborn, on the other, our attitude is symmetrical. Other things equal, we want for them simply the lowest amount of pain. And so there is, in such a case, no future bias.

Matters are less straightforward where the living are concerned. Two revelations do make a difference. When you learn that the person is now fifty, and is you, your preference is for the pain to be past, even if it is therefore greater. There is, as I have agreed, some future bias. But what is your attitude after learning the age but not yet the identity of the person? Here the difference is less clear. Some prefer, even for others, that pain is in the past. But some prefer that others should have the lower amount of pain. Temporal bias, where others are concerned, does exist. But it is seemingly less widespread than when we consider our own situation.

So our attitudes to pain are complex. There is, in our own case, a significant future bias. But this bias tends to be reduced, as we shift away from ourselves and from our times.

What of our attitudes to non-existence? They are relatively simple. Here too we can consider other times. For those alive now, and also the unborn and the dead, my wish is that their death be later. I want for them all a long and happy life. But it is not, as symmetry would demand, that they be born earlier. This further clarifies the point made above. Our asymmetrical attitude to non-existence is not a function of our position in time. It is not, in this sense, a bias. I am in my life. My death is before me, while prenatal non-existence is behind. The difference in attitude does correspond to a difference in temporal direction. Does it depend on this difference? With people who do not exist now, the correspondence is removed. For those as yet unborn, both periods of non-existence are (in part) ahead. And for those who have already died, both periods are (in part) behind. But I still, in each case, have a different kind of concern for the two boundaries to their lives.

Identity

I started with two questions, concerning the possibility and desirability of a longer life. It is possible and often desirable to die later. But now it is both impossible and undesirable to be born earlier. As I have said, someone born earlier would not be me. And we do not want to change the past. Is this right? Consider a seemingly straightforward argument: I could not have been born earlier. This is impossible. And, because it is impossible, I do not want it. It is undesirable. There are several faults with this. Even so, it is not altogether wide of the mark. But I shall first emphasize the faults.

Origins

First, suppose I know or believe something is impossible. Still, I can desire it. Some people will allow this where technological and physical impossibilities are concerned, but have doubts for logical or metaphysical impossibilities. Still, I can seem to desire it. I can desire or seem to desire time travel. Further, I can at least seem to desire what seems to me to be impossible. Perhaps I cannot desire what seems to me to be incoherent. But this is not at issue here. These issues have been discussed earlier, so I have been brief here.

Second, the alleged impossibility here, on at least its standard interpretation, is not something that will seem to most people to be impossible. That standard interpretation makes appeal to the metaphysics of identity. Read Kripke, and you learn that none of us could have originated from a different sperm and egg. The necessity of origin view makes for much less leeway in the circumstances of our birth than might otherwise be supposed. But the problem here is that an abstruse, youthful and somewhat contentious philosophy cannot plausibly be held to lie behind the widespread and perennial asymmetrical attitude concerning death and birth.[19]

Third, what may well be impossible here does not itself render it impossible for me to have been born earlier. Consider Parfit's position. He insists that as a matter of fact, none of us could have been conceived much earlier or later than the time when we were actually conceived.[20] And this is because if that time is altered by as much as a month, a different sperm and a different egg will be involved. Given this wholesale exchange of the originating material, inevitably a different person will come into existence. So even though I could fairly clearly have been born a few days earlier or later, and arguably could as well have been conceived a few days earlier or later, my beginnings are otherwise fixed.

The argument is plainly defective, however. There is just no reason, on the grounds given here, for thinking that we could not have been conceived at a substantially different time. Both sperm and egg can be frozen, and their union delayed. And we could, of course, have been born at a different time. For the embryo itself can be frozen, and its development delayed. Nor is there a way out in noting Parfit's caution, and his insistence on what is in fact true, rather than what is necessarily true. He clearly thinks that even if it is logically possible for someone to be conceived much later than they were, this is not physically possible. But it is. And it is physically possible too for someone to be born much later than they were. The requisite technologies have not been around for long. People born a hundred years ago could not, as things stand, have been frozen as embryos and born later. But things could have stood differently. The technologies could have been developed earlier. That too is physically possible. And earlier births, earlier conceptions, are similarly possible. There may well be people born in 2150 who, had materials not been frozen, would have been born in 2050. So reliance on origin claims, where the question of timing is concerned, is not going to work. We need to look elsewhere.

Psychologies

Consider a radical mid-life change. I am hit by a bus and enter PVS. Do I continue to exist? I say yes, even though many say no. In a variant case I remain conscious, but undergo a sudden and massive personality change, forgetting who I am, where I live, and what I like, and adopting the dispositions, character and beliefs of a rural clergyman. And this change is permanent and irreversible. Do I continue to exist? I am now more inclined to say no. It is one thing to lose my psychology, another for this to be replaced with the psychology of a stranger.

Suppose some mid-life change is identity destroying in this way. Even if you still exist without your psychology, someone with a wholly different psychology just is not you. Then, surely, development of a wholly different psychology from the outset along radically different lines is identity denying. Suppose, as I believe, and evidence from twins notwithstanding, that much of my psychological life is a product of environment, rather than nature. I have just the one brother. As a one-day-old baby my brother's brother is given for adoption to a Japanese family. This child eats fish, speaks Japanese, wrestles sumo. I want to say that if this had happened then I would never have existed.[21] Consider not place, but time. Cryonics works. As a newborn baby my brother's brother is taken from his parents, frozen for two hundred years, with life to be continued late in the twenty-second century. Again, I would not exist, were this to be true.

As with place, so with time. I believe, first, that were the foetus I once was to have been born at any substantially earlier time, I would have been significantly different. Setting exceptional circumstances aside,[22] this is surely true. Second, and unsurprisingly, I do not desire this. Given my interests and concerns, and the life I am leading, I cannot see this earlier birth as offering any sort of benefit. Third, I claim that had there been such a timing shift then I would not have been born. Anyone coming into this world much earlier would not have been me. And so we can revisit, and find the nub of truth, in the straightforward argument. Rather than insisting that as an earlier birth is impossible so I do not desire it, the claim here is that its gross undesirability

169

warrants our holding it impossible that someone born earlier should be me. So it is not so much a deep difference in fact, but a network of superficial differences relating to value, that explains the impossibility.

Three objections

There are several contentious claims here. I shall consider first that just made above: that I could not have been born earlier.

Someone objects that this must surely be false. As I have already explained in relation to Parfit, I could have been born earlier. Granted, this is a remote possibility for most of us today. Nevertheless it is possible. And remoteness will not hamper its being desirable. And, the objection continues, I am simply running together here, and unnecessarily, questions of identity with others of prudential concern. I may have reasons to want to have been born when I was, and reasons to suppose that any radical change here would generate unwelcome changes. Not so, of course, in relation to dying later. And so, given this, I might claim already to have answered Lucretius. The further claim, that I could not have been born earlier, is neither pressing nor persuasive. And it is not persuasive because to grant that this human animal could have come into existence earlier just is to grant that I could have come into existence earlier. For I am that animal.

The first point here reveals a certain misunderstanding. If identity depends only on originating material, then I could have been born earlier. But I question the antecedent. The second point is more promising. I could separate out the undesirability and impossibility claims, and put the latter on hold. And I am disinclined now to be as bullish about the identity claim as I once was.[23] Nevertheless, suppose my embryo had been put on ice, thawed and brought up in a wholly different environment. I still think the claim that I would never then have existed is (a) not false and (b) more defensible than its rival. And as that implies, I doubt that I am identical with a particular human animal. But more of this in Chapter 9.

Second, there might here be noted objections to my earlier conservation claim. We do not desire an earlier birth because that would generate substantial change. And we do not desire change. Fischer and Speak have doubts about this. Although many of us are happy as we are there are many others who are not. And they ask:

> Why wouldn't these people be willing to take the risks involved
> in having a different personality? And of course it is not only

individuals from disadvantaged or troubled backgrounds who suffer from deep, persistent, and unpleasant emotional and mental problems: chronic depression and schizophrenia are not reserved for those who have grown up in poverty or suffered abuse. Why is it so obvious that *almost everyone* would want to keep the past as it is, because they want desperately to keep the basic features of their personality as they are? (Fischer & Speak 2000: 92)

This is, they say, "conservative in the extreme". Nor, apparently, can I concede that significant minorities might be open to such a personality change. For I have said, and "starkly", "We wish to die later. But we don't wish to have been born earlier" (2000a: 317). The last part of this objection surely misses its target. Millions of people might wish for a different past, and a different personality, even while none of them wish to be born earlier. Millions might wish to be born later, even while none wish to be born earlier. To want to be born earlier is either to want to be older, or to want that which, and fairly clearly, results in your being older. And it is a somewhat circuitous route to avoiding poverty or depression.

Are there significantly large numbers of people unhappy enough to want to jettison the accessibility and efficacy of their pasts? Unsurprisingly, I have done no research into this, but I have doubts. It is one thing desperately to want not to be poor, or blind, or depressed, but another to achieve this by a total personality shift.

However, a third objection stems from this. If experience had begun at a substantially different time I would be a very different person today. And we do not wish to have had an earlier, or later, birth. Equally, if experience had had a substantially different content I would be, in a similar sense, a very different person today. Yet we often do wish to have had radically different experiences. Think of two examples. At the age of two, I lose my sight. At forty-two I still wish I had not gone blind. But it is pointed out that had I not gone blind, almost everything today would be different. Or at the age of two, my family emigrates to Australia. I still wish we had stayed in Wolverhampton. But it is pointed out that had we not travelled the globe, almost everything today would have been different. In both cases I seem to be wishing I had lived virtually a different life. But does this make sense? If the desire to have been born at a different time (and to have had more pleasure through having more experience) is so rare, how can the desire to have lived a different life (and to have had more pleasure through having different experience) be so common?

The difficulty will be clear. I have claimed, against others, that there are significant differences in our attitude to past pain, on the one hand, and to past non-existence, on the other. And I have claimed to explain those differ-ences in terms of our legitimate desires to reduce pain and to conserve the time of birth. But the past is the past. If it had been different, in respect of either length or content, we would be different today. The explanation so far offered is threatening to collapse.

Explanation

How, then, are our attitudes to be explained? Brueckner and Fischer believe many of our actual attitudes are rational. Thus it is rational, on their account, to regret death, and rational too to exhibit future bias where pleasures and pains are concerned.[24] Parfit, in contrast, believes that some of these attitudes may be irrational or, more weakly, not rationally, required. Future bias, for example, is on his account irrational, and an attitude we would be better off without. And fear of death is, in large part, accounted for by this irrational bias.[25] But either way, more needs to be said. To claim an attitude is rational is not thereby to explain it. And to question its rationality is not, of course, to throw hope of explanation into doubt.

We can, I think, make progress towards explaining our attitudes if we pay attention to reasons and to causes. For, briefly, attention to causes will help explain how attitudes might in the first place be generated, while attention to reasons will show how our actual attitudes might, when under pressure, be sustained, or how we might, as a result of rational reflection, be led to take up attitudes that we are not initially disposed to adopt. Consider death. We want to die later. And this attitude to death has a causal explanation. First, there are evolutionary pressures. We have, as part of our instinct for survival, a natural fear of and antipathy towards death. These benefit individuals and the species. Second, because our everyday experience generates an awareness of the alter-natives to death – we see around us how some die while others live on, and we see how death is in some cases averted – we are familiar with the thought that death, coming at a particular time, is something that might be avoided. So our desire for a later death is subject to, and in part caused by, both biological and cultural influences. Is it rational to want a later death? I believe this is, at the least, not irrational. Because it is not irrational, our desire here can withstand the pressures of reflection. We do not find (and have no reason to find), in thinking long and hard about it, that our hostility towards death is seriously misplaced. But that we can, in this sense, explain and justify the persistence of the attitude is not yet to account for its initial existence. To account for that, human nature, and human experience, must be invoked.[26]

172

Consider pain. Here, too everyday experience informs our attitudes. We meet older people, and may well think about our own time still to come. Pension companies, doctors, estate agents all encourage us to plan ahead. We see how anxiety, discomfort and unhappiness might be avoided and pleasure increased. Thus it is natural to try to avoid future pain. Similarly for pains of the past. Blind people live among others who have kept or regained their sight. Emigrants hear of the better fortunes of those who stayed at home. We encounter younger people for whom things are now going well, and make invidious comparisons with ourselves at that age.

Thinking of alternatives, and wishing that one had avoided past pain, handicap or tragedy is something we quite naturally do. Hoping to avoid future pain is clearly rational. But it is less clear that we should always think this of past pain. Consider spraining your ankle while hill-walking last year. It would have been better had it not happened. But contrast this with momentous events that happened some years ago. It can be pointed out that if the pains of emigration had not occurred, or if you had experienced all the pleasures of a lottery win, you would be a very different person today. For very little, in the intervening period, would have been the same. A change, apparently for the better, would have had many, and deeply significant, consequences. If you think clearly about what would be involved, it may seem that these consequences are unpalatable. So it may be that with respect to such cases the wish to have avoided past pain, or to have had more past pleasure, will not, in the end, withstand reflection.

Consider, finally, prenatal non-existence. There is a difference here. We are not encouraged to wish that we had been born earlier. There are no biological advantages to so wishing, and nor are there social or cultural influences that might help generate such an attitude. A desire to have been born earlier, although it might in some of us still occasionally surface, will not, in any persistent form, naturally occur. Suppose we do think about an earlier birth. We can easily be brought to see that if we had been born earlier everything would today be different. The wish that might, in casual moments, be expressed will not withstand a process of reflection.

Thus the difficulty that began to threaten my account can be resolved. A desire to have been born earlier is irrational and unnatural. But a desire to have had, in earlier life, more happiness or less pain is, although sometimes irrational, perfectly natural. It is therefore unsurprising that desires of the former kind surface less frequently than those of the latter.

Summary

Our hostility to death does invite questions about our attitudes to further periods of non-existence. Why are we not similarly exercised by non-existence before our births? Suppose we had a simple belief: the more pleasure in our lives the better they are. Then the asymmetry in attitude would be puzzling. One explanation – we are future-oriented pleasure-seekers – fails to convince. There could be creatures like this, but we are not among them.

Our more complex attitudes to our own lives demands a different account. Nor is this particularly difficult to provide. Suppose we were born earlier; then everything now would be different. Suppose we die later; everything now is the same. As we, mostly, care about now, about who we are, how we got here, and care as well to add to and further shape the story of our lives, so our asymmetrical attitudes are to be expected. Death is bad. Prenatal non-existence is not.

8

Numbers

Some deaths are bad, and worse than others. Are more of these bad deaths worse than few? It seems obvious that this is so. It would be good, often, to save someone from death. Would it be better to save more people from death? Again it seems obvious that it would. And these claims are connected. Because more deaths is worse, saving more is better. But, notoriously, these seemingly obvious claims have been denied. It is not true that more deaths is worse. And it is not true that it is better to save more than fewer. I shall consider some of the arguments for these strange views, altogether rejecting those addressed to the first, while acknowledging the force in certain of those addressed to the second.

First efforts

Here are three arguments, the last of which will resurface later. First, it is not worse when more die, as death is not bad at all. The Epicureans will believe this. The argument is valid, but most of us deny the premise. Second, as death is the ultimate evil, and involves each of us in losing infinite amounts of good, then more deaths cannot be worse. It is infinitely bad to lose infinite good. So there is no room for further badness to accrue. Most of us deny the premise. And the argument is not even valid. Third, death is bad for the person who dies. They are worse off being dead. But it is not bad that this person dies. So there is no obligation on us to save lives; it is not better that we do. And it is not worse when more people die. Few of us believe this. It is, often, bad

175

for someone to die. But, further, it is bad that they die. And, almost all of us believe, there is some obligation to save lives. So the more we save, the better it is. Still, the relation between *bad that* and *bad for* needs to be further explored.

Two arguments

John Taurek and Elizabeth Anscombe have both dealt with these controversial views. They claim, or at least are taken to claim, both that more deaths is not worse, and that saving more is not better. Until recently Taurek's argument was by far the better known, but Anscombe's work is being rediscovered and is now more widely acknowledged.[1] Her paper "Who is Wronged?" (1967) is astonishingly brief, and can be fairly fully summarized here.

You can save one patient or five with a drug. Many will say you should save the five, but Anscombe feels "a curious disagreement about this" (1967: 16). She sees nothing wrong in saving the one and letting the others die. It would be wrong, in contrast, not to use the drug at all, for "It was there, ready to supply human need, and human need was not supplied" (*ibid.*). But if it is used, and a life is saved, none of the five can reasonably complain. Imagine one dies. "What is *his* claim, except the claim that what was needed go to him rather than be wasted? So he was not wronged. So who was wronged? And if no one was wronged, what injury did I do?" (*ibid.*: 17).

In another example a boat can rescue either one person from one rock, or many people from another. She makes the same point; if some rescue takes place then no one has grounds for complaint. There may be a small but not unimportant difference between the two cases. About the drug, she says that no one can claim it was owed to them. Hence no one is wronged. But in the boat example she says only that no one is wronged unless help was owed to them. I return to this.

Suppose someone chooses to save the five, or the many. They are asked why. They say, "because they are more". Anscombe allows that this is a reason. And:

> It is a perfectly intelligible reason. But it doesn't follow from that that a man acts badly if he doesn't make it his reason. He acts badly if human need to give what is in his power to give doesn't work in him as a reason. He acts badly if he chooses to rescue rich people rather than poor ones, having ill regard for the poor ones because

they are poor. But he doesn't act badly if he uses his resources to save X, or X, Y and Z, *for no bad reason*, and is not affected by the consideration that he could have saved a larger number of people.   (*Ibid.*: 17)

He is "not affected" by its being pointed out that he could have saved more. It is puzzling as to what this means. It is puzzling, also, as to what is meant in the final cryptic paragraph. I shall come back to it.

In "Should the Numbers Count?" (1977), Taurek makes only passing reference to Anscombe's paper, and appears not to have known of it when writing his. So the parallels are remarkable. He too uses a drug example where we can save either one or five. He uses a rescue example involving a boat and people stranded on an island. And, supposing he saves the one rather than the five, he asks, in phrases redolent of the earlier paper, "Who among them could complain that I have done wrong? And on what grounds?" (1977: 303).[2]

But there are differences. Taurek's paper is far, far longer. It is considerably richer. And it is less clear. So there are two arguments to consider here, with the one very much contained in the other. But there are two arguments in a further sense, corresponding to the pair of questions that I asked at the outset. Anscombe considers only one. Taurek, although they are in serious need of disentangling, deals with both. Most commentators, at least as I read them, fail to clarify the distinctions and the relationships here, focusing on just one of the strands with little or no comment on the other. I need to explain.

One question is about outcomes. Is it, other things being equal, worse if more people die? Another is about action. Ought we, other things being equal, to prevent the more deaths? The questions are connected. Many of us will think that it is because it is worse if more die that we should prevent the more deaths. Some will think that as more deaths is not worse, so there is no obligation to prevent the more deaths. But someone might think that even though more deaths is worse, this does not straightforwardly imply that we should save the greater number. Someone might think, also, that even if more deaths is not worse, still we should save the greater number.

Anscombe deals with only the second question. Nothing in her paper suggests she has any doubt that it is, other things being equal, worse when more die. We hear that ten people have died in a high school shooting. Then the figures are revised; there were fifteen. This is more bad news. Or an earthquake affects two cities on the fault line. In one there are a hundred deaths, while in the other there are a thousand. The greater tragedy has occurred in the second city. Or a car, carrying five people, hits a motorbike. All six are injured. The more that die, the worse it is. There is no hint that she questions

177

any of these everyday judgements about the relative badness of outcomes. Her concern is just with what should, or should not do, to prevent such outcomes. And her point is that we can allow, and do, that which guarantees the worse outcome, and the greater overall harm, without wronging or injuring anyone.

Consider Taurek's title. It is ambiguous. We can ask, should the numbers count in evaluating outcomes? Or, should they count in deciding what to do? Taurek addresses both questions, although in neither case is this as clear as it might be. Take the first issue. There are multiple references, almost from the outset, to bad things, greater evils, worse things, better things. So there is undeniably an interest in outcomes. But someone might think that Taurek wants only to present, and not to question, our ordinary thinking here, and then only to insist, *à la* Anscombe, that this does not straightforwardly bear on what we should do. About halfway through the paper it emerges that he has a further concern:

> The claim that one ought to save the many instead of the few was made to rest on the claim that, other things being equal, it is a worse thing that these five persons should die than that this one should. It is this evaluative judgement that I cannot accept. I do not wish to say in this situation that it is or would be a worse thing were these five persons to die and David to live than it is or would be were David to die and these five continue to live.
>
> (1977: 303–4)

From this point on, I suggest, it is clear that the concern is to deny, at least where deaths are concerned, that numbers count in assessing outcomes.

A natural view is that if it is equally bad when one or five die, then you cannot, special considerations aside, be obliged to save the five. And there is no doubt that this is Taurek's view. But for at least the first half of the paper you might think he is, in contrast, simply reiterating Anscombe's position, and questioning the relation between the two claims. Thus:

> On the view in question, one is morally required to save the five instead of the one, other things being equal, because, other things being equal, it is a very much worse thing that these five innocent people should die than that this one should. But if this fact constitutes a compelling ground for a moral obligation to give the drug to these five rather than to this one, then I too shall have to acknowledge its moral force. (*Ibid.*: 297)

The point here is to question how a difference in outcomes might bear on what we should do. So Taurek does, I think, give us reason to believe he is making a pair of controversial claims: first, that we are not, over a range of cases, obliged to produce the best outcome; and second, that, similarly over a range of cases, there is no such thing as a best outcome. It is, of course, somewhat odd to argue for both claims: if you do not think it is worse if five die, then, fairly uncontroversially, special obligations apart, you do nothing wrong in saving the one. In Taurek's case, as I shall explain, this is less odd than it might first seem.

Criticism: Anscombe

Anscombe is not explicit, but she may have in mind, and want to counter, utilitarian thinking about such life and death matters. The utilitarian will say we should save the greater number. She asks: who is wronged, what injury do we do, in saving the one? A utilitarian might reply in one of two ways. He might say that no one was wronged. But there is more to acting morally than avoiding wrong. We should, other things being equal, maximize overall benefit. So we should save the greater number, whether or not anyone is wronged in not doing so. Or he might say that each of the five was wronged when you chose to save the one. True, had any one of them, individually, been set against the one then they would have had no grounds for complaint if, being unable to save both and having to choose, you had saved the one. But that is not the situation. They are together as a five, gaining from each other's proximity. As you should have chosen to save the five, you wrong each of them by not so choosing.

Anscombe may think she has a reply to this, but it is not fully worked out. Someone can explain their saving the five by pointing to the numbers. That is "a perfectly intelligible reason", but it is not one that has to be utilized. Now someone might agree with that at least this far: it cannot be the case that you have to do what you have reason to do, for you can have reason, or some reason, or even some good reason, for doing each of two things when, however, you can only do one. But if you have reason to do A, and no reason to do B, then it would seem, other things being equal, and assuming you are aware of the reason, that you should do A. Similarly if you have reason to do A, and a lesser reason to do B. The cryptic comment can be brought in here. She says, "when I do action A for reasons R it is not necessary or even usual for me to have any special reason for doing A-rather-than-action-B, which may also be possible" (1965–6: 208).[3] This is clearly supposed to bear on the case, but it is not spelled out how. Still, surely this much is true: there are, for whatever you do, always countless other things you might have done instead, but you do not normally need reasons for not doing those things, or reasons for doing what you do rather than those things. But of these countless other things, most you have no reason whatsoever to do, and most you have not considered doing. We have here in our sights a relatively special situation in which you might, for an apparently good reason, save five lives, and in which the alternative, saving just the one life, is also possible and also something you have reason to do. Suppose you save one, for the reason that he would otherwise die. Someone asks: why did you not do instead the other thing you were thinking of doing, and could have done, namely save five lives? I cannot at all see how there is just no need to answer that question. Nor can I see how the answer, because I had reason to save one, is good enough. I cannot see, that is, how, in a situation like this one can deflect the charge of acting badly without claiming that one did what one had most, or at least equally good, reason to do.[4]

Criticism: Taurek

It is not difficult to find a way forward. Famously Taurek thinks that in choosing between one and five we should toss a coin.[5] Why should we do that? Here is one explanation. Toss a coin and you give everyone a fifty–fifty chance of being saved. And, even though it is, other things being equal, worse if five rather than one should die, it is not the fault of the one that he needs more of the drug. Fairness trumps maximizing benefit. So even though there is reason to save five, there is even more reason to do something else, namely randomly choose between the groups.

That is, as it stands, a pretty straightforward argument. But I might make three points about it. First, it will not get Anscombe what she wants. Even if there is reason to do something other than save the five, there is no reason simply to choose the one instead. Anyone doing that still needs, to my mind, to explain themselves. Second, it is not even close to watertight. Unsurprisingly, it is subject to considerable discussion, parts of which I shall consider below. Third, and perhaps surprisingly, this argument does not play a prominent role in Taurek's case. Even though it features there, it is more or less submerged in something way more convoluted and far less convincing.

Agents

Consider the common-sense view that we should, other things being equal, save the greater number. How might things be unequal? First, there might be some relevant inequality among those to be saved. It may be, as Taurek suggests, that the one is on the point of contributing significantly to medicine, or to peace. Second, there may be some inequality in my relations to those to be saved. If I have promised to save the one, or am her professional bodyguard, or her husband, then things are unequal. Third, surely, if I am the one, I can put myself first, and allow the five to die rather than sacrifice my own life. Notice a difference between these categories. I am permitted, but nor required, to put myself first. Perhaps I am required, and not merely permitted, to put my charge, or promise, or wife first. And the first category? Perhaps, if I am permitted to save one brain surgeon rather than five golfers, I am required to do this.

Taurek is brisk with obligations, but then makes heavy weather of permissions. It is, as he presents it, a more problematic way of making things unequal. So consider the aforementioned David. Suppose he is "someone I know and like". Then, arguably, I might save him, and allow the five to die. So far, perhaps, so good, but Taurek then wants to claim that anyone – other things being equal – might put this one person first: "I am inclined to think, then, that we should either agree that it would be wrong for me to save David in this situation or admit that there are no grounds for a moral requirement on anyone, special obligations apart, to save five instead of David" (1977: 298–9). Someone might say that there are never grounds, special obligations apart, for taking anything other than an agent-neutral perspective on a situation. A utilitarian might say this.[6] Most of us disagree, holding that there are agent-centred permissions. I can save myself, or those close to me. But this permission needs a proper grounding: I can perhaps save David if he is my best friend, but not just because he is cute, or on a whim. And most of us allow one inference here but block another. Suppose I can save him if he is my best friend. Then you can save him if he is your best friend. But *you* cannot save him if, or just because, he is *my* best friend. Now one way to read Taurek, in the above passage, is in offering a *reductio* of this familiar position. If I could put a friend first, anyone could. But this cannot be right. And so it cannot be true that I can put a friend first. But this is not what he intends. It is not clear what knowing and liking David amounts to, but it appears that Taurek is setting something of a low standard here. And, perhaps because the standard is low, it is dispensable. I can put David first. And so someone who does not know and like him might also, and legitimately, choose to save him rather than the five.[7] This is odd. The utilitarian denies agent-centred permissions, holding that each of us should do what any of us should do: maximize benefit. Taurek holds that any of us can do what some of us may do: give someone preferential treatment, and fail to maximize. Or at least, so it appears thus far.

There is a further feature of this odd argument that needs now to be noted. It is not an argument about numbers. For this two-part claim – I can choose an apparently lesser good, so anyone can choose this lesser good, and so no one has to promote the greater good – is perfectly general. This is clear in a later example. I can save my own arm rather than a stranger's life. So a friend can save my arm rather than the stranger's life. And so anyone can save an arm rather than a life. Thus, to generalize:

> If it would be morally permissible for B to choose to spare himself a certain loss H, instead of sparing another person C a loss H′, (in a situation where he cannot spare C and himself as well) then it must be permissible for someone else, not under any relevant special obligations to the contrary, to take B's perspective, that is, to choose to secure the outcome most favourable to B instead of the outcome most favourable to C, if he cannot secure what would be best for each. (Taurek 1977: 301)

This too is odd. It is as if we first assert, and then deny, that anyone can stand in a special relationship to another person. But although we deny it, we still embrace the implications of asserting it. It is not easy to see how, via considerations such as these, there is much hope of avoiding the claim that we should, in general, save the five rather than the one, or the life rather than the arm. But Taurek, although he is down, is not yet out. And he has a more straightforward approach.

Numbers

David is thinking of saving his own life. Someone says that it will be worse if five die. He asks, worse for whom? And he says:

> "It is a far worse thing for me that I should die than that they should. I allow that for each of them it would be a worse thing were they all to die while I continue to live than it would be were I to die and they continue to live. Indeed I wouldn't ask, nor would

I expect, any one of them to give up his life so that I, a perfect stranger, might continue to live mine. But why should you, or any one of them, expect me to give up my life so that each of them might continue to live his?" (Taurek 1977: 299)

There seem to be two strands here. First, there is the now familiar thought that the one cannot be required to put the many first. Second, there is at least the beginnings of a suggestion that outcomes are not additive, or aggregative. This is the theme of the paper's second half.

We think it is bad if one person dies. And it is worse if two die. But, as David asks, worse for whom? Each person loses just the one life. It is bad for each of them if they die. But no one loses more than a life. So if I save David, and let five die, still, no one suffers more than he would suffer, had I chosen differently. Having five deaths, rather than one does not, then, constitute a worse outcome.

We can get a grip on Taurek's position here by way of a contrast that he makes. In another context the question "Worse for whom?" gets an answer. It is bad if one of my paintings is stolen, and worse if two are. For, assuming I value them, it is worse for me (*ibid*.: 306). And similarly if I have particular concerns about people threatened by death; it will be worse, because worse for me, if two of my children die rather than one. So if things are worse, they are worse for someone. What Taurek denies is that it can be, independently of anyone's especial concerns, simply an objectively worse thing if more rather than fewer die. And:

This reflects a refusal to take seriously in these situations any notion of the sum of two person's separate losses … Suffering is not additive in this way. The discomfort of each of a large number of individuals experiencing a minor headache does not add up to anyone's experiencing a migraine. (*Ibid*.: 308)

There are two criticisms to be made here. First, there is some tension between this idea and the argument of the paper's first half. The thought here is that evils do occur, and can be evaluated. Each of the six people is in danger of losing something important. Hence the coin.[8] Anyone neutral between the six people should in this way give them an equal chance. It is not easy to see how to reconcile this with the earlier claim that any of us might, for no reason, choose to save the one.[9] Second, and more importantly, is Taurek not just wrong here? Is it not just obvious that if one death is bad then more deaths is worse? Suffering is not additive in one way – no one gets a migraine, and no one dies twice – but if it is, as Taurek allows, bad when one dies, or suffers, then surely it is worse, and not simply equally bad, when more die, or suffer. So it is additive in another way.

This second strand in Taurek's argument is the main target of Parfit's unrelenting criticisms in a near-contemporary reply (Parfit 1978). Those criticisms are, I believe, all on target. It is worse if more die. Even so, and as I have suggested, there are further comments that might usefully be made.

More is worse

Some will be unpersuaded. They will think that the separateness of persons does stand in the way of their suffering from collective ills. But we can hope to win them round.

Bad and worse

Contrast three comparisons: (i) between one death and five; (ii) between my breaking a finger and your breaking your arm; (iii) between my breaking a finger arm and my breaking an arm. Other things being equal it is clearly worse for me to break my arm than my finger. Neither Taurek nor anyone I know of denies this. We can make intrapersonal comparisons and evaluate the different situations of just one of us. Is it worse for you to break your arm than for me to break my finger? Put this question to David and he will again ask: worse for whom? We can answer this. It is worse for me to break my finger, and worse for you to break your arm. For a detached onlooker, neither fracture is at all bad. But this misses something. This onlooker recognizes that both victims suffer. She either thinks one suffers more than the other, or that they suffer equal amounts, or that no interpersonal comparison can be made. Now it may be that in some particular cases this third option is the one to adopt. But it is hard to see how it can be generally true. One person breaks a fingernail while another is critically injured in a car crash. Perhaps the first suffers more but it seems unlikely. We should agree that, other things being equal, the second suffers more. So we can make, as well, interpersonal comparisons.

Again, Taurek does not want to deny this. He thinks that, at least in the case here, those under threat of death lose equal amounts. And two people could be made to suffer different amounts of pain.

184

The contentious claim is about additivity. Taurek must think that five deaths implies five times the loss of one death. What he denies is that this is five times as bad as, or indeed that it is any the worse than, one death. We can add the bads, but not the badness. But there is surely a problem here. It is worse that I suffer severe pain than that you suffer mild pain. It is worse too that I suffer a given pain for five days than that you suffer a similar pain for one day. Other things being equal, someone should help me rather than you. Suppose my pain is broken up. I suffer on alternate days, with the illness persisting over ten days in all. Still, my situation is worse than yours.[10] The pains are not compacted together into a migraine, but I suffer more in total, just because I undergo more of these pains. But now if the pains of one person over different times can in this way be summed, surely too the pains, or deaths, of different people can similarly be summed. No individual loses more than David, just as there is no time at which my suffering is greater than yours. Still, there is in both cases a collective, and greater, loss. Other things being equal, it is better if that, rather than the lesser loss, be prevented.

For and that

The last point, it might be said, just does not follow. Even if there is one sense in which it is worse when five die, in another sense – and an important one – it is not worse. There is a greater total loss, but we are not obliged to prevent the greater, rather than the lesser, loss. Compare people with trees. I might say that death is bad for trees, but, unless someone is especially attached to them, it is no worse when five trees die than when one dies. And we are not obliged to prevent this greater loss.

There is something in this, but not enough genuinely to help. I might think trees do not matter at all. And so it is not in any way bad when they die. But I might think death is bad for trees. If one tree dies then a bad thing happens. If five die then more bad things happen. But it does not follow that a worse thing happens. For I might think death is bad for trees without thinking it bad that trees die. Badness for trees is not bad for the world, bad in itself, or bad *tout court*. So badness, here, is not additive. If we can understand human death to be bad in a similar way, then that too will not be additive. It will not be worse when more die.

The problem is that if I think death is bad for trees, but do not think it bad that trees die, then I am under no obligation to save, or to attempt to save, trees from death. If, in contrast, I allow that I do have some obligation to prevent the worsening of a tree's condition then, it seems, I must be allowing that badness for trees spills over into some sort of objective badness. It is bad that trees die. Otherwise what would it be to me? Why should I care? So I cannot, I think, both allow that I ought to help trees and at the same time deny that *bad for* implies *bad that*.[11] Similarly, of course, for people. Anyone who grants there is any obligation to prevent deaths ought to think of death not just as an evil for the one who dies, but an evil in itself, or for the world, or some such. It generates ameliorative obligations in passers-by. And anyone who allows that ought to think that more deaths is worse. It is worse in itself, or for the world, or some such, even if there is no one in particular that it is worse for. As we saw, Anscombe is explicit in holding that we have an obligation to help those in need: we cannot just hang on to the drug because we like the packaging. Taurek is less explicit. But he too seems to believe that losses borne by others in death or pain do and should concern us. We should toss a coin and determine who to help. We should not simply walk away. Anscombe does not deny that, other things being equal, more deaths is worse. Taurek should stop denying it, also.

Objections

I shall consider two complaints that might be made. The first considers impersonal bads, the second the prices we might pay.

I am supposing that something might be bad, and yet bad for no one. And that is suspect.[12] But here I am misunderstood. And to explain, I need to clarify the relation between *bad that* and *bad for*. I do not hold that *bad for* implies *bad that*. Our position on trees offers a counter-example. But I do hold that *bad that* implies *bad for*. So although in one way I allow that there are impersonal bads, or objective bads, or things that are bad in themselves, or for the world (for "bad for the world" is just another way of saying something is impersonally bad – it is not like "bad for the planet") there are no bads independently of something's being bad for a person, or for people (or animals, for that matter). In some places Parfit seems to suggest otherwise.[13] So here we will disagree.

I am suggesting that it is worse if five die than if one dies. And I do not mean simply, and trivially, that more bad things happen when five bad things happen. So I must mean that we should make a bigger sacrifice, other things being equal, to prevent five deaths than to prevent one. But it is implausible to suppose we should make sacrifices in strict proportion to the numbers involved. I do indeed think that *bad that* makes demands on us that *bad for* does not. And the bigger the evil the more we should pay to prevent it. But I have made no claims about strict proportionality. I do not want to say that if you should give five minutes to save a life, you should give three or four days to save a thousand lives. But you should give more than five minutes.

Actions

You can save one or five. What should you do? Many will say save five. Taurek says toss a coin. Anscombe says choose, but save at least one. Hers is not a good answer. It is worse if five die. You need to explain why you do not realize the better outcome, and this is not explained simply by pointing out that in saving one you did some good. But Taurek's answer – toss a coin – is not inadequate in the same way. Wanting to give everyone a fair chance appears laudable. And, on the face of, it might explain a reluctance simply to elect to save five. But how far should we take this? Taurek is asked what he would do if it were one or fifty. He says he would toss a coin even there, for "I cannot see how or why the mere addition of numbers should change anything" (1977: 306). So he would toss a coin if it were one or a thousand, and also if it were a thousand and one or a thousand. But this does not seem right. The argument for tossing the coin is that fairness has some intuitive appeal. So it does. But there is intuitive appeal, also, and in no small degree, in saving a thousand lives rather than just one.[14] Most of us think the numbers count, even if they are not the only thing that counts.

Someone might, then, agree with Taurek that we should toss a coin in order to decide whom to save, while disagreeing that it is no worse when more die. But now there are further, and perhaps better, responses to the competing claims of fairness and outcomes. Jens Timmermann rejects the coin in favour of a dice. Each of the six has a number. They each have an equal chance of being the winner. If their number comes up, they are saved. But if any of the five win, then their four neighbours are saved as well, as then there is every reason to save them, and no reason not to. So:

> Depending on the numbers, it is – more, much more, vastly more
> – likely that many will be saved. Being stuck on an island *and*
> losing the lottery, whoever perishes will undoubtedly bemoan his
> ill fortune, but he cannot complain about unfair treatment by the
> person in charge of the ship. (2004: 111)

As with the ship, so with the drugs. Everyone has been given a chance and, although there are inevitably losers, everything has been fair.

Here is another solution. We should, as Iwao Hirose (2004) insists, acknowledge the pulls of both fairness and choosing the better outcome.[15] And we should accept too that there is no easy way of balancing, or adjudicating between, these pulls. But, he suggests, although fairness always counts for something, it is outweighed in the case of one or five and, of course, much more clearly outweighed if it is one or a thousand. And although maximizing benefit always counts, if it is a thousand, or a thousand and one, we should toss a coin. Again, inevitably there are losers, but there will be some occasions on which the chosen procedure is not fair.[16]

Michael Otsuka (2004) offers no solution as such, but wants to argue against those who think the numbers do not count. This numbers sceptic accepts, on Otsuka's reading, that we should save the greater number in no-conflict situations, and thus should save A and B rather than A alone, but he denies that we should save B and C above A. Otsuka endeavours to show that this is an inconsistent position.[17]

There are some uncertainties, perhaps, about Otsuka's target. His sceptic buys into a number of common-sense positions: as well as his stance on no-conflict situations, we should save some rather than none, and prevent, where individuals are concerned, greater rather than lesser harms.[18] But focus on the conflict case. Does this sceptic think that two deaths is worse than one, but nevertheless we are not obliged to save the two, or, further that two deaths is not worse? This is not, I think, ever made clear. Another concern, and one that can be made more general, is that there may be no one other than a straw man around here. Otsuka wants to claim that, although counterintuitive, this scepticism is as reputable as many more familiar forms, and so deserves to be taken seriously. But he never says who these sceptics are, or where they live. And so although we might imagine plenty who worry about the details of Otsuka's argument, it is not clear that anyone will want to take up this sceptic's cause.

We can make some further observations here. Much recent discussion is at least in part motivated by T. M. Scanlon's (1998) attempts to justify saving the greater number on contractualist and non-aggregative terms. He is concerned that no one should have grounds for complaint against the decision.[19] And thus Timmermann's comment above. But this is odd. A loser can always complain. If he says he never had a chance he is straightforwardly in error. But if it were one or five he never had much chance, and if it were one or a thousand he had virtually no chance at all. He can, first, point this out and, second, insist that it would have been fairer to follow Taurek and toss a coin. Whether he is right about this is the point at issue. And then the consequentialist will say that we are always justified in saving the greater number, and the losers should be able to see that. Hirose will make a similar point, saying we are sometimes so justified. One possibility, then, is that we agree we need a fair procedure, but then disagree about what is fair. Another is to construe fairness as giving an equal chance to all concerned, but then we are likely to disagree that the procedure needs to be fair. Either way, I do not see how anyone can hope for their solution to win out over rivals.

There is a final, and different, observation to be made here. As with the discussion of agent-relativity, focusing on numbers appears not to be a critical feature. A doctor has two patients. Both are forty. He can give one five years of extra life, or the other one year. Some will say he should go for the bigger benefit, others that he should toss a coin, others that he should use a dice marking five of the six sides with the first patient's name. What we say here may well vary in so far as the difference between the benefits either increase or decreases. And so on. Once we have admitted that it is worse if five rather than one dies, then the sorts of considerations that might tell against simply saving the five come into play in analogous situations where the differences relate to size of benefits, and not the numbers of players.

Summary

Is it worse if more die? Someone might deny this even while accepting that it is worse to lose an arm than a finger, and worse to lose five years than one. In these cases we are considering different size losses for, or to, the one victim. In the first case we consider the same size loss to different victims. Someone might say that this makes a difference. We can sum the losses, but not the victims. But I have suggested that it is not easy to keep these cases apart. If one death is bad, and something we should be concerned about, then more deaths is worse, and should concern us more. If either death is not bad at all, or if it is bad only for the victim, and so of no concern to us, then of course we should not be more concerned about more. Five nothings is still nothing.[20]

If it is worse, when more die, should we always save the greater number from death? As it is worse, then there is reason to save the greater number. There is not, in the same way, reason to save the smaller number. But there is, also, reason to aim at fairness. And it is legitimate to interpret this as requiring we give everyone at least some chance of being saved. All the options considered in the previous section satisfy this requirement. Thereafter, adjudicating between them calls for artistry.

9

Cheating death

Death comes, and takes from us what we at least think would be good: the continuation of our good lives. Can we avoid this, delay it, make it less bad? Can we hope to cheat death?

Ordinary means

It is already possible to avoid death. We can step out of the way of buses, wrap up warm and do what the doctor says. Take reasonable measures, and we may well extend our lives. It might be objected that here we avoid not death but only particular deaths. All we can do is delay the inevitable. Fair enough, but avoiding particular deaths, and delaying the inevitable, is often worth doing.

Here is another way. Death's badness consists, at least in large part, in depriving us of the good. It stops us from getting what we want. We can take the sting out of death by reducing our attachment to the good. Care less about the future, and death, when it comes, will damage us less. But this self-abnegation is self-defeating. We do not effectively counter death by prior and unforced self-denial.[1]

And another way. Someone might think they can avoid some particular death by choosing instead to die earlier. Rather than face execution a prisoner might take his own life. In some circumstances, perhaps because of illness or disease, life may not be worth living. So an earlier death may be preferable. But, in general, attempts to cheat death by dying earlier are not to be advised. There is little point in interfering unless you thereby stand to gain.

Consider further the first, and seemingly best method, where you aim to extend your life. There are certain complications here. Suppose any extension requires that you succumb to extreme measures: you need to take tablets instead of real food, avoid stress and excitement, live in a plastic bubble. You might reasonably decide that a shorter but richer life is preferable to this. Here there is no question that the longer life, although unattractive, would be yours. In another case there can be a question about this. For suppose the extreme measure involves some rather serious brain surgery. Without it, you will soon die. With it there will be years of life, and a rich life to boot. Even so, this life will not be well connected, psychologically, with your life now. In one version you will suffer serious and irreversible amnesia, retaining your ability to speak, dress yourself, name long rivers and capital cities, but forgetting all the things you ever did, all the people you ever knew. In another version you also lose all aspects of your character. And you seem to take on memories and a character from elsewhere. Of either version you might think: that post-operation person, that – as I shall call him – survivor, is not me. And so this is not a way of cheating death. But it can be objected that no one dies on that operating table: the heart continues beating, the lungs ventilating, and the brain regulating an array of bodily processes all without interruption. It is hard to deny that one human animal survives throughout. Now you might insist that you are something other than, or something more than, merely a human animal, and so insist that its survival does not guarantee yours. Perhaps you will claim you are a person, arguing then either that persons die in a different way, or that persons can cease to exist without dying. But you might instead maintain that whether or not you survive the operation, the psychological disruption means that life thereafter does not offer anything of value to you. Either way, then, the operation is something you can quite reasonably decline, preferring the shorter life to its extension.

Unsurprisingly, I shall need to return to some of the issues raised here. But the interim point is this: of means and technologies currently available some are less effective at avoiding or cheating death than they might at first appear.

Extraordinary means

We should consider as well what are perhaps fanciful ways. They may become less fanciful, or might already be less fanciful than many of us think. We know where we are with science, but do not know where we will be. Perhaps we do not know where we are with religion. The first cases here involve situations where, at least as it seems, we survive intact or whole. The second cases involve, to varying degrees, situations where our survival is compromised.

The mind and body are intact

Our opportunities for avoiding death are, it seems, seriously limited. If all goes well we might live for eighty or ninety years. And then that is it. And often things go wrong long before this time. But perhaps we can hope for more, and perhaps we can explore whether new technologies might, in time, offer us more.

Consider cryonics. Because you are under threat of death it is decided to freeze you. Assume, as suggested earlier, that when frozen before death you exist in suspended animation, neither dead nor alive. You can remain in that state for thousands of years. Cryonics is in its infancy, and thawing techniques are still to be developed. Here you cheat death, but in an altogether worthless fashion. But now suppose the thawing techniques are developed. So the plan is to freeze you until a solution to your problems is found. In one case the threat is internal, and you are already suffering from some disease. After a cure is found you can be thawed and treated. In another it is external. Perhaps those who remain active will succumb to an epidemic, and so we want to freeze you until the threat has passed. Is this a way of cheating death? The same body exists throughout. No one ever dies. When thawed your psychology proves to be intact, with memories, character and dispositions all unchanged. Could it reasonably be doubted that you survive? Someone might argue that a living thing cannot cease to live and then come back to life. And you are not, as I have allowed, alive when in suspended animation. So we have, post-thaw, a survivor who is either a different living thing, or, if it is further claimed that living things come into existence in familiar ways, no living thing at all. But it is hard to see why a living thing should not be frozen and then thawed.

We need to contrast, though, the case as sketched here, with a more familiar account of cryonics, wherein someone who has died is then frozen, in hope of a later cure. A cure is found, effected and the body thawed out. Those engaging in these processes believe this is a way of cheating death. Are they right? The doubts here may be stronger. Someone argues that a thing cannot go out of and come back into existence. And they believe that with death you cease to exist. I reject both claims. But even if I here reject only the latter, I can still hope to silence some part of the doubt. Even if you cannot recover from non-existence, you can recover from death.

Further features of these cases should now be noted. All the bodily parts, down even to the individual atoms, remain in existence throughout the freezing and thawing process. And the connections between them remain in place. It is hard not to agree that the post-thaw body is numerically and qualitatively the very same body that was earlier frozen. In the first case, where freezing occurs pre-death, thawing presents us with a living body. Moreover, the post-thaw person reveals the same memories, beliefs, character and dispositions as the pre-freeze person. Qualitatively, the same psychology is in place. My claim that the very same person survives the procedure is in part based on these observations And now I want to claim that a person picked out at t_1 is the very same person as the one picked out at a later time t_2 if (i) there exists a living human body at both t_1 and t_2 and this body comprises the very same atoms in the very same relative locations throughout[2] and (ii) this body exemplifies qualitatively the same mind at t_1 and t_2. I intend this, of course, as only a sufficient condition of identity over time. In the second case we froze, and will thaw, a dead body. To restore someone to life we need to make certain bodily changes, moving or replacing some of the atoms. Suppose I need only to move around a small number of atoms, replacing none, in order to put the post-thaw body into the same condition it was in five minutes before it died. Then I have restored this person to life. And this even though the body has not comprised the same atoms in the same location throughout.

Consider a different case. Suppose there is a god, and he has the power to do everything that it is logically possible to do with atoms.[3] Can I hope to cheat death by praying hard, and persuading this god – call him God – to resurrect me? I die, say in a car crash, and the atoms that make up my body are dispersed. Six, sixty or six hundred years later God can collect up these atoms and bring them together in just the locations, relative to one another, that they were in the minute before I died. Suppose he does this in a suitably friendly environment and then does whatever is necessary, if anything is necessary, to power them up. A qualitatively identical psychology will then re-emerge. So there will then be present a living human being who at least resembles me both mentally and physically as I was shortly before death. Is it me? I say it is. In this scenario I first die and then cease to exist. Those who think there cannot be two beginnings of existence will insist either that God cannot resurrect us, or that I have misdescribed the case. But we can dismantle and reassemble a watch. I believe that when dismantled, and the parts scattered throughout the workshop, the watch does not exist. Still, it can come back into existence. It does not seem at all right to suppose either that it exists throughout, although scattered, or that the apparently reassembled watch is in fact a new instrument. And similarly for a human being.[4]

193

The case here concerns only a single resurrection. As is well known, it is often and rightly claimed that even God cannot resurrect everyone in this fashion, as different bodies have, over the years, been constituted from the same atoms. If there is to be a multiple resurrection, something other than the thoroughgoing numerical identity of all the parts will have to suffice.

The mind and body are not intact

Although some will have objections to certain of my claims above, the cases described there are in several important respects unchallenging. In both cryonics and resurrection the person identified at the later time is qualitatively identical to the person identified at an earlier time. This is almost never the case. We believe a person can persist through time even though substantial physical and psychological changes occur. Someone can lose memories, or fingers, and nevertheless survive. But what sorts of changes can be endured? What sorts of procedures, offered to you as a way of avoiding death, can deliver what they promise?

I first consider cases where the body remains intact but the mind is altered. Then I consider reverse cases, where the mind remains, but the body is altered. There could, of course, be further cases where we consider alterations to both. But I will not consider these, even though what I say will have fairly clear implications for such cases.

Psychology: fragmented minds

As I have already suggested, some procedures should be rejected. But even more radical procedures are more familiar. The doctors can, or so they say, keep your sister alive even though she will, thereafter, be in an irreversible coma or a persistent or permanent vegetative state. The problem here is not that the psychology is very different. It is that there is no psychology at all. Most of us think that life under such a condition is not worth living.[5] But grant that, and we can still ask whether in such circumstances our lives will continue. Are the doctors right to say that they can keep your sister alive, even when her mind is gone? I think we can agree on this: they can keep a human animal alive, but that animal, having no mind, will not be what we often call a person. So it looks as if the question is this: is your sister an animal or a person?

Now we can think again about the less radical case: that in which a mind survives but is altogether, and abruptly, different. Let us suppose that after

194

the operation you have, apparently, the psychology and memories of an eighteenth-century highwayman. Again we might agree: life with a different mind is not, for you, worth living. But again that leaves open the further question of whether, worthwhile or not, that life is your life, that living thing is you. We can agree: there will be, after the operation, a living human animal. And it will be what we often call a person. It looks here as if the question is: are you a particular animal or a particular person?

I want to make a tentative suggestion, not about what is true, but about what, in fact, many of us will tend to say regarding such circumstances.[6] I might be wrong about this, but I do not think I am completely wrong. I shall say more, later, about why I think these are things we will tend to say, but I shall say something here about what is implied by this. In the first case, where after the operation there is no mind at all, we will mostly think your sister continues to exist. We did not think that Tony Bland and Terri Schiavo ceased to exist when they fell into PVS. In extreme versions of the second case, where, apparently, one psychology is suddenly and non-temporarily replaced with another, we will be more inclined to say that your sister (or whoever) no longer exists. Someone else exists in their place. This is more speculative. Whereas there are many cases where the mind is lost, there are few, if any, where it is so completely changed.

Now one way of describing these situations runs thus: someone can continue to exist without any mind at all, but they cannot continue to exist if they suddenly get a different mind. And what this in turn suggests is that to the question "Am I a person or a human animal?" we do not give a clear and unambiguous reply. For, first, I can continue to exist without a mind, and so without being a person at all. But, second, I can cease to exist (perhaps by, as it were, being invaded by a new psychology) even though the human animal continues to live.

Physiology: fragmented bodies

Why do I say, as if it is clear as crystal, that the human animal continues to live? Because in the cases considered above there is a living human animal, or human being, that survives intact throughout. Sure, if you lose your mind then there are some changes in your brain, but these are, physiologically speaking, minor. All the larger parts are there: the brain, heart, liver, arms and legs. And there are neither gaps in existence, nor, excepting the brain, disruptions in the overall working of these parts. One and the same human animal exists throughout.

In other cases it will be less clear. The doctors say they can extend your life, and stave off death, by performing an operation that will cost you some part of your body. Should you accept? We lose small parts of our bodies – hair, nails, bits of skin – on a regular basis, and it does us no harm. We continue to exist. And we can lose bigger parts. You have a gangrenous finger. If it stays you die, but if it goes you live. Moreover, life without a finger is almost certainly worth living. If you are a pianist then things may be considerably worse, but for most of us this is without doubt a price worth paying to avoid death. But how much of your body could you go without? You could lose an arm or a leg and still remain alive, with a life worth living. You could even lose all your limbs, thus becoming no more than a torso and a head. Could you be reduced to a mere head? Clearly we would need some rather sophisticated technology to keep just a head in reasonable condition, still able to see, hear, think and talk but let us assume that can be developed. And let us agree that the need for such technology does not itself rule out your survival. Even if most of us are in some sense self-sustaining, there are many who already need the assistance of machines in order to remain alive.

Consider three versions of this head case. The first is as here, where your head is sustained by hospital life-support machinery. In the second your head is attached to a different human body. Perhaps this is the body of your identical twin, brain damaged beyond repair in a road crash. In the third the head gets a sophisticated mechanical body, one that behaves like a human body but that is constructed of non-biological material. Of all three cases we can ask, first, does a human being survive this procedure? Second, do you survive? Third, do you now have a worthwhile life, or existence? I shall just sketch answers. Why I prefer these answers to their rivals will become clearer later. Only where your head is attached to another human body am I inclined to say the survivor – the post-operation person – is a human being. But I think that you survive in all three cases. Your life, or existence, is worthwhile in the second and third cases, and considerably less so in the first case. In relation to this I am assuming that your psychology remains more or less intact in all three cases, at least initially. Your changed circumstances will affect your psychology, more so in the first case than in the others. And it is in virtue of this considerable change that the issue is raised as to value of this survival.

In all these cases an obviously important part of your body – your entire head – survives intact. It supports your psychology. Consider now some further cases, involving an even more radical reduction of your old self. In the first you are whittled down to just a consciousness- or mind-supporting upper brain. This is either minimally embodied, existing as a cerebrum in a jar, or it is attached, as above, to either a biological or a mechanical body. In the second scientists take a read-out of your brain and transfer its contents on to a computer. Then, with cameras and microphones they are able to communicate with the survivor. In a more sophisticated version they build a robot or cyborg or android, one that looks a fair bit like you, and transfer the contents to an artificial brain inside it. In a final case scientists offer you a trip in a teletransporter. Rather than linger on in Dagenham they can, or so they say, dematerialize you there and then instantaneously rematerialize you in Solihull, where a second chamber is already primed with the right sorts of particles.[7]

In each case there is a survivor with a psychology pretty much like yours. Again we can ask, is this survivor a human being? Is it you? Is this existence one you might reasonably think is worth having? Again I sketch. Only in the third case is the survivor a human being, although in all three cases you do survive. These responses together imply, of course, that not only can you exist in a non-human form, as in the previous set of cases, but that you can exist without any human parts. Whether this existence is worthwhile might depend on how closely it resembles a normal, or your earlier, human life. Surviving in a laboratory jar would not, for most of us, be much fun. You are faced with imminent death. Scientists offer these procedures, with these futures. Most of them you should accept.

Consider too a religious version. You die. Some time later there comes into existence a being with a ghostly body, perhaps near to a ghostly harp, but with a psychology very much like yours. Is this survivor you? Is it worth praying to God in order to increase the chances of such a resurrection, and so, in an important way, getting the better of death? I think this being would not be a human being, but would be you. Whether this is a worthwhile existence might depend on the rules, and the company.

I have raised questions, and sketched answers. Others will give different answers, as I now explain.

Animalism

An increasingly popular view has it that we are animals, and that each of us is a particular animal of a particular kind, namely a human animal. So each of us came into existence when a particular animal came into existence, and we continue to exist so long as, and just where, that animal continues to exist. Assume that animalism is true. Then it becomes critical to decide, in the above cases, whether the survivor is the animal that you are. For if there is no animal, or the wrong animal, in existence once the operation, or the praying, is over, then assuredly you no longer exist. In some cases it is clear just what survives, in others not.

The best known version of this view is Olson's. As it is widely known, I need only to outline his account here. But I shall focus on those areas I find most troublesome.

I said above that this view is increasingly popular. I meant among philosophers. Olson often suggests that the view that we are animals has long been a part of common sense: we talk of human beings as animals, identify ourselves as belonging to a biological species, *Homo sapiens*, and think of ourselves as closely connected both with other animals and with living things or organisms, generally. But most philosophers have long held a different view, seeing us as in some way essentially mental things. So this flowering of animalism can be seen as bringing philosophical and everyday views better into line.

The supposedly common-sense view that we are animals might be put differently: that people are animals. But this does not, of course, imply that animals are people; some are, most are not. Nor does it imply that all people are animals. There might be gods, or angels, or cyborgs, that are people but not animals. But of course, to say this is to imply that "people" or the singular "person" is not a mere synonym for human being. It means, for Olson as for most of us, something that is or has a mind of the requisite complex kind. And so animalism does not imply, either, that all people that are animals are human animals – dolphins and apes might be counter-examples – or that all human animals are people – embryos and those in permanent vegetative states are not. And what this last point may suggest is something that is in fact true: on Olson's view being a person is a phase that most human beings, or human animals, go through at some stage in their lives. We have, rather than are, minds. This does not rule out the possibility of there being somewhere in the universe people that are minds; there could be free-floating, non-material thinking beings that exist only so long as they are thinking. But none of us are things like that.[8]

So far I have attempted only a part explication of the theory's core belief. Perhaps it does not appear particularly controversial. But animalism can, and in Olson's version does, include further beliefs that, in contrast, do appear controversial. One of these we have encountered already. For Olson holds that animals are essentially alive, that they cease to exist at the moment of death, and so there are no dead animals. This is a strange view, but it does not much matter here. Death is, it seems, often to be avoided, whether or not it brings about non-existence. Controversial too are aspects of Olson's position on what is involved in an animal's persisting, alive, through time.

We all think that some parts can be lost, some replaced even while the same animal continues to survive. Perhaps most of us are unclear on the details here, just as we would be were we considering, say, a ship's survival through time. Olson is not unclear. He seems to think that an animal survives just in case its functioning brainstem survives.[9] This is at least counterintuitive, but it is not an issue that we need to pursue in any detail here. We should note, however, that this component delivers clear verdicts on many of the cases outlined above. You survive in whole-head cases. You do not survive with just an upper brain, or as a computer program, or via teletransportation,[10] or in heaven. Two further components are, perhaps less obviously controversial on the face of it, but they open the door to problems.

First, Olson holds that animalism does not imply that we are *merely* animals. It does not imply that we have "a fixed 'animal' nature" or only biological or natural properties (2003: 321). As he puts it, someone can be an animal and also a philosopher, or tennis player, or cardinal. Second, he fights shy of what someone might think is clearly, and critically, implied here: the claim that we are essentially animals. That depends, he says, on whether animals are essentially animals, and he at least claims not to be sure whether that is true. My reservations about these points are connected. Nevertheless, I shall try to say something about each in turn.

The claim that we are merely animals is, I think, unclear. So too, then, is its denial. Olson believes that we are not merely animals in this sense: to say, of any of us, he or she is an animal, or even a human animal, is not to say all there is to say about us. But there is a sense in which he believes we are merely animals. None of us is a composite, made up of animal and non-animal parts. None of us, for example, consists of both a material animal and an immaterial mind. Now I agree that we are not merely animals in the first of these senses. But then, in this sense, no animal is merely an animal. Some are fish animals, some kings of the beasts, one or two may be prize-winners or garden pests. Of any animal, there is more of interest to say than that it is an animal. What of the claim that our nature transcends that of biological organisms? Again if it is true of us, it is true of other animals as well. But is it true of us? If we are animals nothing that we do is inconsistent with our being animals. So animalists will surely agree that there is an important sense, after all, in which we are merely animals.

Then there is the shilly-shallying about essentialism. Of course, none of us are essentially or necessarily animals in that we are always and everywhere animals. We do not exist always and everywhere. The only plausible claim here is that necessarily we are animals where and when we exist. So necessarily, when we cease to be animals we cease to exist. And this does seem to be what Olson believes. Why, then, the worry about whether animals are essentially animals? Again no animal necessarily exists. But plausibly if an animal turns, or is turned into, something else, it thereby ceases to exist.[11]

Even though it is difficult to see why Olson holds back on the essentialist thesis, he clearly feels he does not need it. For, he insists, anyone who allows that any of us is even contingently an animal is thereby committed to animalism. For suppose your thought is that although you are one now, you could nevertheless cease to be an animal. You could not, though, cease to be yourself. For: "a thing and itself can never go their separate ways ... It follows that you are not that animal, or indeed any other animal. Not only are you not essentially an animal. You are not an animal at all, even contingently" (2003: 324–5). So there is no point fussing about modality – anyone who thinks that it is possible we will not be animals in the future has to concede that we are certainly not animals, even now. There is, though, something odd about Olson's claim here, and I shall return to it below.

Three positions

Animalism is, on Olson's account, sharply contrasted with the rival position allegedly more popular with philosophers. On his view, what he calls the biological approach, we are (i) animals that (ii) do not necessarily think. Are we persons? Yes, but on the biological approach it needs to be understood that being a person is a phase that some animals go through. So we are not necessarily persons. On the apparently prevailing psychological approach we do think, and necessarily so.[12] So in order to track someone through time we should be concerned not with their animal body but with their psychology, or consciousness, or mental states. As Olson characterizes this view, "Roughly speaking, any past or future being that has my mind is me" (1997: 13).

It looks as if we now need to choose between these views, deciding whether we are animals or biological organisms on the one hand, or persons, minds or collections of psychological states on the other. Yet there is an alternative position to be considered. It is one that Olson rejects, often with some passion. But I think there is a good deal that is right about it. This alternative, the so-called constitution view, says that we are constituted by, but not identical with animals. And this is an important difference. For something constituted by one thing could be, and could come to be, constituted by something else. Although I am an animal, and a particular animal, today I might not be that animal tomorrow. Tomorrow I might be (be constituted by) the animal that is now my brother, or I might even be (be constituted by) an android, or cyborg, or robot. I need not think, then, that the death of my body is necessarily the end of me.

Olson is altogether hostile to this constitution view:

> I wish people wouldn't say things like this. If you are not identical with a certain animal, that animal is something other than you. And I doubt whether there is any interesting sense in which you can *be* something other than yourself. Even if there is, expressing a view on which no one is identical with an animal by saying that we *are* animals is badly misleading.   (2003: 319)[13]

But even if there are problems with the constitution view there are also problems with Olson's wholesale rejection of it. And, curiously, the problems are of very similar kind.

Constitutions, substances, phases

Start with some very basic observations. Vases are made from, constituted by, lumps of clay, statues from hunks of marble, cakes from flour, sugar, butter. More generally, material objects are made up from atoms or other microparticles. Is a vase identical with a lump of clay? We shall want to say no. The lump has a longer history, having begun to exist before the vase was formed. And it is contingently true that it was ever made into vase. Is it also contingently true that the vase is made from this lump? Some will find this question harder, and argue for and against the necessity of origin thesis. But take a different example. The revamped St Pancras railway station is constituted by particular bits of glass, metal and stone. It is hard to believe that had the engineers selected a different batch of stones for one platform then this station would not have existed, but there would have existed a different station in its place. More generally, even if all medium sized and larger objects are made from, or constituted by, particular bunches of particles, it seems that those very objects would still have existed even if some different particles had been used instead. Further, those very objects will continue to exist even if some of the particles are lost, or, part way through its history, replaced with others. As I have said, a human animal continues to exist even when fingernails, or fingers are lost.[14]

So far, the constitution view appears fairly innocuous. But it hardly remains so. First, and briefly, the claim that I am constituted by an animal is on the surface significantly different from claiming that a cake is constituted by various ingredients, or a statue from marble. I am not built up from animal parts, and nor do I emerge when an animal is moulded in certain ways. Second, consider a recent account of the constitution view, intended as a self-standing overview of the position, offered by one of its chief advocates, Lynne Rudder Baker. Using the now nonexistent World Trade Center towers as an example, she contrasts three views. On the non-reductionist view she favours, the towers "really existed in their own right, so to speak" and were made up of, constituted by, bunches or aggregates of particles. On two competing views, eliminativism and reductionism, the particles exist alright, but the towers either never existed at all, or did not really exist.[15] Here is some more detail about her view:

> At the time of the collapse, the things that were towers literally went out of existence; they did not just lose the property of being towers and acquire the property of being rubble. The towers were not just fusions that changed shape; they were objects that once existed and then failed to exist. The contents of the world changed … Only a non-reductionist approach allows the extensions of everyday concepts like *tower* to be ontologically significant.
>
> (2006: 314–15)

And:

> The non-reductionist … takes the sentence "The towers collapsed" to imply that in the past there existed entities that were towers (whatever they were made of) and that these entities collapsed and went out of existence. Only non-reductionism takes our everyday discourse to be true on a face-value reading.   (*Ibid*.: 316)[16]

So the non-reductionist view is different, both ontologically and semantically, from its rivals. But Baker's view is not simply non-reductionist. It is, further, the constitution view. And she appears to think this is just one version, albeit the correct version, of non-reductionism. On the face of it, at least, someone could agree that the towers were really real, and so on, without also agreeing with the details of the constitution view. What are these details? Here are some of the things Baker says:

> Constitution is a single comprehensive metaphysical relation that unites items at different levels of reality into the objects that we experience in everyday life: the trees, the automobiles, the credit

cards and the people. These objects are irreducible to the particles that make them up. They are of higher levels of reality than the particles that constitute them ...

On the Constitution view, reality comes in fundamentally different kinds. Each thing is of a primary kind essentially. Objects related by Constitution are of different primary kinds ...

Every object has its primary kind essentially, but not every kind is a primary kind. E.g. *teacher* is not a primary kind, nor is puppy. Teachers may cease to be teachers without ceasing to exist ... Constitution is a relation between things of different primary kinds. So, a person may acquire the property of being a teacher, but a person does not constitute a teacher since *teacher* is not a primary kind.

Alas, I do not have a theory of primary kinds .... But there is a test for a primary kind: x is of primary kind K only if x is of kind K every moment of its existence and could not fail to be of kind K and continue to exist. (*Ibid.*: 318–19)

Baker notes also, in illustrating the difference between constitution and identity, that "a human body may constitute a person at one time, but not at a later time" (*ibid.*: 318). And then, right at the end of the paper, she sketches something of her general approach:

Instead of starting with *a priori* metaphysical commitments, I prefer to start with what is at hand – with what we know and cannot seriously doubt – and try to think clearly about it as unencumbered with antecedent metaphysics as possible. I want the metaphysics to emerge from the reflection on the world, rather than the world to be squeezed into a preconceived metaphysical strait-jacket. (*Ibid.*: 330)

I am, of course, altogether sympathetic to that, but wonder how far it is borne out in what precedes it. What we know and cannot seriously doubt is that there are both particles and larger sized material objects, and that were it not for the former, the latter would not exist. But thereafter much is moot. First, I have some difficulty in understanding what is meant by talk of different levels, and different kinds of reality. Baker's opponents, denying that towers are really real, might buy into this, but it is not easy to see how it fits into the non-reductionist view, or just how it links with what we know and cannot doubt. Second, the meaning of and the test for primary kinds are both puzzling. I once knew a woman who had a skirt made up from men's ties, so it surely looks as if one item of clothing can be constituted by other items. But if "item of clothing" is a primary kind then Baker's claim that constitution relates things of different kinds is false. So perhaps the kinds here are "skirt" and "tie". A problem here is that, on Baker's view, the constituted thing exists at a higher level of reality.[17] But skirts are not more real than ties. So perhaps there is no constitution here at all. Third, and following from this, there are unclarities relating to animals, human beings, persons,[18] human beings. We might agree with aspects of the constitution view – animals, including human animals, are made up of particles – but taking the view further, and fully understanding Baker's position on persons, teachers and the like is not easy. "Teacher" is not a primary kind, as something can cease to be a teacher and yet continue to exist. To put the point in other terms, "teacher" is a phase and not a substance term. But then why is "person" not similarly a phase term?[19] If it is, then persons are not constituted by human bodies, contrary to Baker's claim. Nor does the test help here, either. What does "x" stand for? Suppose it might stand for the name of one of us. Could George Bush fail to be a person and continue to exist? I think so, and so does Olson. Baker evidently disagrees. Perhaps she has a different concept of person? Then even if everyday concepts are a guide to reality, everyday terms are not much of a guide to concepts.

Most of these difficulties for the constitution view derive from its handling of a seemingly basic metaphysical distinction: that between substances, or things, on the one hand, and the phases or stages that a thing might go through, on the other. Baker wants to start out with a common-sense grasp of such terms – towers, like particles, are things, being a teacher is just a phase – and then develop this into some robust metaphysical picture. I doubt that can be done. Go back to the vase. Why is being a vase not just a phase that some lumps of clay go through? Perhaps the answer is that once fired I can no longer get back to the lump of clay I started with. I can, though, make and then destroy a series of vases at the potter's wheel. But perhaps these are not really vases, just vase-like shapes that the lump temporarily acquires. As Baker evidently knows that randomly formed tower-shaped objects would not be towers, or would not be real towers, she may know as well the difference between a real and a seeming vase. Of course, what I really think is that in all these cases we can describe in full detail just what is going on, just what particles are involved, and just what history they have been through. Thereafter the question of which terms to use is relatively unimportant. Call the random construction a tower, or the unfired vessel a vase, and you might be misunderstood, with your interlocutor perhaps jumping to certain conclusions, but talk it through, and everything will become clear.

What we are

Olson is as much a friend of the well-articulated metaphysical picture as is Baker. Like her, he believes that what seems to be real and what is really real can come apart. He too believes that what we fundamentally are and what matters or is important about us need not coincide. And he is at least as attached to the substance–phase distinction as she is, taking it more or less for granted, and relying on it throughout.[20] But he wants to apply it, or believes it is applied, in different ways. For Olson, an animal is a substance, whereas being a person, like having a mind, is just a phase that some animals go through. (Being alive, in contrast is not a phase, but marks the boundary between one kind of thing and another). For Baker a person is a substance, and so itself a thing, constituted by an animal at and for some time in its history. It seems to Olson, then, that the constitutionalist wants it both ways: like defenders of the psychological approach they think of persons as substances, but then they deny free-floatingness and want to ground this person in animal parts – "anyone who assumes that *person* is a substance concept is in effect assuming the Psychological Approach" (1997: 29). A further point of agreement is in thinking that we are things, or substances, rather than merely phases. Indeed, Olson appears even more committed to this than to the animalist thesis itself; for even supposing we are not animals, "There must be *some* sort of thing that we are" (2003: 322–3). And here "thing" is, I am suggesting, bearing some weight. Each of us is strictly identical with one particular thing of a particular kind; we cannot, as some proponents of the psychological approach seem to believe, hop about.

This commitment to and reliance on some rounded idea of thingness is evident in a number of the points that, above, I marked out as warranting further consideration. So our not being mere animals needs to be interpreted, I suggested, consistently with our being only one, and that an animal, thing. And note again the somewhat puzzling point about whether we are essentially or contingently animals. Olson may be right to insist that if we might cease to be animals we cannot be animals at all, not even contingently, for, "a thing and itself can never go their separate ways" (*ibid.*: 324–5). But what lies behind this, surely, is the assumption that if I am contingently an animal then I am one thing that is contingently identical with, the very same thing as, another, animal thing. And certainly that sort of suggestion is always under strain).[21] Then there is Olson's objection to the constitution view. He docs not like the claim that I am (constituted by) an animal, for "If you are not identical with a certain animal, that animal is something other than you". And anyway, "expressing a view on which no one is identical with an animal by saying that we *are* animals is badly misleading" (*ibid.* 319). His point here, again, is that there are either two things or there is one, and anything else is a fudge. And just this point about the number of things in play gets into his main argument also, as I shall now explain.

Intuitions and arguments

Why should we be animalists? Olson's argument can, I think, be best understood thus. First, we are substances rather than phases. And animals are substances. Persons and minds are not. Second, even if the distinctions here are less than perspicuous, our intuitions about certain problem cases support the biological approach, rather than its rival. Both components need explanation.

Suppose I say I am a teacher. Such a claim may well be true. And, contrary to Olson's complaint above, it is not misleading. The English terms "is" and "are" have multiple uses, and Olson cannot insist on their being limited to strict identity. Even so, I am surely not claiming that a teacher is a thing, and that I am strictly identical with that thing, coming into existence when the teaching started, and ceasing to exist on retirement. What I am, rather than what I do, extends beyond such career moves. And so if there is something I am, that I am an animal, a thing, is way more plausible than that I am, in the philosopher's sense, a person. For, like being a teacher, being a person represents just a phase in the history of a thing. And surely I am a thing, rather than a phase. Or think about the mind. Should I say I am a mind? Perhaps that is misleading. Just as my being a teacher can be rephrased, if there is any doubt, in terms of my being a thing that does some teaching, so similarly I am a thing that has a mind. And that thing is an animal.

Suppose someone has some doubts about whether a person, or mind, is simply a phase. Consider some seemingly possible moments in my history, thinking first about relatively familiar turns of events. Was I ever a foetus? Could I come to be in pvs? We are inclined to say yes. This suggests that we do not think of ourselves as necessarily minded things. Rather, we survive when and where a particular member of the species *Homo sapiens* survives. And this supports animalism. But think about the brain transplant case. Your cerebrum is fitted inside your twin's head. The resulting human being remembers, thinks and acts like you. It believes it is you. And, as it is a twin, it looks like you as well. Who is it? Olson concedes that we may well be inclined to think that this is you and that you have moved here from one body to another. If we think that then we think you are a mind. And so we think you were never a foetus, and cannot survive in pvs. So one set of intuitions supports animalism while another, apparently, supports the psychology view. Is it then a stand-off? Not quite. We should, according to Olson, attach more weight to our intuitions about actual and familiar cases, cases that we encounter in real life on a regular basis, than to those concerning fantastical thought-experiments, the inventions of philosophers, and restricted, as we used to say, to the study. So animalism is ahead.

I think Olson overstates the case here. The view that we are minds is not just a philosopher's conceit, wholly at odds with our everyday thinking. Billions of people, over thousands of years, have thought that we are, and begin as, immortal souls, and have bodies only for a short and troubled period in our thereafter endless existence. Of course, billions more have thought that we are necessarily embodied, but few have thought that we have the same body, or even the same sort of body, throughout. And billions have believed that there is some sort of soul or mind, some non-animal essence, contained within the foetus and the comatose, even if it is trapped there, and unable to manifest itself.[22] So even if the view that we are animals is and has been widespread, the view that we are identical with animals, and exist just when they exist, even if mindlessly, is not, and has not been. But even allowing that Olson does not have numbers on his side, he has, I will grant, reasons. If there really is some thing, and some sort of thing that we are, and if the best candidates here are animals on the one hand and minds on the other, then animalism is on strong ground. It seems hard for us, given what we know, to believe that some thing comes into and goes out of existence when an animal begins and ceases to think, or that there really are either disembodied minds, or that minds really can be embodied in a variety of different bodies. It seems hard to believe too, as the psychological approach seems to imply, that I was never a foetus, was never born, and am some several months younger than I think.

And now there is a further argument in animalism's favour. You exist, and you think. Animals exist. And it seems as if many of them think. There is one animal that, at the very least, is closely associated with you, goes where you go, does what you do, thinks what you think and so on. Suppose you are sitting in some chair. Certainly there is an animal sitting in that chair. Look in the mirror. Now either you are that animal or you are not. If you are not then either there are two things in the chair, both of them thinking the same thoughts or, despite many appearances, animals cannot think.[23] Neither is happy. Better to believe that there is one thinking thing sitting there that is both an animal and you. Better to embrace animalism.

Of course, as Olson admits, the conclusion here is resistible. Not a few, for example, will insist that no animal, indeed no material thing, is able to think.

They will hold that there are two things in the chair: a non-thinking animal, and a thinking mind. But I shall accept the premises, and accept also that there is no multiplicity of thinkers in such cases. But I deny that animalism follows.

An alternative to animalism

Olson suffers from an over-attachment to thingness. If we have to plump for one thing, then let it be the animal. But we do not have to plump for one. What we might instead, and better, believe is that although each of us is in some very ordinary sense a thing, there is not some thing, some one thing, that we are. So I am neither an animal, nor a mind. But then if I am not an animal it is on the face of it possible, via a cerebrum transplant, for me to be shifted from one body to another. And if I am not a mind then it is similarly possible for me to have been, as I believe, a foetus, and for me to continue to exist, as I fear, in pvs. Nor is any of this paradoxical, or at odds with common sense. I deny that I am necessarily an animal but not that I am an animal right now, and have a bunch of animal properties. So being an animal is something like being a teacher: if I say that I am contingently an animal I do not mean that I am contingently identical with some thing, but that I contingently have these properties. And so even if I and myself cannot go separate ways, I can lose some of my properties, maybe my animal properties, maybe my mental properties, while retaining others. So, also, although there is only one thing sitting in the chair, and it is me, that thing can be refashioned in various ways and yet still survive.[24]

Consider, then, the cerebrum transplant in more detail. Twins Ron and Reg are injured in a car crash, Ron above the neck, Reg below. Both are near to death. Doctors remove Reg's upper brain and set it to one side. They do what they can to sustain functioning in the remainder of the body, attaching it as necessary to the appropriate machines. Then they remove Ron's mangled cerebrum and replace it with Reg's, hooking it up in the right way. What are the upshots? Consider Reg's body, now empty-headed. Is this body alive? Is it an animal? Given that the lower brain, and with it the brainstem continues to function, Olson thinks the answers here straightforward. I have no difficulty with that, but there are further questions. First, is it the same animal? Olson believes it is, holding that the identity of the animal is determined by the identity of the brainstem.[25] Second, is it Reg? Again Olson believes it is, holding that the loss of the cerebrum and with it the mind is extremely unfortunate, but not identity affecting. Consider, as well, Ron's body, now containing a replacement cerebrum. Is this body alive? Is it an animal? The answers here are if anything even more straightforward. It sits up in bed, asks for a burger, does Sudoku: certainly there is a living animal there. Is it the same animal? Olson believes it is, for again it still has the original brainstem. And so, as it is still Ron, it is not Reg. And this even though, via this particular cerebrum, it thinks it is Reg, remembers what Reg did, acts like Reg.

My response is different, and twofold. Focus just on Reg. I think his body remains where it was, and remains alive, even though now missing some important part. Before the crash there was a particular animal in existence. That animal continues to exist. But just as Reg's cerebrum has been relocated, so too has his mind. That mind, that psychology, now exists in Ron's body. I am pressed. Does Reg still exist, and if so where is he? I respond. As I have explained, Reg has been divided. Most of his body is over there, still alive, still an animal. Part of his body, his mind, is over there. When something is divided up you cannot always expect a straightforward answer as to whether, or where, the thing still exists. And here I have described the situation in full detail. There is nothing to add. That is the first response. But I might respond differently. Although Ron is no longer with us, Reg has been lucky and survived the crash. The doctors were able to save and transplant his cerebrum into Ron's body. So Reg is alive, and over there. His old body is alive too, but not currently of much use to anyone. Maybe he will donate it to science.

The first response is more guarded. It is what I say if I am being quizzed by some philosopher interested in identity and I want an easy life. The second response is the more natural. It marks how I feel when such things happen to friends of mine. Or better, how I guess I would feel were such things to happen. Unlike car crashes, cerebrum transplants are so far only imaginary. So I predict that, at least assuming the procedures become straightforward and reliable, we will generally respond thus, seeing the transplant as a way of avoiding death[26] rather than a mere organ relocation. I will be relieved that Reg has had this lucky escape. Suppose he is not a friend, but a disgruntled neighbour, always complaining about my violin. I will be annoyed that, with his survival, the fighting seems set to continue. But not only will we naturally say such things, what we say will be true. Were my claim that Reg survives to imply certain further, and false, beliefs then that claim itself would be suspect. But it is not as if I believe that a person is an immaterial soul, located in or near a cerebrum, or that a person continues to exist whenever the cerebrum continues, working or not, or that an animal can be reduced to just a cerebrum, and still survive. And, if I neither have, nor am committed to, any false beliefs in so claiming, the claim itself is true. I say that Reg survives, and indeed he does. He, and the animal, have come apart.

Objections

Olson, and hardly he alone, will object. It is not true that Reg survives. And in claiming otherwise, even if I am not making some mistakes, I am making others. First, as Reg does not survive I surely have a false belief in supposing that he does. Second, in so claiming I reject the contention that there is some thing, some substance, that we are. But, according to Olson, I am wrong to reject this. Third, claiming thus commits me to a metaphysics that, on various fronts, leaves me on shaky ground.

These alleged mistakes are, of course, linked. And the last is the key. So what is at risk, in arguing as I do? Olson considers, although briefly, a different view:

> Suppose that this thing is both a person and an animal, and that that thing is also both a person and an animal. Then according to the relative-identity thesis, although we can ask whether this thing and that thing are the same person, or the same animal, we cannot ask whether this thing and that thing are just plain numerically identical, without qualification. In general, from the fact that this thing and that thing are the same F, we cannot infer that this and that are numerically one ...   (1997: 159–62)[27]

But "this way of resolving (or dissolving) problems about personal identity involves certain complications" (*ibid.*) and will demand the rethinking of large areas of philosophy. One example is that the apparently straightforward claim that I might have been six feet tall becomes harder to assess. It depends whether some envisaged world unambiguously contains me.[28] But not only do I tolerate this result, I view it as positively welcome. In most contexts, with most implicit backgrounds, such claims are easily checked. But suppose we think that for Olson to have been taller would have involved his parents feeding him some body-building but mind-altering substances from six months on. Would this gigantic muscle-bound dullard really have been Olson? I am happy to think that that is not clear.

A further objection is related. We have simply overlooked, Olson will say, the distinction between questions of identity, on the one hand, and those of what matters, or is of pragmatic or prudential concern, on the other. Sure, you may well take comfort in knowing that after your death someone will seem to know what you did and wanted to do, and will be as keen as you were to finish your book. You might be annoyed that there is still a belligerent non-musician living next door. And you might well prefer the company of Professor Olson to Big Eric. But whether or not someone speaks to the interests of some former person and whether he or she is that person are different issues. And in the transplant case, where the animal that you were continues to survive, this you-like person assuredly is not you.

Now there is something in this objection, and I shall need to explain why the view advanced here does not altogether collapse the distinction between identity and prudential concern. I shall address this below. But focus for now just on this transplant case. Olson believes that as well as questions about the locations of your mind and your body there is a further question as to where you are. On my view, in tracking the body and the mind we have done, in one important sense, all there is to do. But in another sense I concede that there is a question as to where you are. I answer this, though, differently from Olson. So how is this to be resolved?

An alternative to substances and phases

We should look again at, and, I shall suggest, seriously modify, a distinction that is central to Olson's case.

What we all believe is that there are in the universe aggregates or concatenations of atoms or particles that are in the natural course of things to varying degrees stable. Certain of these aggregates are stable and/or important enough – and I mean important enough to us – to be given names: clouds, trees, butterflies, rocks. There are distinctions here in terms both of stability – clouds are shorter lived, less robust than are rocks – and of complexity – in general living things are more complex and, related, have firmer boundaries, than the non-living.[29] Further, we are able to interfere with these particles and aggregates of particles – these things – in various ways, depending on our own powers, and on the technologies we have to hand. Thus, pulling the wings off butterflies, or dynamiting rocks.

Are any of these things substances? Go back to the lump of clay. Just as we might think of a vase as a phase in the history of this lump, so also might this lump be seen as a phase in the history of clay particles, and the existence of those particles, in turn, as phases in the history of atoms, or indeed of the universe. There are longer and shorter, more or less precarious, captivating or overlooked aggregates of particles. Relative to the construal of some aggregate as a substance, some other aggregate might best be thought of as a phase, but given a different base, it will be thought of differently. And unless we think of atoms as substances, all else as phases, it is hard to see how in reality there can be any more to the so-called metaphysical distinctions than this.

Go back, now, to what we are. And first, note some features of actual and possible situations. Aggregates of particles can give rise to mental properties. And we need not go wrong in talking about the mind. Importantly, throughout all history the mind has been a less stable thing than the animal body. It is more readily altered than the body.[30] And it comes into existence, by degrees, some time after the creation of the animal and ceases to exist, often, and often by degrees, before the animal dies. This, at least, is what most of us not given to religious views now believe. The relations here lend support to the notion that an animal is a substance or thing, a person, the property of being minded, just a phase in the history of that thing. But if, as with the technology envisaged in the transplant case, the mind can outlast the particular animal body, and exist independently of it, then this accounting of the substance–phase distinction loses conviction. Different aggregates here give rise to the same mental properties.[31] And so to speak now of the mind as a thing, albeit not a self-standing mental thing, is not clearly to make any obvious mistake, or to court any serious confusion.

Second, note what Olson will, surely, concede. He allows, of course, that one and the same cerebrum can be transplanted, and survive the death of my body. My personality, my thoughts, can similarly survive. I do not see that he has any grounds for resisting the suggestion that my mind also survives. So one and the same mind has shifted from one animal body to another. Perhaps, given his phase view, he will allow also that one and the same person has relocated also. He allows too that in this sort of survival we have, probably, all that we care about. And, finally, this sort of survival is consistent with the death of what was my body. Now where is the disagreement? In claiming that I have here been transplanted I mean only to refer to ordinary level facts like these. There is nothing further that I think has occurred. And in claiming that I survive I mean only to suggest that this will, as I predict, be found a convenient way of speaking. It seems that in insisting on a contrary view, Olson has either to maintain that there is some further, and deeper, metaphysical fact that has been overlooked, or to claim that our current way of speaking will, as he predicts, lead us, even with transplant technology, to hold that we are animals. Either way, the substance–phase distinction will be in play here. But, as I have argued, that distinction just is not strong.

Closest continuers

What all this may well suggest is that I have considerable sympathy for Nozick's closest continuer account of identity.[32] Here is a ship. Does that ship exist in the future? Find, in the future, whatever is the closest continuer, or best candidate for being that ship. If it is close enough, or good enough, the ship continues to exist. Here is me. Do I exist in the future? Do the same thing. And if someone is close or good enough, then that is me, too.

This account needs some detail. First, as I understand it, and as I have implied above, the name itself is somewhat misleading. For the closest continuer might not be close enough. You die. The closest continuer is your daughter. She is the one who looks and acts most like you, and remembers more than anyone what you did. But you and she are different people. Second, "continuer" does not imply physical continuity. Take an aggregate of particles at t_1, and an aggregate at a later time – say a day later – t_2. Let us assume that both aggregates are stable, distinctive and important enough to be seen as, in the ordinary sense, things. Call the first A, and the second B. Both these things will, uncontroversially, have a degree of persistence through time. Assume that each of them persists for at least an hour before and an hour after, respectively, t_1 and t_2. But it is for some reason and to some degree controversial whether A is B.[33] Suppose that on the closest continuer view it turns out that it is. Now this might in part be because some or all of the particles in A have been tracked through time, and noted to continue into, remain in existence as constituents of, B. But it might be because B has enough of the properties of, enough resemblance to, A to warrant our claiming that it is the same thing, independently of the physical material involved. Third, the account should, I think, be seen as deflationary. In holding that B is A I am not taking the observed continuities as evidence of some deep fact about something's persisting through time. Rather, there is nothing over and above, or indeed below, these ordinary level facts about particles and properties. So "turns out" in the above might be misleading. For it to turn out that B is A involves nothing more than our (i) avoiding ordinary level mistakes about the facts involved and then (ii) deciding, or inclining, to speak of B's being the same thing as A.

There are, notoriously, certain issues about identity over time where, as many believe, the closest continuer account comes unstuck. I shall consider three of these. They are in important respects related.

Gaps

I have said, a number of times, and against some deeply held views, that there can be gaps in existence such that one thing can have two beginnings. And the closest continuer account can readily tolerate such gaps. Take the dismantled watch. For a while the face is hanging from a pin, the case is in a box, and the mechanism is in pieces on the workbench. Later the watch is reassembled. This is the same watch that earlier kept time so well. Why? The reassembled watch very much resembles the original, both in terms of its properties and the stuff from which it is made. It is an extremely close continuer, unchallenged by any rival. But, I say, there was a period when it did not exist. Those who deny that there can be gaps in existence want to say here that either the reassembled watch is merely a replica of the original, or, more likely, that one and the same watch existed throughout, but for some of its history it was scattered, or spatially diffuse. But there is no need for this.

Take a second case, where there is similarly a dismantling, but at least some of the parts are replaced. Imagine there is a ship, or a building in need of considerable repair. It is taken apart, inspected and rebuilt with a mixture of old and new. I shall say again that for a while the thing did not exist. The friends of metaphysics will again deny there can be two beginnings. But here they will see more of an issue about whether the resulting thing is the original or a replica. Is there similarly an issue on the closest continuer account? In one sense yes, in another no. There is a real question as to just which parts have been replaced. There may be question as to their status, with its being unclear, for example, whether some part of the building is itself original or an earlier replacement. Thereafter there is no substantive issue to be decided, and whether to count the resulting thing as original or replica will be determined, in so far as it is determined, via a consultation of our interests.

A third case is merely imaginable. As if magically, your coffee cup suddenly, and before your eyes, disappears. A few seconds later a cup appears, looking for all the world exactly like yours. But suppose it is a few centimetres to the left. Is it the same cup? The metaphysician will either straightforwardly deny this, hostile to gaps, or will hold fire, waiting on further information on what happened to the atoms in the interim. Is it straightforwardly the same cup on the closest continuer account? Here there is a complication. The gap itself is unproblematic, and the new cup resembles its predecessor in all currently discernible respects. But we should consider the future. Suppose after five minutes the cup again disappears, this time for good, or turns into a dragon. That it lacks stable cup properties might give us reason to deny that it really is your cup, in spite of its short-term resemblance. And until we know that it has stable cup properties we might hold off on the identity claim. But suppose that these inexplicable vanishings occur fairly regularly, to a variety of objects, yet always with long-term stability and reliability in the as-if returners. Then, as I predict, we will say that one and the same thing has gone out of, and come back into, existence. And we will not be wrong.

Duplication

Suppose your cup disappears and is, seconds later, seemingly replaced by two cups, each a few centimetres from where the original was located. Now, allegedly, there is a problem. The closest continuer account says that when there is just the one cup it is yours: it is the very same cup. But it cannot continue with this claim after duplication, when there is a pair of equally good candidates. Either your cup has divided, like an amoeba, or it has disappeared, replaced by a duo of replicas. And consider duplication as it might affect human beings. In a variant of the transplant case my cerebrum is divided, with each half being put into the living bodies of my two surviving, although wounded, triplets. On recovery, as, or so we shall suppose, half a cerebrum can perfectly well sustain consciousness, memory and the like, each believes he is, behaves like and looks like me. But evidently they cannot both be me. And so, as there is nothing to choose between them, neither is me.

But there is not yet a problem. Famously, Parfit appeals to such a case to argue that what matters in survival and genuine identity can come apart.[34] But this is far from clear. Uniqueness matters. Life would be very different – in some ways better, in others worse – for my family and for me were I to be duplicated. Much of what matters would remain, but not all. And a defender of the closest continuer account can, and with reason, insist that such duplication means that the relation under investigation is now not close enough. My cup fails to survive, and so do I.

Still, the problem has not altogether gone away. Critics now point out that, on the closest continuer account, whether something survives through time does not depend on its intrinsic or internal properties alone, but also on its relational properties.[35] Being closest obviously depends on what else is around. So a cup that would otherwise have been mine is not mine, just because a second cup pops into existence. And a future person who would have been me is not me just because there is a second person who has an equally good claim to be me. More generally, any candidate's claim to being the continuer of some thing can be overturned, just because some better candidate comes along. And this, or so the critic insists, is clearly intolerable where any viable account of identity is concerned. The survivor either is or is not the very same thing as the original, independently of how things are elsewhere

A defender of the closest continuer account will be unimpressed. Suppose you think I am some indivisible Cartesian soul. Then I am where and when that soul is. And what is happening elsewhere in the universe is irrelevant to the question of my continued existence. But that is not even close to what we believe. Subatomic particles aside, things are complex. We will probably say that the ship taken apart and reassembled with some replacement parts is the same ship. And we will probably say this less readily, or less confidently, if the original parts are added to and themselves fashioned into a ship. Perhaps, if this second ship has many more of the original parts than its rival, we will identify this as the original ship. Someone points out that although it has most of the parts it does not have the figurehead. And that, as all sailors agree, is critical in making a ship the ship it is. In such a case our identification of the second ship as the original rested on a non-trivial error; what we thought was the closest turns out not to be. But failing ordinary factual errors of this kind, it is hard to see how, if we all say that this, rather than that, is the same ship as the original, we might nevertheless be wrong. And so it is hard to see how an identity claim could not depend, in some respects, on the existence of rival candidates and so, in turn, on other than intrinsic properties of the things involved.

It may be that critics of the continuer account suspect that an evidently unwelcome consequence is now in the offing. But they are mistaken. After a car crash you are to some degree both physically and mentally impaired. Still, there is no doubt that you have survived. But now suppose that, as if magically, someone altogether resembling the pre-crash you appears from nowhere and, of course, insists on being you. Surely the claim of the somewhat maimed person to be you cannot be overturned by this rival. Indeed not. But only if attention is focused on intrinsic properties, and the closer resemblance of the rival than the maimed to you, would anyone suspect differently. The closest continuer account can well take non-intrinsic properties – the continuity between you and the maimed, the mystery surrounding the rival – as relevant to the determination of closeness.

Risks

Critics now make a further point. The cup disappears, and is replaced seconds later by a resembling cup, a little to the left. If there had been two cups then neither would have been the original. But it is a matter of luck, surely, that there is just the one. Here, then, is a problem in allowing gaps. In not insisting on physical continuity as a criterion of identity over time, we run the risk of encountering duplication, even when in fact it does not occur. But if duplication is even possible, then our identity claims are already overturned.

There are two problems here. First, a supporter of the closest continuer account can just insist that a possible duplication counts for nothing. If there were equally good candidates we would lose grounds for claiming that the original has survived. But where there is just one, we retain those grounds. Second, the objection is surely too strong. I go to bed at night and get up the next morning. One and the same human being exists both sides of, and indeed through, deep sleep. But I, or the animal that I am, or have, could have divided, amoeba-like, during the night. That is surely at least logically possible. Still, that unrealized possibility represents no challenge to the ordinary view that one and the same person can fall asleep and wake up.

Summary

Can we hope to cheat death? Our options, currently, are limited. But we can at least imagine technologies that permit suspended animation, head swaps, brain transplants, data manipulation and the programming or reprogramming of cyborgs and androids. We can even imagine teletransportation and, independently of machines, the emergence of human-like creatures from dust or ashes. Perhaps, although this may be less clear, we can imagine too some sort of disembodied mind or consciousness. Setting this last aside, none of these other imaginings involve any challenge to the prevailing view that there is, at bottom, just one sort of stuff, and that the mental supervenes always on the physical.

What about the relations between these imagined creatures and ourselves, ordinary human beings, currently in possession of both life and consciousness but under threat of death? Olson insists that we go where the human animal goes. And so, setting one construal of the whole-head transplant aside, he holds that no matter how much any of these creatures might in some important respects resemble us, nor how much they might answer to our, and others', prudential concerns, they will not be us. In many cases they will not be human animals at all; in others they will be numerically different animals from the ones that we, each of us, are. Parfit's position is curiously similar to Olson's here. For he too thinks that identity and prudential concern can come apart.

This is most evident in cases involving duplication. But even concerning a straightforward teletransportation case, Parfit seems to believe that although there will be no question that this is as good as ordinary survival, there is a question about whether the replica person is really you.

I am considerably more optimistic. As I reject much of the attendant paraphernalia of substances and phases, so I reject also the key notion of strict identity over time. There are issues only of how much of what we care about survives, and under what circumstances. And looking to circumstances covers the history and future of this surviving thing, the existence or near-existence of similar surviving things, and the fortunes of what remains of us, and our parts, after the trauma. So it covers quite a lot. But even if detailed, the sorts of investigations needed here are all familiar, We might, thereafter, want to sidestep questions as to whether some resembling creature is really you, preferring instead to give a full description of the base-level facts involved. But consider again an ordinary night's sleep. Can you survive such an experience? Of course we say yes. Is it really you that wakes up the next day? Again, we say yes. And we continue to say yes no matter how much stress is put on "really", and even though we have to acknowledge that you are not in every respect the same. And similarly for the transplant case, and others of that ilk. The differences are only ones of degree. Yet, as I have said, all I am doing here is predicting what we will say, and how we will go on, in this interestingly different world.

Brain death – history and debate

As I noted in Chapter 3, much of the discussion of brain death involves clinical, legal and historical matters on which the mere philosopher has no expertise. In what follows, then, I am in the main concerned only to report on such matters in so far as I understand them. There is some comment and criticism, some taking sides, but this should be understood as provisional.

Some terms

We are sometimes conscious, sometimes not. We are not conscious when asleep, under a general anaesthetic, in a coma, in PVS, when brain dead and when dead. Some of these unconscious states are permanent, others not. Someone who is conscious is very clearly not dead. Some people are very clearly dead. As I have said, most agree that someone who is conscious at some time was never dead before that time. But there are questions about the condition of various of the people who are, for different reasons, permanently unconscious.

PVS is a term of art. It refers most often to a persistent vegetative state. Someone in such a state is permanently and irreversibly unconscious.[1] Those in PVS reveal no self-awareness and engage in no purposive action, but they will show sleep-wake sequences, give reflex responses, yawn, chew and swallow. They breathe unaided. Some now prefer to unpack PVS as a *permanent* vegetative state. But there are not two states that need to be distinguished, one permanent, the other merely long-lasting; and most hold that recovery from what appears to be PVS indicates a misdiagnosis of the condition.[2]

Coma is less obviously a term of art. Some writers use the term widely, covering PVS, brain death and states between, while others seem to view it as picking out a distinctive condition. Some write as if *deep coma* or *permanent coma* are distinctive conditions, while *coma* – unqualified – is much more general.[3] Lamb (1985: 6) suggests that in light of this we simply avoid speaking of an irreversible coma. But this much is true: at least some of those in some forms of coma will never again appear to be awake. And at least some forms of coma involve the loss of unaided breathing.

Brain death is a clinical condition. It has been defined as the "total and irreversible dysfunction of all neuronal components of the intracranial cavity, that is, both cerebral hemispheres, brainstem and cerebellum" (Korein 1978: 21). Someone who is brain dead is permanently and irreversibly unconscious.

Which of the people who have irreversibly lost consciousness are dead? Is it all and only those who have irreversibly lost heart and lung function?

A history

Loss of consciousness will often lead to loss of life. But developments in medical technology have made this less inevitable than it was.

In 1959 French neurologists coined the term *coma dépassé* to indicate an irreversible coma coupled with an irreversible loss of capacity to breathe. That anyone should for more than a few moments be in such a condition depended on resuscitation and ventilation techniques. For the cause – massive and irreversible brain damage – would standardly bring about death: breathing failure would lead immediately to heart failure. But with mechanical ventilation cardio-respiratory function could be sustained for some time, even while the brain was dead. It became possible to sever the link between this brain damage and its natural and immediate consequences. Thus, according to Lamb, "the concept of brain death emerged in France" (1985: 4). Of course, it did not remain there.

In 1968 reflection on developments over the previous decade led to the Ad Hoc Committee of the Harvard Medical School to Examine the Definition of Brain Death (1968) proposing irreversible coma as a new criterion of death. The committee understood by irreversible coma "a permanently non-functioning brain". Thus, according to the committee, those who were brain dead were dead. And they were dead even if, via mechanical ventilation, cardio-respiratory function was sustained.

In 1970 the state of Kansas adopted, at least in part, the new criterion. But this was not unproblematic. Some have claimed that as Kansas was ahead of the game here it was possible for someone to be declared dead in that state, while someone in the same condition would be declared alive elsewhere.[4] Lamb, however, sees the Kansas statute as inherently flawed and as in itself implying that there are two concepts of death. So within the one state someone can die twice over. Lamb's argument here is hard to follow.[5]

In 1981 The President's Commission for the Study of Ethical Problems in Medicine and Biomedical and Behavioral Research was required to propose a coherent and cohesive account of what is involved in someone's being dead. Other states had followed Kansas. Throughout the US as a whole there was now an intolerable pluralism about the conditions under which someone should be declared dead. Hence the Uniform Declaration of Death Act (UDDA). This states that "an individual who has sustained either (1) irreversible cessation of circulatory and respiratory functions or (2) irreversible cessation of all functions of the entire brain, including the brain stem, is dead" (President's Commission 1981: 119). This disjunctive account is, with minor qualifications, now in place throughout the US, with similar legislation in force in many other countries through the developed world. This account has to be distinguished from certain others identified in the main text and elsewhere. The claim here is just that irreversible breakdown of either function is sufficient for death. It does not imply there are two species of death one might suffer. And the point is just to allow that testing directly for brain death is appropriate only in a minority of cases. Yet again Lamb sees problems here.[6]

In 1976 and 1979 the Conference of Medical Royal Colleges published papers indicating their preference for a brainstem account of death. This now provides the standard in both the UK and a number of current and former UK colonies.[7] Is the difference between the UK and the US positions significant? Lamb, and behind him Christopher Pallis, insists that it is, but most US commentators play it down. As noted in the main text, the distinction here does not in practice allow for a situation where someone might be brainstem dead but upper brain alive. And the prevailing view seems to be that it is over the procedures for testing for death where the implications of the distinction are most keenly felt. Here some but not all US commentators hold that the US approach has the edge.[8]

More terms

Discussion of brain death has involved, among both physicians and philosophers, injudicious handling of the terms "definition", "criteria" and "concept".[9]

As many have observed, the Ad Hoc Committee set off on the wrong footing. Proposing irreversible coma as a criterion of death is one thing, defining brain death another, defining irreversible coma as a criterion of death a third. And although the committee is not, strictly, guilty of this, their description of their activities led, not unforeseeably, to the suspicion that they were redefining death. As Karen Gervais observes, the committee went on to make somewhat obfuscating comment on the legal definition or, as she puts it, the legal concept of death.[10]

The President's Commission aimed to do what, exactly? I referred above to the Uniform Declaration of Death Act. This is how Lamb and Gervais gloss UDDA. DeGrazia and Lizza refer to it throughout as the Uniform Declaration of Death Act. And Lizza says that they were asked to provide a "uniform statutory definition of death" (2006: 9). What they did provide, quoted above, looks like two criteria that could be appealed to when determining, and so prior to declaring, that death had occurred. And this is what was needed. But Lizza's claim here is not inaccurate. The commission did address "the matter of 'defining' death at the level of general physiological standards rather than at the level of more abstract concepts or the level of more precise criteria and tests" (President's Commission 1981: 73). The scare quotes are theirs.

A debate

Is brain death a criterion for death? Is a brain-dead patient dead? Is he someone who has ceased, irreversibly, to function as an integrated whole? Defenders of the brain death criterion say yes. Critics says no.

The argument seems not to be about words. Rather, it is about what is going on in the body of a brain-dead patient, when intervention causes that body to behave in certain ways. As such a body is vastly more complicated than a heating system, or even a laptop computer, so what is happening within it is complex and far from easy to understand. I can do little more than report on some of what I read.

Against

Alan Shewmon argues that brain death theorists grossly exaggerate the impor-tance of the brain in maintaining integration. "Integrative unity of a complex organism is an inherently nonlocalizable, holistic feature involving the mutual interaction among all the parts, not a top down coordination imposed by one part upon a passive multiplicity of other parts" (2001: 457; see also Shewmon 1997, 1998). His argument is essentially twofold: most of what the brain does is not critical to bodily integration, and most bodily integration does not depend crucially on the brain.

I. *Most brain-mediated integrative functions are not somatically integrating.* Shewmon's point here is that the notion of integration is ambiguous and wide ranging, and there is a sense in which the brain's many activities, from main-taining body temperature to identifying voices, are integrative. But they are by no means all integrative in the sense under discussion; they do not all involve bodily integration.

Further, as "integration" is somewhat ambiguous, so too are the names of some of those activities over which, the claim goes, the brain exercises a regu-lative role. "Breathing", for example, can be understood in two ways, either as controlling a flow of air into and out of the lungs, or as involving an oxygen and carbon dioxide exchange. The first is clearly brain mediated, the second is not. But it is the second that is more evidently implicated in bodily inte-gration. Is it not farfetched to suppose there is any sense in which we might breathe without the involvement of the brain? Yes, for most circumstances, but Shewmon does not deny that the brain assists in the oxygen regulation and dissipation. Still, the brain is not here "conferring unity but enhancing and preserving a unity *already presupposed*" (Shewmon 2001: 464). And in exceptional circumstances this aspect of brain function can be "grossly substi-tuted" by a machine.

(He makes an important ancillary observation here. There are some respects in which the brain is deeply involved in somatic integration. But now, just as organism death does not require death in every part of the organism, so too for brain death. And such functioning can in part continue, and is brain, or part-brain mediated, even though the patient satisfies the criteria for brain death. So brain death does not always make for thoroughgoing function loss even in cases where the brain controls functioning).

II. *Most somatically integrative functions are not brain mediated*
The second component in the argument appears the more important. Someone might think that, say, seventy per cent of the brain's activity is involved in bodily integration. Then it is shown it is only, say, twenty per cent. Yet that the brain is doing much more than integrating the body does not show that bodily integration can continue independently. But crucially, according to Shewmon, there are many respects in which it can.

There are important senses in which, without the brain, but with of course outside assistance, the body can breathe, digest food, maintain stability in its organs, skin and bones, eliminate waste and poisons, maintain body temperature (albeit lower than normal), heal wounds, fight infection, mature, grow and (to refer back to an example in the text) support life and development in a foetus. Further, it can reveal "spontaneous improvement in general health" and "the overall ability to survive with little medical intervention" (Shewmon 2001: 468). Shewmon's claim is that a body that can do all that is far from non-integrated. And so, on the biological account of death, it is far from being dead. What is needed, then, for all this activity to take place is not brain function but circulatory-respiratory function, however that is arrived at. Machines will do the trick.

Shewmon distrusts the model sitting behind the brain death view. That sees the human body as far too much like a simple machine, in need of some master controller. This is not to deny the uniqueness of the brain among human organs. It is, he allows, irreplaceable, but that "has nothing to do with whether a brain-destroyed body possesses integrative unity" (*ibid.*: 473).[11] And then:

> Integra*tion* does not necessarily require an integra*tor*, as plants and embryos clearly demonstrate. What is of the essence of integrative unity is neither localizable nor replaceable – namely the ant-entropic mutual interaction of all the cells and tissues of the body, mediated in mammals by circulating oxygenated blood. To assert this non-encephalic essence of organismal life is far from a regression to the simplistic traditional cardio-pulmonary criterion or to an ancient cardiocentric notion of vitality. If anything, the idea that the non-brain body is a mere "collection of organs" in a bag of skin[12] seems to entail a throwback to a primitive atomism that should find no place in the dynamical-systems-enlightened biology of the 1990s and twenty-first century.   (*Ibid.*)

For

Although Bernat says, and repeatedly, that the organism cannot function as a whole without the brain, he does not say much to explain this. Much of what he does say – about how the other organs function to support the brain, about the conditions under which brain death occurs – is uncontroversial. And some of what is controversial – the brain is irreplaceable – is not at odds with Shewmon's account. Unsurprisingly, he agrees with Shewmon that certain bodily functions can continue, in spite of brain death, given medical intervention. Thus it is possible to provide "mechanical respiration and, hence, continued support for heartbeat and circulation, despite the loss of the critical system. A brain-dead patient also may retain liver and kidney functions and enteric absorption of food and fluids provided by a feeding gastrostomy tube" (Bernat 2002: 336). The list here is shorter than that provided by Shewmon, but that is neither puzzling nor in itself important. But then Bernat asks what we are to make of this functioning. And he answers, not much. All we have here is something akin to a detached organ awaiting transplant. "They are merely artificially supported organ and tissue subsystems whose overall control, interrelatedness and unity is forever gone because of the loss of the critical system" (*ibid.*). To the lay reader this is less than fully convincing. And the analogy perhaps hurts more than it helps. For the parts of an isolated and sustained organ surely do continue to function as an integrated whole. Otherwise it would not be worth transplanting. And no one can believe that the activities referred to – liver and kidney function, absorption of food, heartbeat and circulation – are not interrelated, or controlled. So perhaps a lot of weight is put on "overall".

Go back to the issue of the brain's irreplaceability. Bernat allows that he can imagine many technological advances, including perhaps mimicry of some of the brain's functions. But "I cannot imagine any machine that will ever reproduce conscious awareness" (*ibid.*: 341).

Adjudication

I want to make three points about this. First, it is difficult not to think that Shewmon has the edge here. Assuming his account is somewhere near correct, it is not at all easy to see how it can be claimed that a brain-dead patient, when appropriately sustained, is to be seen merely as a collection of discrete parts. So it is not easy to see how, on the biological account, she is dead.

But is the account correct? I said at the outset, although tentatively, that this is not about words. Yet even if some of us are ill equipped to assess the various claims it is, first, striking that there does not appear to be disagreement about the basic facts here and, second, surely unlikely that there would be any long-standing dispute of this kind. Even the non-expert might reasonably assume that, were Shewmon seriously wrong in his contentions as to what processes occur in the brain-dead patient, his opponents would be more bullish, and his reputation would not for long be sustained.

Is it, then, not so much a scientific as a philosophical or conceptual question after all? A response here would be easier if we had a good grasp as to what such a question would be, and how, having asked it, we might expect it to be answered. I shall say now only this. It is difficult not to think that, in spite of claims to be giving a biological and species-neutral account of death, the brain death account is inflected by concerns about consciousness. It is here, as Shewmon and Bernat agree, that, in normal circumstances, the brain provides a distinctive and irreplaceable contribution. And I suspect that as we are increasingly prepared to allow that life might, for the person whose life it is, be worthless, and might be ended, so the impetus to hold to the brain death account will fall away.

Notes

1. Death

1. This is not at all original. Similar views include: "permanent cessation of the integrated functioning of the organism as a whole" (A. M. Capron & L. R. Kass, "A Statutory Definition of the Standards for Determining Human Death: An Appraisal and a Proposal", *University of Pennsylvania Law Review* **121** [1972], 87–118, esp. 102); "permanent cessation of the functioning of the organism as a whole" (President's Commission for the Study of Ethical Problems in Medicine and Biomedical and Behavioral Research, *Defining Death: Medical, Ethical and Legal Issues in the Determination of Death* [Washington, DC: US Government Printing Office, 1981], 33); "irreversible loss of integrated function of the organism as a whole" (D. Lamb, "What is Death?", in *Principles of Health Care Ethics*, R. Gillon [ed.], 1027–40 [Chichester: Wiley, 1994], 1033); "the irreversible loss of the capacity of the organism to function as a whole that results from the permanent loss of its critical system" (J. Bernat, "The Biophilosophical Basis of Whole Brain Death", *Social Philosophy and Policy Foundation* **19**[2] [2002], 324–42, esp. 333–4). See also J. Bernat, C. M. Culver & B. Gert, "On the Definition and Criterion of Death", *Annals of Internal Medicine* **94** (1981), 389–94; L. Becker, "Human Being: The Boundaries of the Concept", *Philosophy and Public Affairs* **4**(4) (1975), 334–59; and J. Rosenberg, *Thinking Clearly about Death* (Englewood Cliffs, NJ: Prentice Hall, 1983).
2. This account, as becomes clearer later, is rougher for plants than for higher animals. See Bernat, "The Biophilosophical Basis".
3. It is perhaps surprising how few writers give much space to the question of life, and death, in organism parts. Here, though, are some comments. Bernat claims that, "because the concept of death is biological, it may be applied directly only to organisms: all living organisms must die and only living organisms can die" and so this concept "may not be directly applicable to the death of the subunits of the organism, such as its cells, tissues or organs" (*ibid.*, 330). Although his comment here is not fully embedded in the longer discussion, Fred Feldman seems to disagree: "the concepts of life and death apply univocally to biological entities, whether organisms or not" (*Confrontations with the Reaper* [New York: Oxford University Press, 1992], 70). David DeGrazia appears to be on Feldman's side: "Although individual cells and organs live and die, organisms are the only entities that literally do so without being parts of larger biological systems" ("The Definition of Death", *Stanford Encyclopedia of Philosophy*, http://plato.stanford.edu/entries/death-definition/, §1). I am not sure, though, that I fully understand this. Eric

227

Olson appears to make similar distinctions to mine, holding that individual cells are alive, but that organs are not (*The Human Animal* [Oxford: Oxford University Press, 1997], 130, 132, 137). Yet the second point here is not fully clear: "Suppose we remove one of your kidneys and keep it 'alive' by pumping nutrients through it. Doesn't that detached organ exhibit metabolism, teleology, and organized complexity?" He says it does not, even though the cells that make it up do. Hence it is not literally alive. But this is a detached kidney. What of one *in situ*? I suspect Olson might say here that we cannot coherently ask whether some embedded part of an organism is itself alive. Yet we can ask this of a cell. The difference concerns boundaries (*ibid.*, 130–31).

4. I might add, linguistic rather than metaphysical. But more on this in Chapters 2 and 9.
5. Of course, things that are literally alive might also die metaphorically, and things that are literally dead might still be metaphorically alive. The comedian dies on stage. Mao Zedong lives on in the minds of the Chinese; or used to.
6. See, for example, J. Johansson, *Mortal Beings: On the Metaphysics and Value of Death* (Stockholm: Almqvist & Wiksell, 2005), 59. I say considerably more below about the context within which the point is made.
7. I take this term from Feldman, *Confrontations with the Reaper*, 66.
8. See Rosenberg, *Thinking Clearly about Death*, and discussion in Feldman *Confrontations with the Reaper*, 66–71; J. Lizza, *Persons, Humanity and the Definition of Death* (Baltimore, MD: Johns Hopkins University Press. 2006), 29–31; and Becker, "Human Being: The Boundaries of the Concept", 337. (Curiously, Becker seems to think it clear that a caterpillar is not a butterfly but is nevertheless an insect.)
9. If we did then we would believe that the amoeba is at least potentially immortal.
10. Yet if pushed one way or the other, I probably would say it had ceased to exist. (Part of the resistance comes about because the new amoebae resemble very closely the old. Were division to result in a pair of quite different things then that the original had ceased to exist would be more appealing.) But has it not then died? Olson is interesting here:

> "When an amoeba divides, it seems that it must cease to exist …. But when an amoeba divides, nothing happens that *looks* much like death. Nothing begins to decay, and no corpse results. So we know that an organism *can* cease to exist without interruption of its vital functions, and without leaving behind any lifeless remains – without dying, as it were."

But then he goes on to insist that cell division is a special case: "the biological event we call the cell's life loses its integrity and divides into two independent streams. It seems appropriate to call this event the birth of two new organisms and the demise of the original cell" (*The Human Animal*, 114). I think it is just unclear whether by "demise" he means "death". The idea of amoebae being born is odd, though.

11. See, for example, S. Kripke, *Naming and Necessity* (Cambridge, MA: Harvard University Press, 1980), 110ff. Kripke takes the example from Timothy Sprigge.
12. Here is one example. London Bridge used to exist in London. It now exists in Arizona. In the interim, when it was in pieces, it did not exist. I think that is fairly clearly the natural way to describe this case, and that anyone who resists, holding that it existed but in a dispersed form throughout, or that the Arizona bridge is a replica is, as they say, in the grip of a theory.
13. This example is taken from Feldman, *Confrontations with the Reaper*, 69.
14. I do not mean to suggest that the caterpillar case counters the thesis after all. We should say, one ongoing thing changes its form. It is, in contrast, way more tempting of the fictional case to say that the nymph ceases to exist and is replaced by a bear. If this is resisted it will be because the psychology continues, and we think of Callisto *qua* bear thinking of herself as a trapped nymph. To anticipate, I suggest in Chapter 9 that one of us may suffer, or enjoy, a similar fate, moving, unnaturally, from one body to another.

15. This is meant only as a necessary condition of dying. Feldman denies it: "A giant sequoia might be dying for half a century or more" (*Confrontations with the Reaper*, 76). But this is soon relative to its lifespan.

16. And see, as Bernat suggests, R. Morison, "Death: Process or Event?", *Science* 173 (1971), 694–8, and L. Kass, "Death as an Event: A Commentary on Robert Morison", *Science* 173 (1971), 698–702, for earlier lively discussion.

17. I am assuming here what I argue below is often the case: that the dead exist.

18. For further reading, see J. M. Fischer (ed.), *The Metaphysics of Death* (Stanford, CA: Stanford University Press, 1993), 2–5.

19. Consider, for example, a seed, or a chrysalis. As I noted, Bernat focuses on higher vertebrates and now restricts his account of death accordingly. But even here there are claims made about suspended animation.

20. "…we generally assume that one goes out of existence at death" (DeGrazia, "The Definition of Death", §4.1). But against this see Feldman: that with death things cease to exist "is blatantly inconsistent with common-sense views about death" (*Confrontations with the Reaper*, 95). Philosophers are, of course, prone to such confident assertions about the thinking of the vulgar.

21. So although all the living exist, some, and probably most, of the dead do not.

22. The term is Feldman's (*ibid.*, 89), and see also his "The Termination Thesis", *Midwest Studies in Philosophy* 24, *Life and Death: Metaphysics and Ethics* (2000), 98–115. Johansson, *Mortal Beings*, 44–5, usefully gives names for and against. Terminators include, as well as Johansson himself, Lynne Rudder Baker, Jeff McMahan, Eric Olson, Jay Rosenberg and Harry Silverstein. Early terminators include Epicurus and Lucretius. Believers in souls are opposed, but so too, and more interesting for present purposes, are Michael Ayers, William Carter, Fred Feldman, David Mackie and Peter van Inwagen. Feldman and Johansson both claim to restrict the thesis to people, in Johansson's case to *human* people. But certainly some of those referred to as terminators will not accept this restriction. Surprisingly, Feldman and Johansson need to be included here. Neither of them means what they say.

23. But it should be noted that if we are persons then we often cease to exist before our bodies die.

24. See especially Olson, *The Human Animal*. I think Johansson holds to this view also, and that his claim to restrict the termination thesis to human animals was ill judged.

25. He holds that corpses, unlike the atoms that make them up, come into existence with death. What, in full detail, he thinks about bodies is, for me at least, harder to understand. See Olson, *The Human Animal*, 142–53 and "Animalism and the Corpse Problem", *Australasian Journal of Philosophy* 82(2) (2004), 265–74.

26. Feldman gives a number of scenarios that allegedly make trouble for this view. (*Confrontations with the Reaper*, 93–5). But Olson will be unmoved. (It is because these examples all concern non-human animals that I allege above that Feldman fails adequately to characterize his view.)

27. See especially Olson, *The Human Animal*, 127–31, and "Animalism and the Corpse Problem", 269–70.

28. See Olson, *The Human Animal*, 135ff.

29. See Feldman, "The Termination Thesis", 104–6, for criticism of Olson's position.

30. See Chapter 5 for more on this.

31. For further reading, see Bernat, "The Biophilosophical Basis", 329–32; Lizza, *Persons, Humanity and the Definition of Death*, 1–17.

32. In opposition to this see Lizza, who insists that "death is a metaphysical, ethical and cultural phenomenon *in as equally a fundamental sense* as it is a biological phenomenon" (*Persons, Humanity and the Definition of Death*, 4) and holds, further, that it has always been so understood (*ibid.*, 7). What does this mean? Does he allow that non-biological things can die, or does he not? Does he think that something can die – say, a plant – unnoticed, and so without

exciting metaphysical, ethical or cultural reflection or debate? Or does he deny this? Of course, we have not said all there is to say about death, or all that is extremely important about it, in talking about biology, but we need not, indeed must not, go beyond biology in saying what it is, or in attempting to define it. (Compare Lizza here with Olson, who adds to his insistence that we are animals the claim that we are not merely animals ["An Argument for Animalism", in *Personal Identity*, R. Martin & J. Barresi (eds), 318–34 (Oxford: Blackwell. 2003), 321]. This is, in one sense, right – there are further important things to say – but in another sense wrong – we are not composites, made up of animals and other things.)

2. Definitions

1. See Feldman, *Confrontations with the Reaper*, 11–12.
2. "Definition" is used very loosely. And "criterion" is used in different ways. One way is just that sketched by Feldman here: a criterion of x is a mark by which, in fact, the presence of x can be detected. But there is a second way. Some writers use "criterion" to refer to something necessarily involved in something: see, for example, Parfit on personal identity (*Reasons and Persons* [Oxford: Clarendon Press, 1984], 202). Both uses are legitimate. But in all that follows, in this chapter and beyond, I shall use the term "criterion", and refer to criteria, in Feldman's sense, with an epistemological slant. And this slant, as Feldman notes, involves a species specificity: the signs or marks of death in human beings may well be different from the signs in oak trees, or in amoebae, or in, in an imaginary case, gods or monsters.
3. It may be that Feldman goes some way to acknowledging this in referring to a "really good criterion of death" (*Confrontations with the Reaper*, 15). By implication, some criteria are merely some good.
4. Feldman makes a further point, prior to this summary, that is similarly puzzling. He says that "philosophers and others have set about trying to isolate some clear marks or criteria of death" (*ibid.*, 14). You might wonder why philosophers should be engaged with this. Surely this is a job for doctors.
5. It may seem that I am wrong in attributing the first approach to Feldman. Some of his comments suggest some sympathy for a deflationary account. For example, "Suppose there is such a thing as the concept of death. In other words; suppose the word 'death' has a certain literal meaning in the English language" (*ibid.*, 16–17). If that is all there is to concepts then, perhaps, I should not be sceptical about them. (Or perhaps I should be sceptical about literal meanings?) And he does allow that the meaning of a word, the concept it expresses, can change. So an analysis might need to be amended (*ibid.*, 17). Even so, it still appears that there are discrete concepts, hard edged and unalterable.
6. Feldman numbers his various definitions. As I am not rehearsing the entire argument I have omitted these numbers, here and throughout.
7. Feldman takes this example from N. Smart, "Philosophical Concepts of Death", in *Man's Concern with Death*, A. Toynbee (ed.), 25–35 (London: Hodder & Stoughton, 1968), 29.
8. Thus it is *a posteriori*, rather than *a priori* knowledge.
9. I want, in relation to an earlier point, to emphasize "something" here. We can know more or less about water. But there is no cut off point where we can now unambiguously claim to know what it is.
10. See, of course, Kripke, *Naming and Necessity*, for the basis of this discussion. See also my "Gold", *Theoria* 13(33) (1998), 415–26, for some elaboration of my position.
11. Contrast the other cases. As there are no clear boundaries to what can count as art, so there is not here one thing, a common core, an essence, to be explored. Similarly, although not quite the same, with death. We can certainly study and learn about many of the physiological processes attendant on death. The relevant processes vary across different kinds of living things but,

more so than with art, are present on a regular and long-term basis when death occurs. And so the claim that death has a nature falls, in terms of plausibility, between the other two. All this is far from precise. But only if you think that "nature" can be defined, or that there is a nature to nature, will you find this troublesome.

12. See, for example, J. Ladd, "The Definition of Death and the Right to Die", in *Ethical Issues Relating to Life and Death*, J. Ladd (ed.), 118–45 (Oxford: Oxford University Press, 1979) and W. Chiong, "Brain Death without Definitions", *Hastings Center Report* 35(6) (2005), 20–30. And for further discussion see DeGrazia, "The Definition of Death", §4.2

13. Feldman derives this suggested definition from Rosenberg, *Thinking Clearly about Death*, 106.

14. Although this account does not handle some of the deathless exit problem cases at all well: the amoeba, because of fission; Chlamydomonas, because of fusion; and, allegedly, the caterpillar, because of metamorphosis. See Feldman, *Confrontations with the Reaper*, 66–71.

15. Rosenberg claims that death is "the loss of syntropic capacity or ability. More precisely, an organism dies when it loses its power to preserve and sustain its self-organizing organization permanently and irreversibly" (*Thinking Clearly about Death*, 106). And he adds that such a loss: "is a functional change which constitutes a change of natural kind – from a human being to the remains of a human being – and which, in consequence of our moral practices, also results in a simultaneous change of ethical kind – from a person to a person's corpse" (*ibid.*, 122). So Rosenberg's account here is clearly similar to Olson's. Now Lizza says this is a definition of death, but I do not see that Rosenberg identifies it as such. And the evident concern here with personhood suggests that at least in part he is offering an account of what happens when one of us dies, rather than a definition of death *tout court*.

16. As he notes, his account is similar also to that given by Robert Veatch, who states: "Death means a complete change in the status of a living entity characterized by the irreversible loss of those characteristics that are essentially significant to it" ("Defining Death Anew: Technical and Ethical Problems", in *Ethical Issues in Death and Dying*, T. Beauchamp & S. Perlin [eds], [Englewood Cliffs, NJ: Prentice-Hall, 1978], 22). Like a number of writers, Lizza is mostly concerned with human death. He thinks that we are alive and essentially conscious, and so finds that this account fits well with his view that we die when we lose consciousness. But this does not imply or support this new definition.

17. For Rosenberg, "one requirement which an entity must … satisfy in order to belong to the kind 'animal' is that it be a living organism" (*Thinking Clearly about Death*, 121).

18. Neither of these cases threatens my "definition". It is neutral on ceasing to exist, and it does not claim all organisms die.

19. As I understand it, references to alternative silicon-based organisms sometimes allude to naturally occurring creatures, at other times to things running on microchips (thus the wet and the dry). If so, this is a nice ambiguity. For more on machine life, superorganisms and so on see Olson, *The Human Animal*, 129–30; S. Luper, "Natural Resources, Gadgets and Artificial Life", *Environmental Values* 8(1) (1999), 27–54, and *The Philosophy of Death* (Oxford: Oxford University Press, 2008), ch. 2.

20. It is perhaps worth noting here, as I have noted after several conversations, that professional biologists see no strong need to define, and have little interest in defining, what are surely, for them, key terms.

21. See Chapter 3 for more detail and references.

22. Thus Bernat, in recent work, has seen the need to single out higher vertebrates as the things to which his account refers ("The Biophilosophical Basis", 130). Contrast this with Olson's position, where the *whole organism–organism as a whole* distinction is not pressed. He claims to be talking altogether generally about living things:

> The parts of an organism, like those of a fine watch, are connected together in such a way that each has a role to play in enabling the organism to achieve its ends – survival

and reproduction. No part can fulfil its function without the others; the entire structure will collapse – the organism will die and decay – unless all or nearly all of its parts
do what they are supposed to do. (*The Human Animal*, 128)
This may be true of you and me, cats and dogs, but it is not true of trees, or worms.

23. These matters are discussed in more detail in Chapter 3. But two points might be noted here. First, many supporters of the brain death account are highly sceptical about even the long-term possibility of brain transplants. Second, I have two reversing procedures in mind: repairs to, and replacement of, the damaged brain.

24. Perhaps Hershenov does not make this clear. But I take it the view is that one is not dead so long as self-restarting is possible, and not only that one was never dead when self-restarting is actual.

25. Imagine God does this often, and resurrection is the norm. I think that in such circumstances ordinary notions of death would not survive.

3. Human beings

1. See the Appendix for more detail on these terms.
2. How long? Around ten minutes according to Bernat, "The Biophilosophical Basis", 336, but fifteen to twenty minutes on Lamb's account ("What is Death?", 1035).
3. See, for example, Lamb, "What is Death?", 1034; Olson, *The Human Animal*, 140; R. M. Veatch, "The Death of Whole-Brain Death: The Plague of the Disaggregators, Somaticists, and Mentalists", *Journal of Medicine and Philosophy* 30 (2005), 356. Lamb is perhaps in danger of some circularity here – "Properly understood, criteria for the death of the brain are met only when the individual can no longer function as an integrated whole" (yes, but they are neverthe-less distinct) – and is certainly guilty of making the suspect identity claim: "brainstem death is ... synonymous with the death of the individual ... death of the brainstem is itself death" (*Death, Brain Death and Ethics* [Beckenham: Croom Helm, 1985], 5).
4. For further reading, see Bernat *et al.*, "On the Definition and Criterion", 390–92; Lamb, *Death, Brain Death and Ethics*, ch. 6, and "What is Death?", 1031; A. Halevy & B. Brody, "Brain Death: Reconciling Definitions, Criteria, and Tests", *Annals of Internal Medicine* 119(6) (1993), 519–25.
5. I do not mean to suggest that "we see with our eyes" is analytic. Rather, there is as yet no real replacement mechanism.
6. A third view – the heart functions only when it functions within a living body – might be mentioned and rejected.
7. Some of the earlier reports dealing with brain death were unclear on the distinctions here; see the Appendix. Since then, critics of the brain death account have sometimes tended to characterize it as revisionary, while supporters have emphasized continuities. See J. McMahan, *The Ethics of Killing* (Oxford: Oxford University Press, 2002), 423; Lamb, *Death, Brain Death and Ethics*, ch. 2, and "What is Death?", 1036; J. Bernat, "A Defense of the Whole-Brain Concept of Death", *Hastings Center Report* 28(2) (1998), 14–23 and "The Whole-Brain Concept of Death Remains Optimum Public Policy", *Journal of Law, Medicine and Ethics* 34(1) (2006), 35–43.
8. See, for example, Lamb, "What is Death?", 1039; Bernat, "The Biophilosophical Basis", 325; McMahan, *The Ethics of Killing*, 431. Bernat suggests that although this desire did indeed motivate the change, "'the concept of brain death is not merely a social contrivance" ("The Biophilosophical Basis", 325).
9. See for discussion Bernat, "A Defense of the Whole-Brain Concept of Death"; R. M. Arnold & S. J. Youngner, "The Dead Donor Rule: Should we Stretch it, Bend it, or Abandon it?", in *Procuring Organs for Transplant*, R. M. Arnold, S. J. Youngner, R. Schapiro & C. M. Spicer (eds) (Baltimore, MD: Johns Hopkins University Press, 1995).

10. It should be acknowledged that there is some difficulty in defending the claim that it is good for the patient that their life be ended. Some people desire not to be kept alive on machines. But for those who do not desire this, it is not clearly against their interests to be kept alive in this way.

11. Someone might claim a human organism is alive only when the brain is alive. Then embryos and early stage foetuses present problems. I am not making that claim. But see note 12 below.

12. See, for example, J. McMahan, "The Metaphysics of Brain Death", *Bioethics* 9(2) (1995), 94–5. Yet although it might have been expected, McMahan is not quite making my point. I am envisaging a so far imaginary situation where someone is very obviously alive – let us say they continue to go to work and play football – but are supported by an artificial brain. McMahan is describing a real situation where someone is arguably alive – although not conscious, and this makes for a part of the argument – even though their brain is dead. And I discuss this in more detail later.

13. Brain death is, in fact although not in logic, sufficient for death of the human organism. Is it necessary? Not if an embryo is a human organism and can die before its brain develops. And what about non-human animals? We need to know what sorts of things happen in laboratories, world wide. Nevertheless, in so far as it is construed as a mark or sign of the condition of human patients, defenders of the criterion might wave such considerations aside.

14. See, for example, Lamb, *Death, Brain Death and Ethics*, 34–8; Bernat, "A Defense of the Whole-Brain Concept of Death", 19. M. Green & D. Wikler, "Brain Death and Personal Identity", *Philosophy and Public Affairs* 9 (1980), 105–33, take a different view. What perhaps is not altogether clear is whether the sceptics deny just that there will ever be mechanical brains or, further, that we will ever be able successfully to transplant a brain.

15. Bernat writes: "despite the advances in artificial-intelligence technology and theory, I cannot imagine any machine that will ever reproduce conscious awareness" ("The Biophilosophical Basis", 341).

16. See Olson, *The Human Animal*, 135. Arguing that organisms cannot have inorganic objects as genuine parts – for such objects will not be "caught up in (the) metabolism" – Olson insists that "there is no animal made up of Tom's headless remains together with some mechanical or electronic contraption" (*The Human Animal*, 135). Obviously, this argument does not itself rule out a brain or part-brain transplant.

17. For further reading, see Lamb, "What is Death?", 1029–30; Bernat, "The Biophilosophical Basis", 333.

18. "In 1740 it was suggested by Jean-Jacques Winslow that putrefaction was the only sure sign of death" (Lamb, *Death, Brain Death and Ethics*, 51).

19. This is to some degree plausible for plants. A new plant can, often, be generated from a small bit of material. (And thus it may be that more parts of plants, than of animals, are literally alive).

20. There are not insignificant differences between them, but for versions of such an account see Lizza, *Persons, Humanity and the Definition*; R. M. Veatch, *Death, Dying and Biological Revolution: Our Last Quest for Responsibility* (New Haven, CT: Yale University Press, 1976); McMahan, *The Ethics of Killing*; Green & Wikler, "Brain Death and Personal Identity"; and K. Gervais, *Redefining Death* (New Haven, CT: Yale University Press, 1986). And see, for further discussion, DeGrazia, "The Definition of Death", §2.1

21. For further reading, see S. Luper, "Mortal Harm", *Philosophical Quarterly* 57(227) (2007) 239–51.

22. The term was coined by Richard Ryder.

23. See the study by L. A. Siminoff, C. Burant & S. J. Youngner, "Death and Organ Procurement: Public Beliefs and Attitudes", *Social Science and Medicine* 59(11) (2004), 2325–34. Of a sample population in Ohio, 86.2 per cent thought that the brain-dead patient is dead, while only 34.1 per cent thought this of those in pvs. Is that figure still high? Yes, but this is before education and reflection.

24. For further reading, see J.-D. Bauby, *The Diving Bell and the Butterfly* (New York: Alfred A. Knopf, 1997).
25. Whether it is more extreme depends on the severity. Locked-in syndrome is typically caused by a severe stroke. Its onset is sudden, but even though it may seem that consciousness is gone, there are plenty of signs of life. Guillain–Barré syndrome involves a form of paralysis. It has a gradual onset and often does not progress very far. But in extreme cases it could, at least superficially, be confused with brain death.
26. I have considered here only cases where consciousness initially developed within a living organism. That it is not sufficient for life might be even clearer in cases where it is, from the outset, embedded in a machine.
27. For the description "breathing, warm, and supple" see P. Singer, *Rethinking Life and Death: The Collapse of Our Traditional Ethics* (New York: St Martin's Press, 1994), 21, and for "pink perfused" see D. Lamb, "What is Death?", in *Principles of Health Care Ethics*, R. Gillon (ed.), 1027–40 (Chichester: Wiley, 1994), 1035.
28. See McMahan, *The Ethics of Killing*, 430, for this and further cases.
29. For further reading, see A. Shewmon, "Chronic Brain Death: Meta-analysis and Conceptual Consequences", *Neurology* **51** (1998), 1538–45.
30. For further reading, see Lamb, *Death, Brain Death and Ethics*, 37–9.
31. Stephen Holland makes this point against Lamb. But then: "None the less, Lamb's basic point that either category error has important moral consequences is surely right" (S. Holland, *Bioethics* [Cambridge: Polity, 2003], 69). This may go too far. Whether there are important moral consequences of a temporary waste of resources is moot.
32. DeGrazia may have Alan Shewmon and Josef Seifert – both avowed Catholics – in mind here.

4. Is it bad to die?

1. It should be noted that "for the universe" is one way, perhaps not altogether felicitous, of signalling this concern with intrinsic value. It does not pick out just another form of instrumental bad. (So contrast "for the universe" with "for the planet".)
2. See R. Dworkin, *Life's Dominion* (New York: Alfred A. Knopf, 1993), 71–81, and for further discussion my "Abortion, Value and the Sanctity of Life", *Bioethics* **11**(2) (1997), 130–50. "Personal" here is used somewhat loosely. It is not meant to imply the existence of distinct items we might call persons, and nor is it meant to suggest there is not at least a species of personal bad that can fall to animals.
3. Nagel makes what seems to be a puzzling comment here:
   > The situation is roughly this: There are elements that, if added to one's experience, make life better; there are other elements that, if added to one's experience, make life worse. But what remains when these are set aside is not merely *neutral*: it is emphatically positive. Therefore life is worth living even when the bad elements of experience are plentiful and the good ones too meagre to outweigh the bad ones on their own. The additional positive weight is supplied by experience itself, rather than any of its contents.   (*Mortal Questions* [Cambridge: Cambridge University Press, 1979], 2)

   The claim here is not that death is always bad. First it is experience, rather than life itself that is always good. Second, the claim is only that mere experience has some positive value. So it is allowed that enough bad experience can make life not worth living. Perhaps Nagel's view is strange, but it is not a sanctity view.
4. This is inadequate as it stands. There is normally something identifiably evil about the lesser of two evils – amputation is preferable to death, but there is something clearly bad about losing your leg – but the problem here is in finding any residual evil in death, in the case where it is

preferable to life. We might agree that in such a case we can at least imagine a better alternative – a miracle cure – but that does not in itself rule out death's being, in certain circumstances, either good or neutral. Suppose we say that when death is for the best there is still something bad about it, in that it puts an end to the possibility, no matter how remote, of your living a good life. We can equally say that when it is bad there is still something good about it, in that it forecloses on the remote possibility of your being captured by bandits and then tortured. So there is still some explaining to do. If death, as we seem mostly to think, can ever be straightforwardly a bad thing, and bad for you, why cannot it ever be equally straightforwardly a good thing? And there is a further dimension to this puzzle. Many people – and I am among them – are at least tempted by the Epicurean position. There is some difficulty in seeing just what is bad, or what is so bad, about the unannounced and painless death. But there is no corresponding difficulty in seeing what might be good about it. That death might be better than life is, then, more clearly true than that it might be worse than life. The difference here relates to a more general asymmetry concerning goods and bads, and links here in particular with the view that although there seems to be a clear duty not to start a wretched life, there is no parallel duty to start a happy life.

5. See John Broome's "Goodness is Reducible to Betterness", in his *Ethics out of Economics* (Cambridge: Cambridge University Press, 1999).
6. As I have suggested, there may be room for reservations about "intrinsically bad for you". But as the end thought here is that death is *not* intrinsically bad, we might not worry too much about this.
7. Life might be good, or bad, or neutral. Suppose it is good, or neutral. If death is not worse, death is not bad. Suppose you think life is bad. Then it is on the face of it possible for death not to be worse, not something to avoid or regret, but still itself bad.
8. Someone might think that to compare two states we need to know what it is like to be in those states. So although we can compare different good lives, and further compare a good life with a (conscious) life of neutral value, we cannot compare life with death. Similarly, we cannot say it is better to be a person than a tree.
9. One puzzle here, to be mentioned and then set aside, is why materialists should think that our ceasing to be sentient, and our ceasing to exist, should go hand in hand. But perhaps Epicurus believed that as an artefact, say a table, can be destroyed, and so cease to exist even while the individual particles continue, so similarly for a human being.
10. I take the phrase from Fischer, *The Metaphysics of Death*, 4.
11. See, usefully and recently, J. Warren, *Facing Death: Epicurus and his Critics* (Oxford: Oxford University Press, 2004).
12. People say we grieve because we will never see them again. But we used never to see again those who emigrated. Our grievings at death and at departure have always been different.
13. There is a reply. Someone might think the highest good is being free of pain. But there is no further good in acquiring pleasure. So being dead is not worse than living a good life, but it is better than living a bad life.
14. Again, Johansson (*Mortal Beings*, 69) usefully provides names. Critics include Bradley, Broome, Draper, Feit, Feldman, Fischer, Kamm, Luper, McMahan and Nagel. Perhaps the best known defender of Epicurus (after Lucretius) is Stephen Rosenbaum.
15. See again Chapter 1, n.21.
16. For further reading, see Feinberg, "Harm to Others", 90; G. Pitcher, "The Misfortunes of the Dead", in Fischer, *The Metaphysics of Death*, 161.
17. So some ways of making this point are suspect. For example, "After Socrates is dead, 'Socrates' continues to refer to the living Socrates. Hence 'Socrates was harmed at time *t*' can only mean that the living Socrates is what is harmed at *t*" (Luper, "Mortal Harm", 243). If there is such a thing as the dead Socrates, then, I think, "Socrates" refers to him also. He does not, after all, have some different name. And see Johansson, *Mortal Beings*, 97, for some appropriate impatience with such distinctions.

18. "One that was a woman, sir; but, rest her soul, she's dead" (*Hamlet*, V.i).
19. At this point the so-called problem of the subject slips over into that of harm. For now the question "Who is harmed by death?" is difficult, if at all, not because we cannot identify the person who is allegedly harmed, but because we cannot see how, given that he does not now exist, he can be the subject of, or subject to, harm.
20. See, for example, J. Feinberg, "Harm to Others", in his *Harm to Others*, 79–96 (Oxford: Oxford University Press, 1984), 80; J. McMahan, "Death and the Value of Life", *Ethics* 99(1) (1988), 39. Of course, Epicurus' dictum "Where death is, there we are not" invites this error.
21. See S. Luper, "Posthumous Harm", *American Philosophical Quarterly* 41 (2004), 63–72, for distinctions between and discussion of *priorism, subsequentism, concurrentism, eternalism* and *indefinitism*. Several other writers (e.g. Bradley, Johansson) have taken up at least parts of this terminology.
22. See for similar positions W. Grey, "Epicurus and the Harm of Death", *Australasian Journal of Philosophy* 77 (1999), 358–64; N. Feit, "The Time of Death's Misfortune", *Noûs* 36 (2002), 359–83; and B. Bradley, "When Is Death Bad for the One Who Dies?", *Noûs* 38 (2004), 1–28. And notice that this answer requires a combining of two of Luper's options. And this mix – concurrentism *and* subsequentism – avoids at least some of the objections that can be levelled at the separate components.
23. A similar passage is in Feldman, *Confrontations with the Reaper*, 154.
24. I hope this is not misleading. I am assuming here that in one way pain is always bad, always a misfortune, even if it is sometimes instrumentally good. Feldman's claim is not that death is always or eternally bad. It is rather that if there are times or circumstances where death is bad, it is always bad, at those times, or in those circumstances.
25. Feit also picks up on this problem in Feldman. But I am not fully persuaded by his account, even though Bradley ("When Is Death Bad for the One Who Dies?") thinks it very clear:

    > Consider again the question: When is Abe Lincoln's death bad for him? Feldman takes the question to be equivalent to this: when is it true that his death is bad for him? Hence Feldman is led to his version of eternalism about the evil of death. On the other hand, I take the question to be asking this: At which times *t* is it true that his death is bad for him at *t*? … (Compare: "he is a good person" could be true at all times, but "he is a good person at *t*" might be true of some times during his life and false of others).   (Feit, "The Time of Death's Misfortune", 372–3).

26. This represents a résumé (and compression – the ellipses are the author's) of Silverstein's "The Evil of Death", *Journal of Philosophy* 77(7) (1980), 401–24. See Bradley, "Eternalism and Death's Badness" (forthcoming), for extensive criticism of Silverstein's position.
27. Feinberg acknowledges the problem here: "a conclusion that does not at first sight carry much conviction" ("Harm to Others", 92).
28. The first sentence is odd. A life might be overall good. If it is, then at each moment in life, and indeed both before and afterwards, it can be so described. But life might be overall good without being good at every moment.
29. Indeed, the critics of Epicureanism mentioned earlier are all supporters of the deprivation account.
30. This may be false. It may be that only premature deaths are bad, as inevitably, we tire of life, such that more of it would not be better. Some will say, but then this is bad. It may be. But it is a separate issue. All this is discussed further in Chapter 5.
31. See, against this, B. Bradley, "How Bad is Death?", *Canadian Journal of Philosophy* 37(1) (2007), 11–128, esp. 120. This seems unduly sceptical about medicine.
32. See Bradley: "death causes us not to have any sensations, which is worse for us than having good sensations" ("When Is Death Bad for the One Who Dies?", 5).
33. I think the example is from Feldman.
34. This is from Nagel, *Mortal Questions*, 5–6.

35. See R. Cigman, "Death, Misfortune, and Species Inequality", *Philosophy and Public Affairs* **10** (1981), 47–64. But against this, see Bradley's views on animal death, in his forthcoming book *Well-Being and Death* (Oxford: Oxford University Press, 2009).

36. See J. Rachels, *The End of Life* (Oxford: Oxford University Press, 1986) on lives, and B. Williams, "The Makropoulos Case: Reflections on the Tedium of Immortality", in his *Problems of the Self*, 82–100 (Cambridge: Cambridge University Press, 1973) on desires.

37. Nagel makes a curious comparison between coma and death. He notes that: "most of us would not regard the *temporary* suspension of life, even for substantial intervals, as in itself a misfortune" (*Mortal Questions*, 3). This is puzzling. You have some remaining years: with death you lose them all; with coma you lose some. Some will think that death is therefore the greater evil. Others, swayed by Epicurus, will think coma worse. For when you recover you are aware of time lost, and that brings with it pain and regret. But it seems that either way, a coma, or temporary suspension is bad. Yet by "in itself a misfortune" Nagel means to exclude those cases where, as a consequence, life is shortened. You have forty years ahead. Like Rip van Winkle, you fall asleep, waking three hundred years later to live those years. But this too is an evil. There is a particular life you were in the business of living. And that life is taken from you by this coma. Does he want to exclude these cases too? Perhaps it is true that we would not regret a temporary suspension that has absolutely no unwelcome consequences. But then the same is true of a permanent ending.

38. For a good account of hedonism's resources, see F. Feldman, *Pleasure and the Good Life: Concerning the Nature, Varieties, and Plausibility of Hedonism* (New York: Oxford University Press, 2004).

39. See also Robert Nozick, "On the Randian Argument", reprinted in *Reading Nozick*, J. Paul (ed.), 206–31 (Totowa, NJ: Rowman & Littlefield, 1981), 221.

40. Rosenbaum may disagree. For he expresses difficulty in seeing how death, construed as a momentary event, can be bad for one. But, as he says, "death is the portal between the land of the living and the land of dead" (S. Rosenbaum, "How to be Dead and not Care: A Defense of Epicurus", in Fischer, *The Metaphysics of Death*, 121). And I have difficulty seeing how someone could be unconcerned about going there. As I have said, death, *qua* moment, cannot be characterized by its intrinsic features alone.

41. See also Fischer, *The Metaphysics of Death*, 20–23.

42. See Chapter 6 for more on this.

43. For this discussion see McMahan, "Death and the Value of Life", 34–5.

44. "the hypothetical cases in which people who long to be loved and admired and believe they are, when in fact they are ridiculed and despised behind their backs" (J. McMahan, "Death and the Value of Life", 33).

5. Circumstances and degrees

1. Remember, death might be overall bad in some circumstances, not in others, but nevertheless always bad in one way.

2. See Feldman, *Confrontations with the Reaper*, 153. The phrase, as he notes, derives from H. Silverstein, "The Evil of Death Revisited", *Midwest Studies in Philosophy* **24**, *Life and Death: Metaphysics and Ethics* (2000), 116–35, esp. 119, and "The Evil of Death", 414. Others, notably Bradley and McMahan refer instead to the *life comparative account* (See McMahan, *The Ethics of Killing*, 105ff.).

3. It is suggested here, even if it is not clearly spelled out, that S does not, as a result of this, receive some compensating benefit from elsewhere. That is, it is not just some, but all better lives that he fails now to live.

4. There may be a worry, however, about the moral and non-moral connotations of badness. It is worse not to get an expected promotion, but is it bad for you if you do not deserve it? The

Mafia boss is worse off if the drug deal is busted, but is it a misfortune for him if this happens? I owe the point here to Carolyn Price.

5. In the last section of this chapter it is precisely this that I question.
6. As discussed in Chapter 4, some will want to deny this. It is perhaps worth noting (although of course it settles nothing) that K. Draper, "Disappointment, Sadness, and Death", *Philosophical Review* **108**(3) (1999), 387–414, esp. 404, is unimpressed by these objections.
7. Although, as I have said, I am sympathetic to hedonism, I mean by this that it is bad when your life gets worse, not that it is bad whenever there is some reduction in levels of pleasure. There are many intense pleasures – think of your own example – where it is good that their intensity is short-lived. Related, there are situations in which it is inappropriate that you feel a great deal of pleasure. Your life might be worse if your pleasure levels were higher.
8. This is not to say it gets a yes/no answer.
9. Thus it is not quite as clear as McMahan has it: "It seems, indeed, a necessary truth that, in the absence of death one would live forever" (*The Ethics of Killing*, 99).
10. It is not clear, though, that losing merely possible goods is enough to give us a bad end.
11. For further reading, see Williams, "The Makropoulos Case".
12. I address them in *10 Good Questions about Life and Death* (Oxford: Blackwell, 2005).
13. Although Draper finds this a little glib. This case – and it is Nagel's – is special, he thinks, as "inevitable agony merits distress. But agony inherently involves distress, whereas deprivations do not. And … I have been unable to discover a deprivation that is inevitable in the strong sense of being humanly unavoidable and is, nevertheless, unquestionably a genuine evil" ("Disappointment, Sadness, and Death", 399–400). As the main text suggests, I do not find this persuasive.
14. Again, Bradley's point about different biological laws just seems wrong.
15. See Draper, "Disappointment, Sadness, and Death", 402–3.
16. For McMahan's investigations, see *The Ethics of Killing*, 103ff. and "Death and the Value of Life". I follow McMahan's discussion in the latter in the main, but note places where the accounts vary significantly.
17. He is not searching for this in the later work: "I do not mean to imply that there is always, or ever, a single, uniquely correct identification of any particular death" (*The Ethics of Killing*, 112).
18. Consider McMahan's account of the bus crash here:

    we naturally evaluate the death by comparing it to the life he would have had if every-thing had been the same except that he had not stepped in front of the bus. It is equally possible, of course, that he might not have died if, for example, he had taken a shorter step, so that the bus would have struck him a glancing blow rather than hitting him head-on. Suppose, if that had happened, he would have survived but with permanent brain damage and painful physical disabilities. Compared with that way in which he might not have died, his actual death may not seem so bad. But even though this was a possible alternative, we do not consider it. (*Ibid.*, 111–12).

    But I wonder who the "we" are here? If a friend of yours had recently been brain-damaged in a crash you might well consider it. (Think about reactions to bike and motorbike accidents. People often wonder whether it would have been better had the victim not worn a helmet, and had been killed outright). Further, the objection to the glancing blow scenario cannot be that it represents a possible but unlikely alternative. If we ask, what would have happened if he had stepped out a fraction later, this alternative is highly likely.
19. But in some weak(ish) sense. It was not physically necessary that she died, as, presumably, a cure or a life-prolonging treatment were both physically possible.
20. See McMahan's extended discussion in *The Ethics of Killing*, 127–45.
21. One I have not mentioned concerns expectation. Two people, both thirty, equally hope to live to eighty, but one expects only to make sixty. They both die at fifty.

22. Compare Wilfred Owen, dying close to the end of the war, with Rupert Brooke, dying early on.
23. Is her death more, less or as bad as Jane's? We cannot, I think, expect to answer this question. One reason for thinking this is that we cannot, in this case, meaningfully ask the related question: which of these two lives should we save?
24. Feldman ("Some Puzzles About the Evil of Death", in Fischer, *The Metaphysics of Death*, 307–26) and Bradley ("The Worst Time to Die", *Ethics* **118** [2008], 291–314) hold to at least versions of this view.
25. For further reading, see F. Kamm, *Morality, Mortality*, vol. 1 (Oxford: Oxford University Press, 1993).
26. For further reading, see G. Harman, *Explaining Value* (Oxford: Oxford University Press, 2000), pt. II.
27. People have said this about, for example, Gustave Eiffel and also, although less persuasively, of Coleridge.
28. For further reading, see A. MacIntyre, *After Virtue* (London: Duckworth, 1981); McMahan, *The Ethics of Killing*; J. Kekes, *Pluralism in Philosophy: Changing the Subject* (Ithaca, NY: Cornell University Press, 2000) and *The Art of Life* (Ithaca, NY: Cornell University Press, 2002).
29.   If the future that a person loses could reasonably be expected to round out his life or bring it to completion, the death is tragic for a particular reason: it leaves the life in suspension without resolution or closure. If, by contrast, the future life that death excludes would have been unlikely to provide a fitting conclusion to the person's life story, the death will lack this particular tragic dimension. Indeed, if the death prevents what would have been a jarring, inappropriate or inharmonious conclusion to the life, it may not be bad at all, or might even be good for the person … Suppose that two people each suffer a stroke. Each can be expected to live for another year in bovine contentment. One implication of the concern with narrative unity is that whether and to what extent that further year of life would be good depends on its relation to the person's previous life. Thus even if the additional year of each person's life would be much the same in terms of its intrinsic features, it might be good in one life but bad in the other.   (McMahan, *The Ethics of Killing*, 175)
30. McMahan appears to be sympathetic, if not fully committed, to the one version. He claims:
      Many people believe, for example, that what a person deserves depends in part on what he has achieved or what he has contributed to the common good. Others believe that a person is more deserving the more virtuous he is or the better he is morally. If either of these views is right, death may be worse, other things being equal, for those who have been unusually productive or virtuous.   (*The Ethics of Killing*, 181)
    See, for further discussion of desert, Feldman, *Confrontations with the Reaper*, 182–5, 201–4; Bradley, "The Worst Time to Die", 299.
31. For further reading, see Williams, "The Makropoulos Case".
32. Consider a related case. Ann desires death as she falsely believes she has some terminal disease. Although she desires death she desires also to travel to Venice, to see her younger sister grow up, to finish her degree. She has various categorical desires. Death now is bad for her. Suppose now that dwelling on her supposed condition she loses these desires. Still, death is bad for. Were she to learn the truth her life would regain its coherence.
33. There are further considerations: we can know of the man's plans and projects and so better sympathize with them, and with him. And, avoiding death now, he is more likely to succeed in controlling his fate than someone who, so young, is so subject to vicissitudes. He has friends, relatives and dependants, all of whom will suffer should he die. But then the baby has parents, who will similarly suffer. And there is nothing worse than the loss of an innocent life. These further considerations are irrelevant. They bring in badness for others, or challenges to our assumptions about the length of life ahead, or suspect claims about desert.

34. A roughly equal divide, so far as I can tell, between both philosophers of death and the public at large.
35. Nor am I going to insist that only present or past desires matter. Your project is to have no further projects, but to exist as an unthinking animal, wallowing in sensual pleasure. If that is the aim, then death now robs you of nothing worth having. We agree, then, that death's badness consists in preventing your having worthwhile, coherent, well-structured human life.
36. Although, as I have noted, Bradley wants elsewhere to hold that an animal's death is, often, bad for the animal. And, as will emerge, there is one sense in which I might be sympathetic to this.
37. For the Time Relative Interest Account see McMahan, *The Ethics of Killing*, 194ff.
38. Matthew Hanser has suggested, in correspondence, that the question may be not who to treat now, but who to benefit now. The benefit now, if I treat the baby, is preventing death in thirty years. But if the baby is not a person, how is she benefited now?
39. Notice that I am not inclined, as a result of these considerations, to suggest that it is always bad for a human being to die. It is not bad for someone in PVS to die. Here is a quick explanation. Death is not bad when it ends a life that is no longer worth living. Similarly with trees. If a tree is near death as a result of drought, it is not then bad for the tree that it is cut down. Is it *ever* bad for a human being to die, in circumstances when it is not bad that they die? We can say yes. Someone may deserve to die.
40. So I disagree with Philip Larkin. See his "Aubade".
41. For further reading, see S. Rachels, "Is it Good to make Happy People?", *Bioethics* 12(2) (1998), 93–110, and my "More Lives, Better Lives", *Ethical Theory and Moral Practice* 6(2) (2003), 127–41.
42. For me, it is sometimes thus: I wake up and, still half asleep and very comfortable, realize I have to stir myself and get going for another day at work or, worse, travel to an airport and beyond. I sometimes think it would be better just to die. Similarly this: "Robert Lowell once remarked that if there were some little switch in the arm that one could press in order to die immediately and without pain, then everyone would sooner or later commit suicide" (A. A. Alvarez, *The Savage God: A Study of Suicide* [Harmondsworth: Penguin, 1971], 158). Earlier in the book Alvarez reports on two ancient suicides: Zeno, who hanged himself out of sheer irritation after twisting his finger, and Cleanthes who, ordered to starve in order to cure a gumboil, found that once having set out on the road to death it was far easier to continue. All this proves nothing. But it may be that our strong aversion to death is in no small part shaped by culture.
43. Another example. Two people, both thirty, are in a car crash. I can help only one, either saving A, who is already unconscious, from a quick and painless death, but leaving him maimed, or assisting B so that she lives on in good health rather than maimed. So in the first outcome two people live, but both are thereafter maimed. In the other, one lives on in good health and the other dies. Many think the first outcome is evidently preferable. I find it less than evident.
44. McMahan then refers to Dworkin, *Life's Dominion*, chs 7 & 8, where these matters are, he says, "admirably discussed" (McMahan, *The Ethics of Killing*, 175).
45. For a further somewhat sympathetic discussion of the Epicurean view, and the suggestion that death is in some sense an innocent evil, see Johansson, *Mortal Beings*, ch. 6.

6. Posthumous harms

1. See M. Hanser, "The Metaphysics of Harm", *Philosophy and Phenomenological Research* 77 (2008), 421–50, for a recent account that is much fuller than can be provided here. And see, of course, Feinberg, "Harm to Others" and *Harm to Self* (Oxford: Oxford University Press, 1986), for comprehensive discussion.

2. Nagel, Pitcher and Levenbook offer similar views.
3. Against, for example, Peter Singer. He supports the claim thus:

> It would be nonsense to say that it was not in the interests of a stone to be kicked along the road by a schoolboy. A stone does not have interests because it cannot suffer .... A mouse, on the other hand, does have interests in not being tormented, because mice will suffer if they are treated in this way.
>
> (*Practical Ethics* [Cambridge: Cambridge University Press, 1993], 57)

Fair enough, but plants fairly obviously constitute an intermediate case.
4. I do not mean to suggest that all living things can be harmed. It may be that someone in PVS has no interests in remaining alive, and so will not be harmed by being killed. A salient difference between someone in this condition and a plant is in their relation to normal instances of their kind. We might say that someone in PVS is only unnaturally alive.
5. Suppose someone objects that it is natural for a body to decay, and so cease to exist, slowly. But, just as we might say that exposed stone will naturally weather, this only means that such things typically occur within a given environment.
6. Someone might object that this is simply question-begging. Believers in posthumous harm may well claim that among the things having interests, moral status, or a good of their own are dead persons. But the objection here is somewhat tangential to my claim. The thought that dead trees, dead animals, dead human beings are interest-bearers is, I say, hard to believe. But I did not mention persons. If "person" is another word for human animal then I shall include it here. If "person" is a separate entity then, as before, I doubt there are dead persons.
7. The qualification is intended. Although we use both, perhaps we talk more often of hurting people than harming them. And much talk of harm occurs in legal contexts. (See Feinberg's anticipation of the murderer's response: "Harmed him? Hell, no; I killed him outright!"; "Harm to Others", 80).
8. M. Hanser, "The Metaphysics of Harm", *Philosophy and Phenomenological Research* 77 (2008), 421–50, offers a further account of harm that is not comparative in either of these ways.
9. I return to and refine the points made here towards the end of the chapter. In the interim I make some further distinctions that allow for those later refinements.
10. See Feinberg's references to Pitcher ("Harm to Others", 89). See also Joan Callahan's good objections:

> [Feinberg and Pitcher's account] terminates in the ironic position of having to allow that the very events it sets out to show are harmful to the dead are not and cannot be harmful to the dead. What seems to have happened here is that a provocative thesis – that the dead can be harmed – has itself been mortally injured by the proverbial thousand qualifications. ("On Harming the Dead", *Ethics* 97[2] [1987], 346)

Also, "when we say we feel sorry for the dead Smith because of some posthumous event, we generally do mean it is the *dead* Smith we feel sorry for, even if ... we are confused about this" (*ibid.*).
11. I take this last example from Parfit, *Reasons and Persons*, 356.
12. Luper employs a different terminology: "Let us say that an event that is responsible for our coming to be in a bad condition is an indirect harm, while the bad condition itself is the direct harm" ("Posthumous Harm", 70). This seems to me a less than intuitive use of these terms.
13. Curiously he acknowledges Nagel for the first case, Nozick for the second. But both occur in Nagel.
14. For further reading, see Nagel, *Mortal Questions*, 5; J. O'Neill, "Future Generations: Present Harms". *Philosophy* 68 (1993), 44.
15. See Pitcher, "The Misfortunes of the Dead", 160.
16. See Feinberg:

> When a promise is broken, someone is wronged, and who if not the promisee? When a confidence is revealed, someone is betrayed, and who, if not the person whose confi-

dence it was? When a reputation is falsely blackened, someone is defamed, and who, if not the person lied about? If there is no "problem of the subject" when we speak of wronging the dead, why should there be when we speak of harming them, especially when the harm is an essential ingredient of the wrong? ("Harm to Others", 89)
But that is precisely what is in question.

17. For further reading, see Nagel, *Mortal Questions*, 5.

18. See D. Portmore, "Desire Fulfillment and Posthumous Harm", *American Philosophical Quarterly* 44 (2007), 27–38, for a good discussion of pointless sacrifice. I have some reservations, however. Some activity may be pointless if there is, and there should be known to be, no chance of success, as with the flowers. But surely more than later bad luck is needed to render current activities pointless.

19. See the discussion in Feinberg, Harm to Others", 84, and Luper, "Posthumous Harm" , 67–8.

20. It is a small town and I am not a professional, so their fortune does not affect my career prospects.

21. I take the skeleton of the example from Parfit, *Reasons and Persons*, 151.

22. There are, of course, some exceptions. I might desire that I be famous, or desire that my body be preserved.

23. This view was, as Feinberg acknowledges, robustly criticized by Ernest Partridge, "Posthumous Interests and Posthumous Respect", *Ethics* 91 (1981), 243–64.

24. For further reading, see F. Feldman, "Hyperventilating about Intrinsic Value", *Journal of Ethics* 2 (1998), 339–54.

25. As Pitcher puts it, the postmortem person, the dead and rotting corpse, the dust, cannot itself be harmed by such things ("The Misfortunes of the Dead", 161–2). One who thinks otherwise is Geoffrey Scarre:

    [I]f we are uneasy about pulling forward into his life all the harm of an event that takes place following Jack's death we can opt for the more "natural" dating of the harm at the posthumous point in time when Jack undergoes the Cambridge change of becoming a person whose wishes have been flouted by his executors.
    (*Death* [Stocksfield: Acumen, 2007], 112–13)

    But it seems more needs to be said here. For it is one thing to say that a person who exists at *t* can undergo some relational or Cambridge change at *t*, and another to say that this can happen to a non-existing person.

26. Quoted approvingly by Feinberg, "Harm to Others", 91.

27. Thus we should distinguish between different sorts of relational changes. Some do, others do not, lead to intrinsic change. You stand close to a big bomb and then move away before it explodes. Or not. Someone places a bomb in your room. Then they lock the door. Five minutes later the bomb explodes. A harming event occurs five minutes before the harmed condition. Suppose you escape. Then there was no harm. Nor are you harmed by the bomb, or the bomber, if you coincidentally die of a heart attack before the bomb explodes. Similarly when the dead and nonexistent are prevented from regaining existence, and life. A harming event occurs when you lose the possibility of regaining life, on condition that you would not have lost that possibility anyway.

28. McMahan makes, and discusses, a similar point (*The Ethics of Killing*, 129–30).

29. See Scarre, *Death*, 116.

30. If it is better for us to think with the vulgar and hold that respecting the dead, keeping our promises to them and so on are important, then, arguably, there are reasons for us to acquire the relevant dispositions both to believe and act in ways that are supportive of this. So perhaps I should say, that the dead can be harmed is false, whether or not we believe, and indeed have reasons to acquire the belief, that it is true.

7. An asymmetry

1. See A. Brueckner & J. Fischer, "The Asymmetry of Early Death and Late Birth", *Philosophical Studies* **71** (1993), 327–31; "Death's Badness", *Pacific Philosophical Quarterly* **74** (1993), 37–45; and "Being Born Earlier", *Australasian Journal of Philosophy* **76**(1) (1998), 110–14. See also J. Fischer, "Death, Badness, and the Impossibility of Experience", *Journal of Ethics* **1** (1997), 341–53, and J. M. Fischer & D. Speak, "Death and the Psychological Conception of Personal Identity", *Midwest Studies in Philosophy* **24**, *Life and Death: Metaphysics and Ethics* (2000), 84–93.
2. In order to achieve a more uniform presentation of the different cases, I have slightly simplified Parfit's original example.
3. Much more might be said. So described these experiences are not thoroughly inaccessible. They are inaccessible only after they have occurred. Parfit (*Reasons and Persons*) considers, but rejects, the need for thorough inaccessibility, wherein experiences are, by a double dose of amnesia, neither anticipated nor remembered. But there is room for a suspicion that inaccessibility of the limited kind introduced here might skew the structure of the overall argument. In these cases there is a kind of symmetry. Past pains are anticipated, occur, but are then forgotten. Future pains similarly are anticipated, occur, and are then forgotten. In non-existence cases there is a different kind of symmetry. In the past non-existence was followed by existence. In the future existence will be followed by non-existence. As the symmetries differ so connections between the cases appears to be reduced. It is, however, inappropriate to pursue these matters here.
4. Perhaps Parfit uses the term differently (*Reasons and Persons*). He says he would not be *distressed* to be reminded of a past operation. If he thinks that distress is somehow a condition of our not being indifferent, such that I can be indifferent even while very much regretting the operation occurred, then he does use the term differently. So used, the indifference claim may be true. But so used, some needless distortion of ordinary language occurs. Brueckner and Fischer give it an ordinary use (A. Brueckner & J. Fischer, "Why Is Death Bad?", *Philosophical Studies* **50** [1986], 213–21). So used, the claim is false.
5. And it is a mistake I made in an earlier paper; see my "Asymmetry and Non-Existence", *Philosophical Studies* **70** (1993), 103–16.
6. See Brueckner & Fischer, "Why Is Death Bad?", 216–19. They say, immediately after giving the hospital case, that "we are indifferent to past pleasures and look forward to future pleasures" (Brueckner & Fischer, "Why Is Death Bad?", 227). They are somewhat cagey about Parfit's view: "His position could be put as follows. We have a (not irrational) bias towards the future to the extent that there are cases where we are indifferent toward (or care substantially less about) our own past suffering" (*ibid.*). And they later revive their own position in the direction of caginess: "it is rational to welcome future pleasures while remaining relatively indifferent to past pleasures" ("The Asymmetry of Early Death", 328). Parfit shifts from a claim about future bias (*Reasons and Persons*, 166) to past indifference (*ibid.*, 173) without, so far as I can tell, explaining that shift.
7. Although, as noted above, Brueckner and Fischer refer, I think unhelpfully, to our being "relatively indifferent" to past pleasures ("The Asymmetry of Early Death", 328).
8. Thus, "Death deprives us of something we care about, whereas prenatal nonexistence deprives us of something to which we are indifferent" (Brueckner & Fischer, "Why Is Death Bad?", 226). Their efforts to ground a distinction between these periods of non-existence on our different attitudes towards them is criticized by Ishtiyaque Haji ("Pre-Vital and Post-Vital Times", *Pacific Philosophical Quarterly* **72** [1991], 171–80). They reply in "Death's Badness".
9. See Parfit: "If we often think about, and view serenely, the blackness behind us, some of this serenity may be transferred to our view of the blackness before us" (*Reasons and Persons*, 175).
10. Although unlikely, this combination of attitudes is possible. Someone could think existence is good, while not caring at all what happens once we exist.

11. This may be a little unfair. A legitimate question might be: what attitude to non-existence ought we to have, if we are to be consistent? But then, first, other attitudes – principally here to experience – need themselves to be correctly identified and, second, there needs to be a case for achieving consistency via one route, rather than the other.

12. Remember, the concern is with our actual attitudes. Attitudes differ. So I should be taken, in all these remarks, as referring to a general or prevailing pattern. I do not want to deny that there can be exceptions.

13. For a fuller account see my "Asymmetry and Non-Existence", 109–12. A similar point has been made more recently by Frederick Kaufman, "Death and Deprivation; Or Why Lucretius' Symmetry Argument Fails", *Australasian Journal of Philosophy* **74**(2) (1996), 305–12, and "Pre-vital and Post-mortem Non-existence", *American Philosophical Quarterly* **36** (1999), 1–19.

14. Some say that if offered a later death we assume the birth date is fixed. So it represents an extension to life. But if offered an earlier birth we assume that death is then correspondingly earlier. So it represents only a relocation of a life. Unsurprisingly, then, we much prefer the later death. This is not a good explanation. It needs to be – and surely is – made clear that life is longer in both cases. See here Feldman, *Confrontations with the Reaper*, 154–6, for an example of appeal to the bad explanation.

15. I have written "or so they say" because I am not yet convinced that this limited claim was evident in the earlier paper.

16. The passage is puzzling in one respect. While it is clear enough why the authors should allow we might care about present and future effects of past experiences, it is less clear how a concern for the total pattern is to be accommodated. For the total pattern could be improved, presumably, simply by enhancing the past.

17. Parfit's mother is not, in relation to Parfit, simply some other. And he is concerned here, in particular, to make a point about our attitude to the pains of those closest to us. There may be further differences between attitudes to family and friends on the one hand, and strangers, on the other. But I shall not explore these further differences.

18. A further difficulty here is that the explanation fails to engage with our different attitude to our own past and future pain. Neither is experienced now. So why worry about future pain? It explains nothing to say that this, unlike past pain, will be experienced. As Parfit asks, why does *will be* count for more than *was*?

19. See Kripke, *Naming and Necessity*, 110–15, and Nagel, *Mortal Questions*, 8 n.3.

20. See Parfit, *Reasons and Persons*, 351–2.

21. Parfit might appear to take a different view. In *Reasons and Persons*, 522–3 n.6, he resists the claims of those who say of such cases that different persons are involved. But in fact the case he considers – moving to Italy at age three – is importantly different from mine. Wholly different psychologies are one thing, branching psychologies with common origins another.

22. Here is an example. Suppose the embryo is put on ice and birth is delayed by two centuries. But scientists replicate in every respect the environment that the resulting foetus would have been born into. Then, given that there is physical and psychological qualitative identity, we should say here there is numerical identity also.

23. For example, see my "Identity and Disability", *Journal of Applied Philosophy* **17**(3) (2000), 263–76.

24. For further reading, see Brueckner & Fischer, "Why Is Death Bad?", 220, and "The Asymmetry of Early Death", 327–8.

25. For further reading, see Parfit, *Reasons and Persons*, 174–86,

26. Suppose we all lived to eighty. Suppose too that entire populations live and die together, as do (most of) some plants and many insects. We would still be able to imagine living longer. It would not be irrational to desire this. But in such circumstances it might be unnatural to desire it.

8. Numbers

1. This is, I think, in part attributable to her work's having recently become much more readily available, and also to her role in the revival of virtue ethics.

2. He refers to Anscombe's paper in a footnote to the point here.

3. See also: "The nerve of Mr. Bennett's argument is that if A results from your not doing B then A results from whatever you do instead of doing B. While there may be much to be said for this view, still it does not seem right on the face of it" (G. E. M. Anscombe, "A Note on Mr. Bennett", *Analysis* **26** [1965–6], 208).

4. For considerably more discussion of this, see V. Munoz-Dardé, "The Distribution of Numbers and the Comprehensiveness of Reasons", *Proceedings of the Aristotelian Society* **105**(2) (2005), 207–33, esp. 210ff.

5. For the discussion, see J. Taurek, "Should the Numbers Count?", *Philosophy and Public Affairs* **6** (1977), 303.

6. A utilitarian might also claim that special obligations cannot be binding.

7. Here is some evidence of the low standard: "In securing David's survival I am acting on a purely personal preference", and "the only relevant consideration here is that I happen to like David more than I like any of them", and "the mere fact that I know and like him" (Taurek, "Should the Numbers Count?", 297).

8. In introducing the suggestion that we should toss a coin Taurek claims only that we should give the relevant people an equal chance of being saved. In developing the suggestion he appears to suggest also that this is because they are threatened by equal losses.

9. It might be objected that this misrepresents Taurek's position. But I do not see any significant difference between saving the one for no reason and saving him just because one prefers to do that.

10. See Parfit: "Those who believe that suffering is 'additive' do not believe that many lesser pains might be the same thing as one greater pain. What they believe is that the lesser pains might be together as bad" ("Innumerate Ethics", *Philosophy and Public Affairs* **7**[4] [1978], 293).

11. We need a further point. Suppose trees are good for people. Then I might be obliged to help trees without thinking it bad in itself, or *tout court*, that trees die. But this merely pushes the problem back a step. That trees are good for people does not bear on me unless it is good that people flourish. (Compare trees being good for people with their being good for aphids).

12. See Taurek: "I cannot give a satisfactory account of the meaning of judgements of this kind" ("Should the Numbers Count?", 304).

13. For further reading see Parfit, *Reasons and Persons*, 351–79.

14. For Parfit there is indeed an argument for deciding between David and the five by flipping a coin, "But I believe it is outweighed". There follows an important parenthetical remark:

    Much more needs to be said. I will add this. David's death is undeserved. So is the loss of Y's arm. It is simply their misfortune that their claims are outweighed. In a way, this is unfair. It involves a kind of natural injustice. But such injustice cannot be removed by flipping coins. It could only be transferred. Natural injustice is bad luck. Making more depend on luck will not abolish bad luck.　　　("Innumerate Ethics", 300–301)

15. See also Broome, "Fairness", in his *Ethics out of Economics*, 162–73.

16. Hirose's view is perhaps more puzzling than my sketch implies. For he thinks that we only achieve fairness by an equal distribution of goods. It is fair, although "stupid", to let all six die but unfair to one to save five, even when saving five is the result of tossing a coin. Now he distinguishes between a strict and moderate account of fairness, and so it might not be unsurprising that this view figures in the strict account. But it figures in the moderate account also. A second puzzle is in claiming that coin tossing is the least unfair device for choosing between one and five. Timmermann's dice alternative might seem to be fairer.

17. Otsuka states: "numbers skepticism is irrational insofar as it gives rise to a choice-defeating cycle of intransitive preferences. More precisely, the combination of the skeptic's endorsement

of the principle of non-aggregation and her affirmation of pairwise comparisons of harms give rise to this intransitivity". ("Skepticism about Saving the Greater Number", *Philosophy and Public Affairs* **32**[4] [2004], 416).

18. As he says, neither Anscombe nor Taurek "necessarily subscribe" to all such views (*ibid.*, 414 n.6).

19. As Timmermann puts it, "The decision procedure employed must be one that can be justified even to those who eventually lose" ("The Individualist Lottery", *Analysis* **64**[2] [2004], 107). This is odd. The losers can always complain. Whether their complaints are reasonable depends on what counts as a justification. The consequentialist will say that we are justified in saving the greater number, and the losers should be able to see that.

20. It took me a while, as a schoolboy, to learn that multiplying by zero was different from not multiplying.

9. Cheating death

1. See Nagel, *Mortal Questions*, 22. Bradley makes an odd comment: "there is no point in trying to make your death less bad" ("How Bad is Death?", 125). In contrast, I think there is a point, even though some methods are not to be recommended.

2. Although I suspect this may not be possible. Perhaps inevitably there is at least some small scale movement, even over short periods of time, in the parts of a living body.

3. This may be too generous. People will say that God cannot do evil things with atoms.

4. But distinguish this claim – a watch can cease then begin again – from another that may be made here – a watch can continue to exist, even when irreparably damaged. See D. Mackie, "Personal Identity and Dead People", *Philosophical Studies* **95** (1999), 219–42, for emphasis on the latter claim. Johansson (*Mortal Beings*, 54–61) is altogether unimpressed, distrusting the analogy and questioning Mackie's claim.

5. No one, I think, will claim that you should sacrifice a period of (worthwhile) conscious life for a longer period of unconscious life. Perhaps there is here some sort of counter to some versions of the sanctity of life view.

6. This is not simply speculative. I have found that students appear to hold such views.

7. There may be two versions of the teletransporter. In this one it is clear that different matter is involved: the second chamber needs priming, the first cleaning out after use. In another the original matter disappears, and qualitatively identical matter appears in the second chamber. Here it is not clear whether the matter is the same or different. Parfit's account (*Reasons and Persons*, 199) implies the first version.

8. For discussion, see Olson, *The Human Animal* and "An Argument for Animalism".

9. I argue that this is his position in my "Animalism: Some Shortcomings" (unpublished manuscript). It should be noted, however, that Olson, in correspondence, has denied that this is his view.

10. The distinction I made in note 7 is relevant here. The new matter version seems fairly clearly to involve a replica head. On the second version this is just unclear.

11. There is a qualification. The plausible point is about animals in general. But can a particular animal turn into another animal, or an animal of a different kind, and continue to exist? Could the Queen, who is a human animal, turn into a swan, and still exist? I think Olson's view would be that if the Queen turns wholly into a swan she ceases to exist. If she turns into some composite then either she ceases to exist or she retains essential human parts, that is, the head.

12. I talk here of our thinking. We might, as well or instead, talk about our having minds or psychologies. Olson puts the points thus: "The Biological Approach makes two claims. First, you and I are animals … second … Psychological continuity is neither necessary nor sufficient for a human animal to persist through time" (*The Human Animal*, 17). "The Psychological Approach is the view that some psychological relation is both necessary and sufficient for one to survive" (*ibid.*, 13).

13. See also Olson, *The Human Animal*, 101–2.
14. Whether we, like stations, could have had different parts from the outset is perhaps less clear. Think of the sperm and egg as atomic and the answer is no. But in fact those small parts themselves have parts.
15. It should be noted that Lynne Rudder Baker's "Everyday Concepts as a Guide to Reality", *Monist* 89(3) (2006), 313–33, is presented as a self-standing account of the constitution view, and its supposed merits. For more detail on her view, see her *Persons and Bodies: A Constitution View* (Cambridge: Cambridge University Press, 2000).
16. There is a puzzling claim here. Baker takes the reductionist as holding that towers are just arrangements of particles. But "a random arrangement of particles – even if it happened to be shaped tower-wise – would not be a tower" ("Everyday Concepts as a Guide to Reality", 316). I am not sure this is true, nor that it is a point against the reductionist. He could accommodate it.
17. See L. R. Baker, "Big Tent Metaphysics", *Abstracta*, special issue 1 [2008], 12.
18. Baker notes: "As a terminological point, I take 'human being' to denote human *persons*" ("Big Tent Metaphysics", 8). So perhaps there are, for Baker, only two terms to consider.
19. Further, if Baker can, as she believes, cease to be an animal without ceasing to exist, then *human animal* is not a primary kind. But now give the animal that presently constitutes Baker a name. Call it Fido. Fido is (constitutes) a person. But it can cease to be a person. So *person* is not a primary kind.
20. See, for example, Olson, *The Human Animal*, 27–31. A related similarity is in their believing in ontological hierarchies: Baker has her concern with primary kinds, Olson with what we most fundamentally are. And see, for much of the metaphysical back story here, D. Wiggins, *Identity and Spatio-Temporal Continuity* (Oxford: Blackwell, 1967) and *Sameness and Substance* (Oxford: Blackwell, 1980).
21. For further reading see Kripke, *Naming and Necessity*.
22. It is worth noting in passing that Olson's view that animals cease to exist with death has a kind of parallel here. On many religious views death, ushering in this disunity, does plausibly involve a change in kind.
23. See Olson, "An Argument for Animalism", 325–6, and *The Human Animal*, 100–109. He considers and unsurprisingly quickly rejects a third alternative, namely that there are no human animals at all.
24. The view here is not dissimilar to Rosenberg's (*Thinking Clearly about Death*, 97), mentioned but rejected early on by Olson: "a person" is a living organism. Luper similarly advances a disjunctive account in *The Philosophy of Death*.
25. Now I think the question of animal identity is not as clear as Olson makes out. And just as one vase, or ship, or item of clothing can be turned into another, so too for an animal.
26. There is an ambiguity to avoiding death here. I might avoid death even though a death occurs by ceasing to be an animal. Or I might avoid it by continuing as an animal, but by preventing any animal death from occurring. In the case described here I continue as an animal, but another animal dies.
27. On this issue of relative identity see also, as Olson suggests, P. Geach, "Identity", *Review of Metaphysics* 21 (1967), 3–12.
28. See Olson, *The Human Animal*, 161–2. What Olson sees as a problem, the conversion of seemingly metaphysical questions into a string of linguistic and semantic points, I see as a virtue.
29. I do not mean that a lump of rock has a blurry edge. But we might think that while to cut off parts of a living thing will clearly destroy, or not, that thing, the question of when one rock, or cloud, or river turns into another and/or is obliterated is inherently vague.
30. Of course, it is extremely likely that every mental alteration involves some physical alteration of microparticles in the brain. All I mean is that gross and readily detectable mental change is more common and more easily produced than a corresponding physical change.

31. Again, it may be that there is inevitably some difference in mental content if a cerebrum is differently situated. But I am supposing these may be trivial differences.
32. For details of this theory see Nozick, "On the Randian Argument", esp. 29–70.
33. Some people will prefer that the question here be refined and reformulated. Perhaps they will say, with Butler, that everything is what it is and not another thing. I think the meaning is clear, but if it helps to think of A and B as names of stages in the longer-term existence of some thing or things, and then ask whether A and B are stages in the same thing, or some such, then do so.
34. This way of putting the point is Parfit's (*Reasons and Persons*, esp. ch. 12), but I find it misleading. If no future person is, strictly, me – no one then is identical with me now – then, I want to say, I do not survive. So there is not, in division, a double survival. But I might have what matters in survival without survival.
35. For further reading, see B. Williams, "The Self and the Future", *Philosophical Review* 79(2) (1970), 161–80; H. Noonan, *Personal Identity* (London: Routledge, 1991), esp. chs 7, 11.

Appendix: Brain death – history and debate

1. Are they unconscious? Most writers say they are without explaining why this is so. Hence, often, the surprise among lay people in discovering in detail how those in PVS behave.
2. Given the distinction that Feldman rightly insists on between permanence and irreversibility (*Confrontations with the Reaper*, 60–64), one might wonder whether the suggested terminological shift is adequate to the supposed task.
3. For further reading, see, for example, DeGrazia, "The Definition of Death", §1; McMahan, *The Ethics of Killing*, 440ff.
4. For example, see Lizza, *Persons, Humanity and the Definition of Death*, 8.
5. For Lamb's argument see Lamb, *Death, Brain Death and Ethics*, 20–23.
6. See Lamb, *Death, Brain Death and Ethics*, 24–8. Lamb asks, following C. Culver & B. Gert, *Philosophy in Medicine: Conceptual and Medical Issues in Philosophy and Psychiatry* (New York: Oxford University Press, 1982) whether the reference is to loss of *spontaneous* or *artificially supported* circulatory and respiratory functions. It cannot be the former for otherwise even those with pacemakers would be dead. And it cannot be the latter since this, although providing a sufficient condition for death, is not a necessary one. Hence it is not a definition of death (Lamb, *Death, Brain Death and Ethics*, 24–5). It is difficult to see what the problem is supposed to be. See also Gervais, *Redefining Death*, 199.
7. For further reading see DeGrazia, "The Definition of Death".
8. For support for the brainstem criterion see Lamb, *Death, Brain Death and Ethics*, chs 4, 5; C. Pallis, "ABC of Brainstem Death", *British Medical Journal* 285 (1983), 1487–90. For criticism see Bernat, "The Biophilosophical Basis", 338–9. DeGrazia notes that the brainstem standard "has the practical advantage of requiring fewer clinical tests".
9. See, for example, Lamb, *Death, Brain Death and Ethics*, ch. 2. Summing his discussion, he insists that "brain death is a radical reformulation of traditional concepts of death rather than a new concept, since there is no new way of being dead … It is not so much a new concept as the formulation of a definition of death where previously none existed" (*ibid.*, 18).
10. See Gervais, *Redefining Death*, 23–5. Gervais goes on to talk about the concept of death more generally, taking the discussion further away from the committee's brief.
11. A. Shewmon, "The Brain and Somatic Integration: Insights into the Standard Biological Rationale for Equating 'Brain Death' with Death", *Journal of Medicine and Philosophy* 26 (2001), 457–78, claims that any unity imposed by a master controller is only a pseudo-unity. That is, I think, unnecessarily contentious.
12. Shewmon is referring here to Jonathan Glover, whose views he criticizes earlier in the paper.

Bibliography

Ad Hoc Committee of the Harvard Medical School to Examine the Definition of Brain Death 1968. "A Definition of Irreversible Coma: Report of the Ad Hoc Committee of the Harvard Medical School to Examine the Definition of Brain Death". *Journal of the American Medical Association* **205**: 337–40.

Alvarez, A. A. 1971. *The Savage God: A Study of Suicide*. Harmondsworth: Penguin.

Anscombe, G. E. M. 1965–6. "A Note on Mr. Bennett". *Analysis* **26**: 208.

Anscombe, G. E. M. 1967. "Who is Wronged?". *The Oxford Review* **5**: 16–17.

Arnold, R. M. & S. J. Youngner 1995. "The Dead Donor Rule: Should we Stretch it, Bend it, or Abandon it?". In *Procuring Organs for Transplant*, R. M. Arnold, S. J. Youngner, R. Schapiro & C. M. Spicer (eds), 219–34. Baltimore, MD: Johns Hopkins University Press.

Baker, L. R. 2000. *Persons and Bodies: A Constitution View*. Cambridge: Cambridge University Press.

Baker, L. R. 2006. "Everyday Concepts as a Guide to Reality". *Monist* **89**(3): 313–33.

Baker, L. R. 2008. "Big Tent Metaphysics". *Abstracta*, special issue **1**: 8–15.

Bauby, J.-D. 1997. *The Diving Bell and the Butterfly*. New York: Alfred A. Knopf.

Becker, L. 1975. "Human Being: The Boundaries of the Concept". *Philosophy and Public Affairs* **4**(4): 334–59.

Belshaw, C. 1993. "Asymmetry and Non-Existence". *Philosophical Studies* **70**: 103–16.

Belshaw, C. 1997. "Abortion, Value and the Sanctity of Life". *Bioethics* **11**(2): 130–50.

Belshaw, C. 1998. "Gold". *Theoria* **13**(33): 415–26.

Belshaw, C. 2000a. "Death, Pain, and Time". *Philosophical Studies* **97**: 317–41.

Belshaw, C. 2000b. "Identity and Disability". *Journal of Applied Philosophy* **17**(3): 263–76.

Belshaw, C. 2003. "More Lives, Better Lives". *Ethical Theory and Moral Practice* **6**(2): 127–41.

Belshaw, C. 2005. *10 Good Questions about Life and Death*. Oxford: Blackwell.

Belshaw, C. 2006. "My Beginnings". *Monist* **89**(3): 371–89.

Belshaw, C. "Animalism: Some Shortcomings". Unpublished manuscript.

Bernat, J. 1998. "A Defense of the Whole-Brain Concept of Death". *Hastings Center Report* **28**(2): 14–23.

Bernat, J. 2002. "The Biophilosophical Basis of Whole Brain Death". *Social Philosophy and Policy Foundation* **19**(2): 324–42.

Bernat, J. 2006. "The Whole-Brain Concept of Death Remains Optimum Public Policy". *Journal of Law, Medicine and Ethics* **34**(1): 35–43.

Bernat, J., C. M. Culver & B. Gert 1981. "On the Definition and Criterion of Death". *Annals of Internal Medicine* **94**: 389–94.

Bernstein, M. 1998. *On Moral Considerability: As Essay on Who Morally Matters*. Oxford: Oxford University Press.

Bradley, B. 2004. "When Is Death Bad for the One Who Dies?". *Noûs* **38**: 1–28.

Bradley, B. 2007. "How Bad is Death?". *Canadian Journal of Philosophy* **37**(1): 11–128.

Bradley, B. 2008a. "The Worst Time to Die". *Ethics* **118**: 291–314.

Bradley, B. 2009. *Well-Being and Death*. Oxford: Oxford University Press.

Bradley, B. forthcoming. "Eternalism and Death's Badness".

Broome, J. 1993. "Goodness is Reducible to Betterness: The Evil of Death is the Value of Life". In *The Good and the Economical: Ethical Choices in Economics and Management*, P. Koslowski & Y. Shionoya (eds), 70–84. Berlin: Springer. Reprinted in his *Ethics out of Economics*, 162–74 (Cambridge: Cambridge University Press, 1999).

Broome, J. 1999. *Ethics out of Economics*. Cambridge: Cambridge University Press.

Broome, J. 2004. *Weighing Lives*. Oxford: Oxford University Press.

Brueckner, A. & J. Fischer 1986. "Why Is Death Bad?". *Philosophical Studies* **50**: 213–21.

Brueckner, A. & J. Fischer 1993a. "The Asymmetry of Early Death and Late Birth". *Philosophical Studies* **71**: 327–31.

Brueckner, A. & J. Fischer 1993b. "Death's Badness". *Pacific Philosophical Quarterly* **74**: 37–45.

Brueckner, A. & J. Fischer 1998. "Being Born Earlier". *Australasian Journal of Philosophy* **76**(1): 110–14.

Callahan, J. C. 1987. "On Harming the Dead". *Ethics* **97**(2): 341–52.

Capron, A. M. & L. R. Kass 1972. "A Statutory Definition of the Standards for Determining Human Death: An Appraisal and a Proposal". *University of Pennsylvania Law Review* **121**: 87–118.

Carter, W. R. 1999. "Will I be a Dead Person?". *Philosophy and Phenomenological Research* **59**(1): 167–71.

Chiong, W. 2005. "Brain Death without Definitions". *Hastings Center Report* **35**(6): 20–30.

Cigman, R. 1981. "Death, Misfortune, and Species Inequality". *Philosophy and Public Affairs* **10**: 47–64.

Culver, C. & B. Gert 1982. *Philosophy in Medicine: Conceptual and Medical Issues in Philosophy and Psychiatry*. New York: Oxford University Press.

DeGrazia, D. 2005. *Human Identity and Bioethics*. Cambridge: Cambridge University Press.

DeGrazia, D. 2007. "The Definition of Death". *Stanford Encyclopedia of Philosophy*. http://plato. stanford.edu/entries/death-definition/

Diogenes Laertius 1925. *Lives of Eminent Philosophers*, vol. 2, R. D. Hicks (ed. and trans.). Cambridge, MA: Harvard University Press.

Draper, K. 1999. "Disappointment, Sadness, and Death". *Philosophical Review* **108**(3): 387–414.

Dworkin, R. 1993. *Life's Dominion*. New York: Alfred A. Knopf.

Feinberg, J. 1984. "Harm to Others". In his *Harm to Others*, 79–96. Oxford: Oxford University Press. Reprinted in Fischer (1993), 171–90.

Feinberg, J. 1986. *Harm to Self*. Oxford: Oxford University Press.

Feit, N. 2002. "The Time of Death's Misfortune". *Noûs* **36**: 359–83.

Feldman, F. 1992. *Confrontations with the Reaper*. New York: Oxford University Press.

Feldman, F. 1993. "Some Puzzles About the Evil of Death". See Fischer (1993), 307–26. Originally published in *Philosophical Review* **100**(2) (1991): 205–27.

Feldman, F. 1998. "Hyperventilating about Intrinsic Value". *Journal of Ethics* **2**: 339–54.

Feldman, F. 2000. "The Termination Thesis". *Midwest Studies in Philosophy* **24**, *Life and Death: Metaphysics and Ethics*: 98–115.

Feldman, F. 2004. *Pleasure and the Good Life: Concerning the Nature, Varieties, and Plausibility of Hedonism*. New York: Oxford University Press.

Fischer, J. M. (ed.) 1993. *The Metaphysics of Death*. Stanford, CA: Stanford University Press.

Fischer, J. 1997. "Death, Badness, and the Impossibility of Experience". *Journal of Ethics* **1**: 341–53.

Fischer, J. M. & D. Speak 2000. "Death and the Psychological Conception of Personal Identity". *Midwest Studies in Philosophy* **24**, *Life and Death: Metaphysics and Ethics*: 84–93.

Geach, P. 1967. "Identity". *Review of Metaphysics* **21**: 3–12.

Gert, B. 1995. "A Complete Definition of Death". In *Brain Death*, C. Maxhado (ed.), 23–30. Amsterdam: Elsevier.

Gervais, K. 1986. *Redefining Death*. New Haven, CT: Yale University Press.

Green, M. & D. Wikler 1980. "Brain Death and Personal Identity". *Philosophy and Public Affairs* **9**: 105–33.

Grey, W. 1999. "Epicurus and the Harm of Death". *Australasian Journal of Philosophy* **77**: 358–64.

Griffin, J. 1986. *Well-Being*. Oxford: Clarendon Press.

Haji, I. 1991. "Pre-Vital and Post-Vital Times". *Pacific Philosophical Quarterly* **72**: 171–80.

Halevy, A. & B. Brody 1993. "Brain Death: Reconciling Definitions, Criteria, and Tests". *Annals of Internal Medicine* **119**(6): 519–25.

Hanser, M. 2008. "The Metaphysics of Harm". *Philosophy and Phenomenological Research* **77**: 421–50.

Harman, G. 2000. *Explaining Value*. Oxford: Oxford University Press.

Hershenov, D. 2003. "The Problematic Role of 'Irreversibility' in the Definition of Death". *Bioethics* **17**(1): 89–100.

Hirose, I. 2004. "Aggregation and Numbers". *Utilitas* **16**(1): 62–79.

Holland, S. 2003. *Bioethics*. Cambridge: Polity.

Johansson, J. 2005. *Mortal Beings: On the Metaphysics and Value of Death*. Stockholm: Almqvist & Wiksell.

Kamm, F. 1988. "Why Is Death Bad and Worse than Pre-Natal Non-Existence?". *Pacific Philosophical Quarterly* **69**: 161–4.

Kamm, F. 1993. *Morality, Mortality*, vol. 1. Oxford: Oxford University Press.

Kass, L. 1971. "Death as an Event: A Commentary on Robert Morison". *Science* **173**: 698–702.

Kaufman, F. 1996. "Death and Deprivation; Or Why Lucretius' Symmetry Argument Fails". *Australasian Journal of Philosophy* **74**(2): 305–12.

Kaufman, F. 1999. "Pre-vital and Post-mortem Non-existence". *American Philosophical Quarterly* **36**: 1–19.

Kekes, J. 2000. *Pluralism in Philosophy: Changing the Subject*. Ithaca, NY: Cornell University Press.

Kekes, J. 2002. *The Art of Life*. Ithaca, NY: Cornell University Press.

Korein, J. 1978. "The Problem of Brain Death". *Annals of the New York Academy of Sciences* **315**: 19–38.

Kripke, S. 1980. *Naming and Necessity*. Cambridge, MA: Harvard University Press.

Ladd, J. 1979. "The Definition of Death and the Right to Die". In *Ethical Issues Relating to Life and Death*, J. Ladd (ed.), 118–45. Oxford: Oxford University Press.

Lamb, D. 1985. *Death, Brain Death and Ethics*. Beckenham: Croom Helm.

Lamb, D. 1994. "What is Death?". In *Principles of Health Care Ethics*, R. Gillon (ed.), 1027–40. Chichester: Wiley.

Levenbook, B. 1984. "Harming Someone After His Death". *Ethics* **94**: 407–19.

Lizza, J. 2006. *Persons, Humanity and the Definition of Death*. Baltimore, MD: Johns Hopkins University Press.

Luper, S. 1985. "Annihilation". *Philosophical Quarterly* **37**(148): 233–52. Reprinted in Fischer (1993), 269–90.

Luper, S. 1999. "Natural Resources, Gadgets and Artificial Life". *Environmental Values* **8**(1): 27–54.

Luper, S. 2002. "Death", *The Stanford Encyclopedia of Philosophy (Winter 2002 Edition)*, Edward N. Zalta (ed.), URL = http://plato.stanford.edu/archives/win2002/entries/death/

Luper, S. 2004. "Posthumous Harm". *American Philosophical Quarterly* **41**: 63–72.

Luper, S. 2007. "Mortal Harm". *Philosophical Quarterly* **57**(227): 239–51.

Luper, S. 2008. *The Philosophy of Death.* Oxford: Oxford University Press.

MacIntyre A. 1981. *After Virtue.* London: Duckworth.

Mackie, D. 1999. "Personal Identity and Dead People". *Philosophical Studies* 95: 219–42.

McMahan, J. 1988. "Death and the Value of Life". *Ethics* 99(1): 32–61. Reprinted in Fischer (1993).

McMahan, J. 1995. "The Metaphysics of Brain Death". *Bioethics* 9(2): 91–126.

McMahan, J. 2002. *The Ethics of Killing.* Oxford: Oxford University Press.

Morison, R. 1971. "Death: Process or Event?". *Science* 173: 694–8.

Munoz-Dardé, V. 2005. "The Distribution of Numbers and the Comprehensiveness of Reasons". *Proceedings of the Aristotelian Society* 105(2): 207–33.

Nagel, T. 1970. "Death". *Noûs* 4(1): 73–80. Reprinted in his *Mortal Questions*, 1–10 (Cambridge: Cambridge University Press, 1979), and in Fischer (1993), 59–70.

Nagel, T. 1971. "The Absurd". *Journal of Philosophy* 68: 716–27. Reprinted in his *Mortal Questions*, 11–23 (Cambridge: Cambridge University Press, 1979).

Nagel, T. 1979. *Mortal Questions.* Cambridge: Cambridge University Press.

Noonan, H. 1991. *Personal Identity.* London: Routledge.

Nozick, R. 1981. *Philosophical Explanations.* Cambridge, MA: Harvard University Press.

Nozick, R. 1981. "On the Randian Argument". Reprinted in *Reading Nozick*, J. Paul (ed.), 206–31. Totowa, NJ: Rowman & Littlefield. Originally published in *The Personalist* 52 (1971): 282–304.

Olson, E. 1997. *The Human Animal.* Oxford: Oxford University Press.

Olson, E. 2003. "An Argument for Animalism". In *Personal Identity*, R. Martin & J. Barresi (eds), 318–34. Oxford: Blackwell.

Olson, E. 2004. "Animalism and the Corpse Problem". *Australasian Journal of Philosophy* 82(2): 265–74.

O'Neill, J. 1993. "Future Generations: Present Harms". *Philosophy* 68: 35–51.

Otsuka, M. 2004. "Skepticism about Saving the Greater Number". *Philosophy and Public Affairs* 32(4): 413–26.

Pallis, C. 1983. "ABC of Brainstem Death". *British Medical Journal* 285: 1487–90.

Parfit, D. 1978. "Innumerate Ethics". *Philosophy and Public Affairs* 7(4): 285–301.

Parfit, D. 1984. *Reasons and Persons.* Oxford: Clarendon Press.

Partridge, E. 1981. "Posthumous Interests and Posthumous Respect". *Ethics* 91: 243–64.

Pitcher, G. 1993. "The Misfortunes of the Dead". See Fischer (1993), 157–68. Originally published as The Misfortunes of the Dead". *American Philosophical Quarterly* 21(2) (1984), 217–25.

Portmore, D. 2007. "Desire Fulfillment and Posthumous Harm". *American Philosophical Quarterly* 44: 27–38.

President's Commission for the Study of Ethical Problems in Medicine and Biomedical and Behavioral Research 1981. *Defining Death: Medical, Ethical and Legal Issues in the Determination of Death.* Washington, DC: US Government Printing Office.

Rachels, J. 1986. *The End of Life.* Oxford: Oxford University Press.

Rachels, S. 1998. "Is it Good to make Happy People?". *Bioethics* 12(2): 93–110.

Rosenbaum, S. 1989. "The Symmetry Argument: Lucretius Against the Fear of Death. *Philosophy and Phenomenological Research* 50(2): 353–73.

Rosenbaum, S. 1993a. "How to be Dead and not Care: A Defense of Epicurus". See Fischer (1993), 117–34. Originally published in *American Philosophical Quarterly* 23 (1986): 217–25.

Rosenbaum, S. 1993b. "Epicurus and Annihilation". See Fischer (1993), 293–304. Originally published in *Philosophical Quarterly* 39(154) (1989): 81–90.

Rosenberg, J. 1983. *Thinking Clearly about Death.* Englewood Cliffs, NJ: Prentice Hall.

Scanlon, T. M. 1998. *What We Owe to Each Other.* Cambridge, MA: Harvard University Press.

Scarre, G. 2007. *Death.* Stocksfield: Acumen.

Seifert, J. 1993. "Is "Brain Death" Actually Death?". *Monist* 76: 175–202.

Shewmon, A. 1997. "Recovery From 'Brain Death': A Neurologist's Apologia". *Linacre Quarterly* 64: 30–96.

Shewmon, A. 1998. "Chronic Brain Death: Meta-analysis and Conceptual Consequences". *Neurology* **51**: 1538–45.

Shewmon, A. 2001. "The Brain and Somatic Integration: Insights into the Standard Biological Rationale for Equating 'Brain Death' with Death". *Journal of Medicine and Philosophy* **26**: 457–78.

Silverstein, H. 1980. "The Evil of Death". *Journal of Philosophy* **77**(7): 401–24. Reprinted in Fischer (1993), 95–116.

Silverstein, H. 2000. "The Evil of Death Revisited". *Midwest Studies in Philosophy* **24**, *Life and Death: Metaphysics and Ethics*: 116–35.

Siminoff, L. A., C. Burant & S. J. Youngner 2004. "Death and Organ Procurement: Public Beliefs and Attitudes". *Social Science and Medicine* **59**(11): 2325–34.

Singer, P. 1993. *Practical Ethics*. Cambridge: Cambridge University Press.

Singer, P. 1994. *Rethinking Life and Death: The Collapse of Our Traditional Ethics*. New York: St Martin's Press.

Smart, N. 1968. "Philosophical Concepts of Death". In *Man's Concern with Death*, A. Toynbee (ed.), 25–35. London: Hodder & Stoughton.

Taurek, J. 1977. "Should the Numbers Count?". *Philosophy and Public Affairs* **6**: 293–316.

Timmermann, J. 2004. "The Individualist Lottery". *Analysis* **64**(2): 106–12.

Van Inwagen, P. 1990. *Material Beings*. Ithaca, NY: Cornell University Press.

Veatch, R. M. 1975. "The Whole-Brain-Oriented Concept of Death: An Outmoded Philosophical Formulation". *Journal of Thanatology* **3**: 13–30.

Veatch, R. M. 1976. *Death, Dying and Biological Revolution: Our Last Quest for Responsibility*. New Haven, CT: Yale University Press.

Veatch, R. M. 1978. "Defining Death Anew: Technical and Ethical Problems". In *Ethical Issues in Death and Dying*, T. Beauchamp & S. Perlin (eds), 18–38. Englewood Cliffs, NJ: Prentice-Hall.

Veatch, R. M. 2005. "The Death of Whole-Brain Death: The Plague of the Disaggregators, Somaticists, and Mentalists". *Journal of Medicine and Philosophy* **30**: 353–78.

Warren, J. 2004. *Facing Death: Epicurus and his Critics*. Oxford: Oxford University Press.

Wiggins, D. 1967. *Identity and Spatio-Temporal Continuity*. Oxford: Blackwell.

Wiggins, D. 1980. *Sameness and Substance*. Oxford: Blackwell.

Williams, B. 1970. "The Self and the Future". *Philosophical Review* **79**(2): 161–80. Reprinted in his *Problems of the Self*, 46–63 (Cambridge: Cambridge University Press, 1973) and in *Personal Identity*, J. Perry (ed.), 179–98 (Berkeley, CA: University of California Press, 1975).

Williams, B. 1973. "The Makropoulos Case: Reflections on the Tedium of Immortality". In his *Problems of the Self*, 82–100. Cambridge: Cambridge University Press.

Youngner, S. & R. M. Arnold 2001. "Philosophical Debate about the Definitions of Death: Who Cares?". *Journal of Medicine and Philosophy* **26**: 527–37.

Index